D1557200

Frank J. Fabozzi / Gifford Fong

Advanced
Fixed Income
Portfolio Management
The State of the Art

IRWIN
Professional Publishing®
Chicago • London • Singapore

ISBN 1-55738-568-8

Printed in the United States of America

BB

3 4 5 6 7 8 9 0

CB/BJS

FJF
To my father
Alfonso Fabozzi

HGF
To the staff of Gifford Fong Associates
whose dedicated effort, team spirit and hard work
have made this book possible and the contents relevant

Table of Contents

Acknowledgments

We wish to thank the following individuals at Gifford Fong Associates for their able assistance and special contributions: H. Clifford Fong (Senior Vice President), Daihyun Yoo (Research Associate), and Theresa S. Conroy (Manager). Dunmu Ji (Vice President, Director of Research) provided support and insight throughout this project. Oldrich Vasicek made critical contributions to this book.

The following individuals provided assistance at various stages of this project: Stephen Arbour (Alex. Brown & Sons), T. Dessa Fabozzi (Merrill Lynch), Frank Jones (The Guardian Life Insurance Company), Frank Ramirez (Alex. Brown & Sons), Chuck Ramsey (Alex. Brown & Sons), and Scott Richard (Miller Anderson & Sherrerd).

Chapter 1

Introduction

Fixed income investment management has undergone a remarkable evolution. As the range of portfolio strategies has expanded, the technology of portfolio analysis has developed to match it. This broadened capability enhances efficiency and effectiveness, and encourages introduction of innovative strategies. Perhaps most remarkable is the prospect of a new dimension of fixed income portfolio strategy that dramatically extends the traditional notions of management.

The purpose of this introductory chapter is threefold. First, we provide an overview of the investment management process. Second, we provide an overview of fixed income portfolio management. Third, we describe the changes that have occurred in fixed income portfolio management over the last 25 years. Here we trace the emergence of various quantitative tools that have helped shape today's world of fixed income portfolio management. We end the chapter with an overview of the book.

OVERVIEW OF THE INVESTMENT MANAGEMENT PROCESS

The investment management process consists of five steps: (1) setting investment objectives; (2) establishing investment policy; (3) selecting the portfolio strategy; (4) selecting the assets; and (5) measuring and evaluating performance. Each of these steps is described below.

Setting Investment Objectives

The first step in the investment management process is the setting of investment objectives. The nature of an institutional investor's liabilities will largely dictate the investment strategy it requests its money manager to pursue. Depository institutions, for example, seek to generate income by the spread between the return they earn on their assets and the cost of their funds. Life insurance companies have a variety of policies (e.g., guaranteed investment contracts and single-premium deferred annuities) for which they seek to earn a spread over their crediting rate. Sponsors of defined benefit plans seek to cover the cost of pension obligations at a minimum cost. While investment companies do not face such liability obligations, they do seek to outperform or match a designated benchmark.

By the "liabilities" of an institutional investor, we mean both the *amount* and *timing* of the cash outlays that must be made to satisfy the contractual terms of the obligations issued. The liabilities of any institutional investor can be classified as one of four types, as in Exhibit 1.1. Any such categorization assumes that the entity that must be paid the obligation will not cancel the institutional investor's obligation before any actual or projected payout date.

The descriptions of cash outlays as either known or uncertain are undoubtedly broad. When we refer to a cash outlay as uncertain, we do not mean that it cannot be predicted. For some liabilities, the "law of large numbers" makes it easier to predict the timing and/or amount of cash outlays. This work is typically done by actuaries, although even

Exhibit 1.1

Classification of Liabilities of Institutional Investors

Liability type	Amount of cash outlay	Timing of cash outlay
Type I	Known	Known
Type II	Known	Uncertain
Type III	Uncertain	Known
Type IV	Uncertain	Uncertain

actuaries have difficulty predicting natural catastrophes such as floods and earthquakes.

The important thing to note in our illustrations of each type of risk category is that, as for assets, there are risks associated with liabilities. Some liability risks are affected by the same factors that affect the risks associated with assets.

For Type-I liabilities, both the amount and the timing of the liabilities are known with certainty. An example is a liability of $50,000 to be paid by an institution six months from now. Banks and thrifts know the amount they are committed to pay (principal plus interest) on the maturity date of a fixed-rate deposit, assuming that the depositor does not withdraw funds prior to the maturity date. Another Type-I example is a guaranteed investment contract (GIC) issued by a life insurance company.

For Type-II liabilities, the amount of the cash outlay is known, but its timing is uncertain. The most obvious example of a Type-II liability is a basic life insurance policy insuring against death. For an annual premium, a life insurance company agrees to make a specified dollar payment to policy beneficiaries upon the death of the insured.

For Type-III liabilities, the timing of the cash outlay is known, but the amount is uncertain. A two-year floating-rate CD whose interest rate resets quarterly based on three-month LIBOR is an example. Another example is a floating-rate GIC.

Type-IV liabilities are those with uncertainty as to both the amount and the timing of the cash outlay. The most obvious examples are damage payments on automobile and home insurance policies issued by property and casualty insurance companies. When, and if, a payment will have to be made to a policyholder is uncertain. Whenever damage is done to an insured asset, the amount of the payment that must be made is uncertain. Another example is defined benefit plans, because retirement benefits depend on the participant's income for a specified number of years before retirement, along with the total number of years the participant worked. These factors will affect the amount of the cash outlay. The timing of the cash outlay depends on when the employee elects to retire, as well as whether the employee remains with the sponsoring plan until retirement. Moreover, both the amount and the timing will depend on how the employee elects to have payments made—over only the employee's life or those of the employee and spouse.

Establishing Investment Policy

The second step in the investment management process is the establishing of policy guidelines to satisfy the investment objectives. Setting policy begins with the *asset allocation decision*. That is, the investor must decide how the institution's funds should be distributed among the major classes of assets in which it may invest. The major asset classes typically include stocks, bonds, real estate, and foreign securities.

Client and regulatory constraints must be considered in establishing an investment policy. Examples of constraints that a client might impose are the amount that may be invested in a bond of an issuer whose credit rating is below some specified level, or a restriction that no more than a predetermined percentage of the assets may be invested in a particular industry.

For state-regulated institutions such as insurance companies, regulators may restrict the amount of funds allocated to certain major asset classes. Even the amount allocated within a major asset class may be restricted, depending on the characteristics of the particular assets.

Tax and financial reporting implications must also be considered when adopting investment policies. For example, life insurance companies have certain tax advantages that make it generally unappealing for them to invest in tax-advantaged assets. Pension funds, which are exempt from taxes, are also typically not particularly interested in such investments.

Financial reporting requirements affect the ways that many institutional investors establish their investment policies. Unfortunately, such reporting considerations sometimes cause institutions to establish investment policies that, in the long run, may not be in the best economic interest of the institution.

Selecting a Portfolio Strategy

Selecting a portfolio strategy that is consistent with the objectives and policy guidelines of the client or institution is the third step in the investment management process. We describe the various types of portfolio strategies later.

Selecting Assets

Once a portfolio strategy is chosen, the next step is to select the specific assets to be included in the portfolio. This requires an evaluation of individual securities, which will include trying to identify mispriced securities. It is in this phase that the investment manager attempts to construct an *efficient* portfolio. An efficient portfolio is one that provides the greatest *expected* return for a given level of risk, or, equivalently, the lowest risk for a given *expected* return.

Measuring and Evaluating Performance

The measurement and evaluation of investment performance is the last step in the investment management process. Actually, it is misleading to say that it is the last step, as the investment process is never ended—it is ongoing. This step, however, involves measuring the performance of the portfolio, then evaluating that performance relative to some benchmark or bogey.

While a portfolio manager's performance may look superior to the performance of a benchmark portfolio, this does not necessarily mean that a portfolio satisfies its investment objective. Suppose, for example, that a financial institution establishes as its objective the maximization of portfolio return, and it then allocates 75% of a fund to stocks and the balance to bonds. Suppose further that the portfolio manager responsible for the stock portfolio earns a return over a one-year horizon that is considerably higher than the established benchmark portfolio. Assuming that the risk of the portfolio is similar to that of the benchmark portfolio, we would say that the portfolio manager outperformed the benchmark portfolio. If, despite this performance, the financial institution cannot meet its liabilities, however, it has failed to meet its established investment objectives.

OVERVIEW OF FIXED INCOME PORTFOLIO MANAGEMENT

Given this background, let us now look at the area of concern to us in this book—fixed income portfolio management.

Active Management Strategies

The range of active fixed income portfolio management strategies is wide and immensely varied. To establish a basis for discussion, we can identify three broad categories. Keep in mind, however, that this general categorization serves merely a pedagogical function. In practice, strategies are subject to significant combination and permutation.

The first category includes strategies that seek to benefit from temporary market price disequilibriums. As bonds trade over time, it may happen that switching from one bond to another will result in either a price appreciation or increased return. A bond may be swapped or exchanged, for example, for another that is identical in all respects except for price. In effect, a lower-priced bond is acquired by selling off the identical bond with a higher price. In a similar approach, instead of exploiting a price discrepancy, differences in yield may be sought. More complicated strategies include evaluating the perceived normal spread relationship between two segments of the bond market. When these relationships become distorted, a trade may be made in anticipation of re-establishment of a normal spread. Such a strategy would result in a capital appreciation as the price of the acquired security conforms to the "correct" spread.

A basic assumption of this sort of analysis is a belief that some "correction" in bond price or yield will occur before overall market conditions change the underlying relationship. This premise is akin to the stock valuation assumption that the price of an undervalued stock will reach its proper valuation before the overall influence of the market changes the relationships among groups of stocks, thus mitigating the superior return of the undervalued stock. The focus of this type of analysis is on the unique characteristics of bonds, particularly those relating to creditworthiness, and individual bond valuation is stressed apart from the expectations of the overall market. The period of time over which the undervaluation is corrected is called the "work-out time." It is over this horizon that the effects of market influences are assumed to be insignificant. We can call this approach the *valuation approach* to bond analysis.[1]

A second management strategy focuses on the effects of overall changes in the market environment, whose prime component is overall changes in interest rates. The key is to anticipate the direction of changes in interest rates. When rates are projected to drop, the longer maturities are sought in order to maximize capital appreciation. While maximum enhancement of total return can be achieved, forecasting interest rate movements consistently is extremely difficult to achieve.

---

[1] This parallels closely the process of achieving the "alpha" or risk-adjusted return in stock valuation terms. This component is sought independent of the effect of overall market movements; its emphasis is on analysis of individual bonds relative to each other. The problems are proper timing of a swap before market conditions swamp its potential and the need to make a large number of swaps to achieve a meaningful contribution to return.

The third approach is actually a combination method of evaluating the previous two. Bond sensitivity analysis combines the influences of unique bond characteristics and the effect of market environment changes so that unique characteristics can be evaluated in the context of overall market influence. To overcome the difficulty in interest rate forecasting, multi-scenario projections may be used to test the behavior of securities in response to alternative outlooks.

Passive Management Strategies

Basic to all passive portfolio management strategies is the minimal expectational input required. In fact, this is the distinguishing feature of passive compared to active strategies. Minimizing expectational requirements limits the total return potential but enhances the ability to be responsive to other needs of the client. That is, seeking the maximum return is tempered by other client-specified requisites.

As the ability to generate expectational inputs is the key to active management strategies, the possibility of fulfilling alternative investment objectives is the measure for passive approaches. The diversity of these other objectives suggests that there may need to be a variety of strategies to accommodate these alternatives. Furthermore, as the needs of the client change, so will the requirements of passive approaches.

Finally, no single strategy is appropriate across the board, and the degree of client responsiveness to a strategy will vary from situation to situation. Unique risk preferences are an example. In some circumstances, a fund sponsor may be satisfied with or even require a portion of a portfolio to be committed to long-term, fixed income securities, and be satisfied by the rate of return realized by long-term bonds over a long horizon.

There are two types of passive strategies—*buy-and-hold* and *indexing*. A buy-and-hold strategy is the simplest strategy for passive portfolio management. As the term implies, securities are bought and held to maturity. The main considerations are to be assured that there will be no default and to achieve the highest yield-to-maturity possible. In the face of fluctuating or rising interest rates, a buy-and-hold approach has a potentially severe disadvantage because there will be a tendency to miss opportunities from anticipated changes in interest rates as well as subjecting the portfolio to a lag in yield-to-maturity as rates rise. Credit analysis is essential to minimize default risk. Advantages include low transactions costs, a better resolution of return over near-term horizons, and minimal expectational requirements.

An indexing or index fund strategy aims to replicate the performance of the bond market using a proxy, which is frequently a designated index. Any of the Lehman Brothers, Salomon Brothers, or Merrill Lynch bond indexes is used. Capital market theory suggests that a portfolio including every outstanding issue held in proportion to its relative market value will be the efficient portfolio. Efficiency is defined here as the least amount of risk assumed for achieving the overall market return. It follows that holding a portfolio of securities reflecting the same portfolio characteristics as the market (in the form of an "index") would result in a favorable risk/return trade-off. It is presumably difficult to outperform the index through expectational inputs, and combining securities in a portfolio with characteristics similar to the market allows capturing of the efficiency of the market. A fundamental issue in indexing is identification of the appropriate index.

Immunization and Cash Flow Matching Strategies

Immunization and cash flow matching strategies can be thought of as a hybrid of active and passive portfolio management strategies. At one extreme, they have a similarity to passive strategies in that there is minimal requirement for expectational inputs, and there are unique characteristics that allow addressing a number of investment objectives. At the other extreme, many of the same expectational inputs of active management can be integrated to enhance the expected return. Between these extremes, there is a range of alternatives.

Exhibit 1.2 provides a schematic representation. At one corner is active management, as exemplified by two specific activities, rate anticipation and sector valuation. At another corner is passive management, where risk control is the primary emphasis, as exemplified by buy-and-hold and indexing strategies.

The basic difference between active and passive management is the use of expectational inputs. Active management derives its returns from expectational inputs, and as a consequence also experiences higher expected risk. Passive management, in contrast, emphasizes risk control; the expected return may be lower, but the expected associated risk is also lower because of reliance on nonexpectational inputs.

Exhibit 1.2

Fixed Income Management

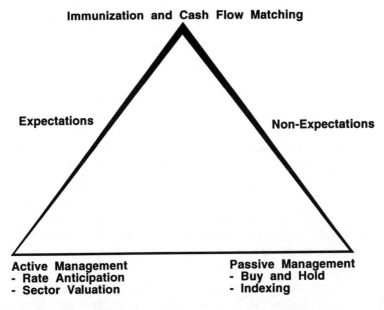

Immunization and cash flow matching management can be pursued with either emphasis, so if return maximization is the objective, using expectational inputs would be called for. Alternatively, maximum risk control immunization will make use of nonexpectational inputs.

Immunization can be defined as the process of creating a fixed income portfolio having an assured return for a specified time horizon, irrespective of interest rate changes. When a portfolio must be constructed to fund a number of liabilities over time, a hybrid management strategy known as a *dedicated portfolio strategy* is appropriate. A dedicated portfolio is a portfolio with a structure designed to fund a schedule of liabilities through portfolio return and asset value, with the portfolio's value diminishing to zero after payment of the last liability. Multi-period immunization and cash flow matching are two approaches for dedicating a portfolio.

HISTORICAL PERSPECTIVE

From a historical perspective, the early quantitative tools starting from
the 1970s were first used to support active management. Sensitivity
analysis, allowing evaluation of the implications of the expectations on
portfolio returns, became a fundamental tool in active strategies. Expected scenarios of interest rate change could be applied to the current
portfolio, and prospective returns calculated. Extensions of this analysis included evaluating the implications of the expected returns.

Quantification has traditionally been informal. It allowed the portfolio manager to pursue a more systematic and structured approach to
portfolio decision making. It is not the case that quantification requires
a foreign step. It is instead an alternative path freeing the time of the
portfolio manager. In effect, automation of a computational task allows
more time to be devoted to tasks that cannot be automated. Given the
demands on the time of the portfolio manager, quantitative methods
leverage the ability of the manager to focus on the expectational inputs
that are central to the active management process.

While the principles of portfolio immunization were conceived in
the 1930s, the widespread use of this strategy did not occur until the
1980s when the following factors came together to encourage its use.
First, relatively high interest rates in relationship to the typical actuarial
assumption used in pension plans meant that locking in a higher rate
would minimize pension contributions. Second, the application of
portfolio immunization was fostered by the relatively poor performance results of traditional active management. Finally, the practical use
of the strategy awaited a series of theoretical and empirical develop-
ments, which were realized by the 1980s.[2]

In the 1980s, the portfolio strategy tended in the direction of dura-
tion-controlled approaches.[3] Investor aversion to unexpected exposure
to changes in interest rates prompted monitoring the duration of the
portfolio to control interest rate risk. Out of this trend emerged index-

---

2 Important advances in the nature of immunized portfolios were made by Lawrence
   Fisher and Roman Weil, "Coping with Risk of Interest Rate Fluctuations: Return to
   Bondholders from Naive and Optimal Strategies," *Journal of Business* (October 1971),
   and H. Gifford Fong and Oldrich A. Vasicek, "A Risk Minimizing Strategy for
   Portfolio Immunization," *Journal of Finance* (December 1984), provided explicit risk
   measures for immunized portfolios.

3 Duration is a measure of the price sensitivity of a security or a portfolio to changes
   in interest rates.

ing, where the portfolio duration became targeted. Indexing is an extreme case of quantification which minimizes the need for expectational input.

Concurrent with the evolution of strategy over the last 25 years has been the changing role of quantitative methods. What started out as primarily a means of portfolio measurement and monitoring has become an important source of portfolio strategy.

Early applications were mere alternatives to traditional practice, which allowed the automation of basic tasks. As concern for unconstrained use of expectational inputs increased in active strategies, quantitative methods provided a way to identify new strategies that relied less on expectational inputs and focus the attention of the portfolio manager's judgment on those factors specifically deemed appropriate. For example, a targeted-duration portfolio removes interest rate forecasting from the manager's judgment yet still allows expectations to be applied in the selection of the market sector and individual bonds. However, as the use of quantitative methods has increased so has the potential for return decreased. The question now becomes, "How can we expand the horizons of return in the face of quantitative control?"

Exhibit 1.3 is a representative listing of quantitative applications to fixed income portfolio management, all of which we discuss in this book. The cornerstone of quantitative analysis has been the identification and measurement of the relevant factors that provide analytical insight into the investment management process.

OVERVIEW OF BOOK

This book is divided into three sections. In Section I, we focus on the risks associated with investing in a fixed income security and a fixed income portfolio. Chapter 2 explains the various sources of risk and return. In Chapter 3, we demonstrate how to measure two important sources of risk: interest rate risk and yield curve risk.

The three chapters in Section II are dedicated to techniques for valuing fixed income securities. The starting point for all such analysis is the term structure of interest rates. It is the term structure that provides the benchmark interest rates for the valuation of cash flows of all financial instruments. Chapter 4 explains the term structure of interest rates. Of the various valuation methodologies that are used to value securities with embedded options, Chapter 5 describes the tech-

---

Exhibit 1.3

Quantitative Applications

Active Management

Return Simulation: Predicts bond and portfolio behavior given alternative interest rate scenario projections.

Immunization

Immunization Model: Creates and maintains a portfolio that will have an assured return over a specified horizon irrespective of interest rate change.

Passive Management

Indexing System: Creates and maintains a portfolio that will track the performance of a given bond index with a manageable set of securities.

Individual Security Analysis

Swap System: Allows comparison of individual securities with the objective of identifying historical price (or basis point spread) relationships.

Term Structure Analysis: Evaluates the current level of yields by producing spot, discount, and forward rate structures. Also values Treasury securities.

Bond Valuation Model: Develops a normative value for corporate and mortgage-backed securities based on the evaluation of those characteristics of the security that contribute to overall price.

Contingent Claims Model: Evaluates the embedded option in a security without forecasting interest rates.

Other

Performance Attribution System: Calculates the total return for a bond portfolio and attributes the return to its components.

Risk Analysis Report: Calculates option-adjusted average duration, convexity, and yield for a portfolio.

nique we use, contingent claims analysis. Chapter 6 explains how contingent claims analysis is applied to mortgage-backed securities.

Portfolio management strategies are the subject of Section III. The strategies discussed are active strategies (Chapter 7); indexing (Chapter 8); and immunization, cash flow matching, and combination strategies (Chapter 9). Chapter 10 shows how interest rate derivatives (futures, options, and interest rate swaps) can be used in managing a fixed income portfolio. Models for making the asset allocation decision between equity and fixed income are explained in Chapter 11. Finally, Chapter 12 shows how to measure and evaluate the performance of a manager.

Section I

Risks Associated with Investing in a Fixed Income Security and a Fixed Income Portfolio

Chapter 2

Sources of Risk and Return

The most distinguishing features differentiating fixed income securities from equities are the priority of lien position and, generally, the size and certainty of the cash flows. Fixed income securities have specified, contractually guaranteed interest payments during the period to maturity that are typically larger, in percentage (yield) terms, than the dividends paid on stocks. They also have a defined maturity date as opposed to stocks, which have a perpetual existence. Finally, fixed income securities have relatively large assured cash flows, permitting the accommodation of particular objectives, as will be discussed throughout this book.

In this chapter we discuss the characteristics of fixed income securities that affect their risk and return parameters. In the next chapter, we explain how to measure two of these risks. An understanding of the sources of risk and how they can be measured provides the foundation for understanding how to control a portfolio's exposure to these risks and the wide range of portfolio strategies that either seek to exploit the potential returns associated with these risks or minimize the risks in attempting to accomplish an investment objective.

SOURCES OF RETURN FROM
HOLDING A BOND TO MATURITY

There are three potential sources of return from holding a fixed income security to the stated maturity date: (1) the coupon (or interest) payments, (2) capital gains or losses (i.e., price change), and (3) reinvestment income from interim cash flows that are reinvested until the original security matures.

The relative contribution of each of these components of return for a security held to maturity depends on two factors. The first is the maturity of the security. All other factors constant, the longer the maturity, the greater the relative importance of the reinvestment income. The second factor is the level at which the security is trading, in terms of the coupon rate relative to the prevailing market rate. For a bond selling at a discount from par, the contribution of reinvestment income is less than for a bond selling at a premium. The extreme case is a zero coupon bond. None of the return for this bond comes from the reinvestment income component.

Investors who buy a coupon bond and hold it to maturity face *reinvestment risk*. That is, the total amount that is realized from holding a bond to maturity is unknown, because the amount of reinvestment income that will be realized is uncertain. This amount depends on the interest rates at which interim cash flows can be reinvested. There is no uncertainty about the capital gain or loss that will be realized at the maturity date (assuming the issuer does not default). Nor is there any uncertainty about the total coupon income that will be realized if the security is a fixed-rate instrument and the issuer does not default.

The problem with the conventional yield-to-maturity as a measure of the relative attractiveness of a fixed income security is that it assumes that the coupon payments can be reinvested at a rate equal to the computed yield-maturity. That is, if the yield-to-maturity of a given bond is 8%, it is assumed that each coupon payment can be reinvested at a rate of 8%. Thus, reinvestment risk can be defined as the risk that the investor will have to reinvest any interim cash flows at a rate that is less than the computed yield-to-maturity. In addition to assuming realization of a reinvestment rate equal to the yield-to-maturity, the yield-to-maturity measure also assumes that the entire amount of any interim cash flow can be reinvested, which is not a plausible assumption for fixed income securities in a portfolio that is subject to income taxes or minimum purchase sizes. Finally, it assumes that the bond will not be redeemed prior to the stated maturity.

MARGINAL IMPACT ON RETURNS FOR SHORT-TERM INVESTMENT HORIZONS

The dominant source of fixed income portfolio return and risk arises from the effect of interest rates. Although fixed income securities derive return from the three sources described, the most important source of return and risk impact for typical management time horizons of up to two years arises from changes in interest rates over the investment horizon or holding period. As the horizon lengthens, the reinvestment return becomes the most important return source, dominating the level and change in rates as the controlling source of risk and return.

Yield Curves

A popular indicator of the level and changes in interest rates is the *yield curve* for U.S. Treasury securities, where the percentage yield is plotted as a function of maturity. Any change in rates across the maturity spectrum can be observed by comparing the position and shape of the curve for different periods.

Yield curves have several uses. Consider, for example, the change in rates between two times, as illustrated in Exhibit 2.1. At the starting time, a plot of Treasury bond yields versus term to maturity results in the curve labeled "Yield curve 1." The yield of a specific (not necessarily Treasury) bond at this time is shown at point A_1. At a later time, rates have moved to the new curve labeled "Yield curve 2," and the specific bond we are considering has shortened in maturity and increased in yield to point B_1.

We can use this basic illustration to identify the three major and one additional minor sources of the return from this bond over the period between the two yield curves. They are:

1. The return due to the yield level as the bond moves closer to maturity from point A_1 to point B_3. That is, if there is no change in either the slope or the level of the market yield curve—rep-

resented by curve 1—or in the bond's valuation relative to the market, this bond will "ride the yield curve" from A_1 to B_3.

This return source has also been called the *return from the impact of time*, because it is based on no change in interest rates, merely on the effect of the passage of time.

2. The return due to the impact of changes in the slope and/or the level of interest rates, such as from yield curve 1 to yield curve 2. This is illustrated by the movement from A_1 to B_1.

3. The return implied by the yield curve position when a cash flow must be reinvested. Suppose a coupon is paid at A_1. The return of position A_1 would be the reinvestment rate for that cash flow if it is reinvested in the same type of investment; or, if the coupon were to be held in cash equivalents, the relevant yield would be a point on the short maturity portion of yield curve 1.

4. The return due to the impact of changes in market valuation that arise from the characteristics of the bond itself. This is illustrated by the movement from A_1 to B_4 as the yield-to-ma-

Exhibit 2.1

Yield Curve Analytical Framework

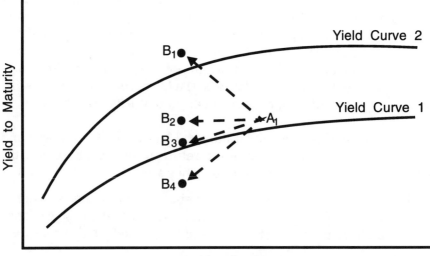

turity changes from a premium relative to the market—again represented by curve 1—to a discount, with a consequent increase in market value relative to the market. A widening of the yield premium and the consequent lower valuation relative to the market are reflected in the movement from A_1 to B_2.

Both the capital changes and the reinvestment return of fixed income assets will be directly affected by changes in interest rate levels. Interest rate changes can be characterized by various yield curve shifts, as shown in Exhibits 2.2 and 2.3. Parallel changes are those having equal basis point moves across all maturities (see Exhibit 2.2); nonparallel changes are exemplified by unequal basis point shifts (see Exhibit 2.3).

Term Structure Analysis

The term structure of interest rates is a collection of data that describes the dependence of interest rates, generally of U.S. Treasury issues, on their term to maturity date. As we explain in Chapter 4, while these data may be expressed in different forms, probably the most useful is

Exhibit 2.2

Parallel Yield Curve Shift

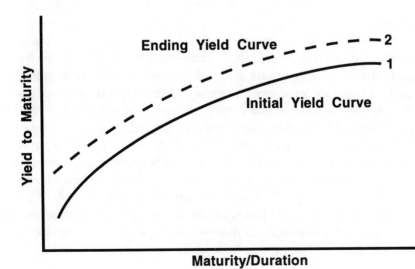

Exhibit 2.3

Nonparallel Yield Curve Shift

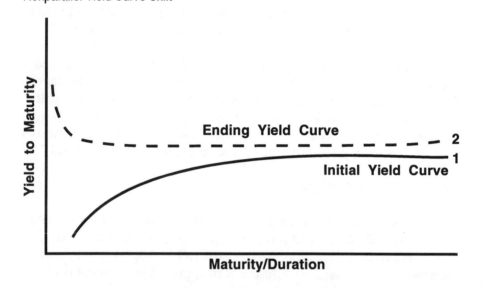

as *spot rates*. A spot rate may be defined as the yield on a pure discount (zero coupon) security. The term structure, then, may be expressed as a series of such rates for each maturity within the range of maturities of a homogeneous universe of bonds. In its most common form, the universe would be made up of default-free U.S. Treasury issues. These interest rates are, in effect, yields that have been adjusted to remove the complicating effects of coupons and default risk. The term structure also may be expressed in terms of forward rates: interest rates appropriate to the period between two future dates. Commonly, forward rates are expressed over regular intervals of time: a day, month, or year.

All of the theoretically pure spot rates located on the spot rate curve can be converted mathematically into a set of one-period spot forward rates based on the expectations theory. That is, the n-period spot rate in the term structure is equal to the compound average (nth root) of the current one-period spot rate times all the successive one-period forward rates out to the maturity of the n-period spot rate. For example, the five-year maturity spot rate would be equal to the compound average (geometric mean) of the current one-year spot rate and each of the four succeeding one-year forward rates, or the fifth root of the product of these five rates.

In effect, each of the spot rates and, taken together, all of the spot rates in the total term structure imply a continuum of the one-period future reinvestment rates that are expected at each future maturity date if the term structure created remains constant. When compounded, this continuum of forward rates or expected yields on pure discount zero coupon bonds provides the bond investor with a basic market-implicit return regardless of maturity. That is, it is the equilibrium expected compound rate of return for the entire term structure such that no maturities or payment schedules are preferred ex ante (before the fact) to any others. Why? Because it encompasses all that the market is currently requiring in the way of return across the entire spectrum of future maturities.

If this is so, how then can the market-implicit rate so derived be most effectively used? It has not been an accurate estimator of future rates in an absolute sense, but it does provide a most likely scenario for decision making. This scenario is then bracketed by less probable optimistic and pessimistic rate forecasts to produce a probability distribution of returns. The approach can also be used in sensitivity analysis measuring the effect of "what if" changes in assumed rates. This use of the term structure should provide a more comprehensive perspective of potential rate changes and can serve as the basis for further analysis, such as for bond performance analysis as discussed in Chapter 12.

Sector and Individual Security Effects

The fourth source of risk and return that we identify in the discussion of Exhibit 2.1 is the yield differences attributable to sector and individual security effects. Sectors are segments of the bond market classified on the basis of some common characteristics such as industry, maturity, issuer, or combinations thereof. Because the yield differential or "spread" (as measured by the number of basis points from a comparable U.S. Treasury) changes over time, this has been a source of incremental risk and return for fixed income portfolios. The risk/return component associated with yield spread changes can occur over holding periods ranging from several days to perhaps a few months.

Measuring Potential Return

The conventional yield-to-maturity measure does not provide insight as to the potential return from holding a bond over some investment horizon for two reasons. First, it does not take into consideration the price that the bond will have to be sold for prior to the maturity date. That price will depend on the prevailing yield on comparable bonds at that time. Second, it assumes that all coupon payments can be reinvested at the calculated yield-to-maturity.

A measure that considers reinvestment risk and interest rate risk over some investment horizon is called the *total return*. The procedure for calculating the total return requires an assumption about future reinvestment rates and the future required yield for the security at the end of the investment horizon. The total future dollars at the end of the investment horizon is then calculated on the basis of these assumptions.

The total return assuming semiannual coupon-paying bonds and an investment horizon of h semiannual periods is then either:

Total return (on a bond-equivalent yield basis) =

$$2\left[\left(\frac{\text{Total future dollars}}{\text{Purchase price} + \text{Accrued interest}}\right)^{1/h} - 1\right]$$

Total return (on a semiannual compounded basis) =

$$\left[\left(\frac{\text{Total future dollars}}{\text{Purchase price} + \text{Accrued interest}}\right)^{2/h}\right] - 1$$

FACTORS THAT HAVE HISTORICALLY DRIVEN RETURNS

Empirical studies have investigated the factors that affect the historical returns on Treasury portfolios. A study by Robert Litterman and José Scheinkman identify three factors that explain historical bond returns.[1] The first factor is changes in the level of rates; the second factor is

---

1 Robert Litterman and José Scheinkman, "Common Factors Affecting Bond Returns," *Journal of Fixed Income* (June 1991), pp. 54–61.

changes in the slope of the yield curve; and the third factor is changes in the curvature of the yield curve.

Litterman and Scheinkman use regression analysis to determine the relative contribution of these three factors in explaining the returns on zero coupon Treasury securities of different maturities. Exhibit 2.4 summarizes their results. The second column of the exhibit shows the coefficient of determination, popularly referred to as the "R-squared," for each zero coupon maturity. In general, the R-squared measures the percentage of the variance in the dependent variable explained by the

Exhibit 2.4

Factors Explaining Treasury Returns

Factor 1: Changes in the level of interest rates
Factor 2: Changes in the yield curve slope
Factor 3: Changes in the curvature of the yield curve

Zero coupon maturity	Variance of total returns explained (R^2)	Proportion of total explained variance accounted for by		
		Factor 1	Factor 2	Factor 3
6 months	99.5%	79.5%	17.2%	3.2%
1 year	99.4	89.7	10.1	.2
2 years	98.2	93.4	2.4	4.2
5 years	98.8	98.2	1.1	.7
8 years	98.7	95.4	4.6	.0
10 years	98.8	92.9	6.9	.2
14 years	98.4	86.2	11.5	2.2
18 years	95.3	80.5	14.3	5.2
Average	98.4	89.5	8.5	2.0

Source: Robert Litterman and José Scheinkman, "Common Factors Affecting Bond Returns," *Journal of Fixed Income* (June 1991), p. 58.

independent variables. The R-squared will have a value between 0% and 100%.

In this exhibit, the R-squared measures the percentage of the variance of historical returns explained by the three factors (i.e., the independent variables). The R-squared in this case is very high for all maturities, meaning that the three factors had a very strong predictive or explanatory effect.

The last three columns in Exhibit 2.4 show the relative contribution of each of the three factors in explaining the return on the zero coupon maturity bond. In the case of the 18-year zero, for example, 95.3% of the variance of the return is explained by these three factors. The first factor, changes in the level of rates, holding all other factors constant (in particular, yield curve slope), contributes about 81% of the explanatory power. For all the maturities, this factor has the greatest explanatory power, averaging about 90%. The clear implication is that a portfolio manager should control for exposure to changes in interest rates by adjusting the market risk or interest rate risk of the portfolio. For this reason it is important to have a way to measure or quantify this risk.

The second factor, changes in the yield curve slope, is the second largest contributing factor. For the 18-year zero coupon bond, the relative contribution is 14.3%. For all maturities, the average relative contribution is 8.5%. Thus, changes in the yield curve slope are, on average, about one-tenth as significant as changes in the level of rates. While this may not seem very significant, remember that Litterman and Scheinkman are examining a portfolio containing a series of Treasury zero coupon bonds, which typically have much less yield curve slope risk than securities such as collateralized mortgage obligations (CMOs). Moreover, while the relative contribution of the yield curve slope is only 8.5%, a variance of this degree can still have a significant impact on the return for a portfolio, and a portfolio manager must control for this risk.

Notice that the third factor, changes in the curvature of the yield curve, contributes relatively little to explaining historical returns. For simplicity we can therefore ignore this factor.

Michael Schumacher, Daniel Dektar, and Frank Fabozzi replicate the Litterman-Scheinkman study for mortgage-backed securities considering only two factors: changes in the level of interest rates and

Exhibit 2.5

CMO Bond Returns versus Changes in Level and Slope of the Yield Curve:
Regression Results 12/83 through 12/92

Dependent variable	R^2	Coefficients		T-statistics	
		Level	Slope	Level	Slope
Current coupon fixed-rate mortgage	79%	−4.01	−1.20	−18.5	−5.7
1-Year CMT adjustable-rate mortgage	30	−1.30	.3	−4.9	.1
Principal-only strip	64	−11.43	−2.66	−10.2	−2.4
High-coupon interest-only strip	32	12.47	1.13	5.0	.5
7-Year PAC	86	−6.70	−1.15	−14.0	−2.8
10-Year VADM	95	−8.00	−2.31	−9.6	−2.9
Short average life floater	11	− .43	− .22	−1.9	−1.1
Long average life floater	13	− .64	− .51	−1.1	− .9

Source: Michael P. Schumacher, Daniel C. Dektar, and Frank J. Fabozzi, "Yield Curve Risk of CMO Bonds," in Frank J. Fabozzi (ed.), *CMO Portfolio Management* (Summit, NJ: Frank J. Fabozzi Associates, 1994).

changes in the yield curve slope.[2] Exhibit 2.5 reports the regression results for current coupon fixed-rate passthroughs; one-year constant maturity Treasury (CMT) adjustable-rate passthroughs (ARMs); a principal-only strip; a high-coupon interest-only strip; and four CMO bonds (a seven-year PAC, a ten-year VADM, a short average life floater, and a long average life floater). The dependent variable in the regression is the return on the particular mortgage-backed security. The independent variables are the level of rates and changes in the yield curve slope. The time period studied was December 1983 through December 1992.

The second column shows the R-squared. The third and fourth columns report the estimated regression coefficient for the two factors,

2   Michael P. Schumacher, Daniel C. Dektar, and Frank J. Fabozzi, "Yield Curve Risk of CMO Bonds," in Frank J. Fabozzi (ed.), *CMO Portfolio Management* (Summit, NJ: Frank J. Fabozzi Associates, 1994).

and shown in the last two columns are the corresponding T-statistics. The results are quite interesting.

With the exception of the two floaters, the ARM, and the high-coupon interest-only strip, the R-squareds are reasonably high. While not reported here, the R-squareds for the short average life and long average life floaters have been much higher in other periods. The level and slope variables explain a very high fraction of the variance of the PAC and VADM returns.

The R-squared gives the explanatory power of the two factors collectively. The T-statistics shown in the last two columns indicate the statistical significance of each factor separately. Generally, a T-statistic with an absolute value greater than two is considered statistically significant at the 5% level of significance. The T-statistics reported for changes in the level of interest rates are statistically significant for all but the short and long average life floater. The T-statistics reported for changes in the yield curve slope are statistically significant for the PO strip, the PAC, the VADM, and the current coupon mortgage. The only instruments for which changes in the yield curve slope were not statistically significant are the IO strip, the floaters, and the ARM. These results further support the importance of yield curve risk. Thus, in addition to measures of market risk or interest rate risk, a measure to quantify yield curve risk is needed.

OVERVIEW OF RISKS ASSOCIATED WITH INVESTING IN FIXED INCOME SECURITIES

Our discussion of the factors that affect the return has introduced several risks. In this section, we discuss those risks more thoroughly and introduce several others. How several of these risks are measured is discussed in the next chapter.

Interest-Rate Risk

The price of a typical fixed income security will change in the opposite direction from a change in interest rates: As interest rates rise, the price of a bond falls.[3] If an investor has to sell a bond before the maturity date, an increase in interest rates will mean the realization of a capital

---

3 We say "typical" security, because there are bonds in the mortgage-backed sector whose prices may move in the same direction as the change in interest rates.

loss (i.e., selling the bond below the purchase price). This risk is referred to as *interest-rate risk* or *market risk*. This risk is by far the major risk that investors in the bond market face. The actual degree of sensitivity of a bond's price to changes in market interest rates depends on various characteristics of the issue, such as coupon and maturity. It also depends on any options embedded in the issue (e.g., call and put provisions).

Reinvestment Risk

As we noted earlier, the "yield" of a bond assumes that the cash flows received are reinvested at the calculated yield. The additional income from such reinvestment, sometimes called "interest-on-interest," depends upon the prevailing interest rate levels at the time of reinvestment, as well as on the reinvestment strategy. Variability in the reinvestment rate of a given strategy because of changes in market interest rates is called *reinvestment risk*. This risk is that the interest rate at which interim cash flows can be reinvested will fall below the yield calculated at the time of purchase. As we noted earlier, reinvestment risk is greater for longer holding periods, as well as for bonds with large, early cash flows, such as high-coupon bonds.

It should be noted that interest-rate risk and reinvestment risk have offsetting effects. That is, interest-rate risk is the risk that interest rates will rise, thereby reducing a bond's price. Reinvestment risk is the risk that interest rates will fall. A strategy based on these offsetting effects is called *immunization*, a topic covered in Chapter 9.

Call Risk

Many bonds include a provision that allows the issuer to retire or "call" all or part of the issue before the maturity date. The issuer usually retains this right in order to have flexibility to refinance the bond in the future if the market interest rate drops below the coupon rate.

From the investor's perspective, there are three disadvantages to call provisions. First, the cash flow pattern of a callable bond is not known with certainty. Second, because the issuer will call the bond when interest rates have dropped, the investor is exposed to reinvestment risk; that is, when the bond is called the investor will have to reinvest the proceeds at lower interest rates. Finally, the capital appreciation potential of a bond will be reduced, because the price of a callable bond may not rise as much as an otherwise comparable non-callable bond.[4]

Even though the investor is usually compensated for taking call risk by means of a lower price or a higher yield, it is not easy to determine whether this compensation is sufficient. In any case, the returns from a bond with call risk can be dramatically different from those obtainable from an otherwise comparable noncallable bond. The magnitude of this risk depends upon various parameters of the call provision, as well as on market conditions. Call risk is so pervasive in bond portfolio management that many market participants consider it second only to interest-rate risk in importance. Techniques for analyzing callable bonds are presented in later chapters.

In the case of a mortgage-backed security, call risk takes the form of *prepayment risk*, the risk that homeowners prepay their mortgages. Thus, an investor in such a bond is exposed to reinvestment risk and call risk.

Yield-Curve Risk

Changes in the shape of the yield curve as well as changes in the level affect returns and therefore are a source of risk. For example, consider two Treasury portfolios. Portfolio I includes a 20-year issue, and Portfolio II a five-year and a 30-year issue. It is easy to construct the two portfolios so that they have the same interest-rate risk for a small change in the yield curve. That is, if the yield curve shifts by a small but equal amount for all maturities, the performance of the two portfolios would be the same. Note that this will not be the case if the yield curve does not shift in a parallel fashion.

For example, suppose that the yield curve shifted so that: (1) the five-year rate declined by 50 basis points; (2) the 30-year rate increased by 50 basis points; and (3) the 20-year rate did not change. These changes would result in a steepening of the yield curve. The result would be that Portfolio II would underperform Portfolio I because, as we explain in the next chapter, the price decline for the 30-year issue would more than offset the price appreciation of the five-year issue, resulting in a decline in the value of Portfolio II.

---

4 This characteristic of a callable security is referred to as "negative convexity."

Volatility Risk

The price of a bond with certain types of embedded options depends on the level of interest rates and the factors that influence the value of the embedded option. One of these factors is the expected volatility of interest rates. Specifically, the value of an option rises when expected interest rate volatility increases. In the case of a bond that is callable, or a mortgage-backed security, where the investor has granted the borrower an option, the price of the security falls, because the investor has given away a more valuable option. The risk that a change in volatility will affect the price of a bond adversely is called *volatility risk*.

Default Risk

Default risk, also referred to as *credit risk*, refers to the risk that the issuer of a bond may default, i.e., will be unable to make timely principal and interest payments on the issue. Default risk is gauged by quality ratings assigned by commercial rating companies such as Moody's Investors Service; Standard & Poor's Corporation; Duff & Phelps; and Fitch Investors Service, as well as the credit research staffs of securities firms. Because of this risk, bonds with default risk trade in the market at prices lower than comparable U. S. Treasury securities, which are considered free of default risk. In other words, a non-U.S. Treasury bond will trade in the market at a higher yield than a Treasury bond that is otherwise comparable.

Except in the case of high-yield or junk bonds, the investor is normally more concerned with the changes in perceived default risk and/or the cost associated with a given level of default risk than with the actual event of default. Even though the actual default of an issuing corporation may be highly unlikely, investors reason that a change in perceived default risk, or in the spread demanded by the market for any given level of default risk, can have an immediate impact on the value of a bond.

Exchange-Rate Risk

Our illustrations assume that the cash flows from a bond are in U.S. dollars. For bonds whose cash flows are not denominated in U.S.

dollars, there is another potential source of return: changes in the exchange rate between the U.S. dollar and the currency in which the cash flows are denominated. If the foreign currency appreciates relative to the U.S. dollar, the cash flow in U.S. dollars will be greater; the reverse is true if the foreign currency depreciates relative to the U.S. dollar.

The risk associated with a decline in the relative value of the foreign currency is called *exchange-rate* or *currency risk*. The total return for nondollar-denominated bonds can be calculated on the basis of an assumed spot exchange rate at the time of receipt of each cash flow.

Inflation Risk

Inflation risk or *purchasing-power risk* arises because of changes in the value of cash flows through the effect of inflation, as measured in terms of purchasing power. For example, if investors purchase a bond on which they can realize a coupon rate of 7%, but the rate of inflation is 8%, the purchasing power of the cash flow actually has declined. For all but floating-rate bonds, an investor is exposed to inflation risk because the interest rate the issuer promises to make is fixed for the life of the issue. To the extent that interest rates reflect the expected inflation rate, floating-rate bonds have a lower level of inflation risk.

Liquidity Risk

Liquidity or *marketability risk* depends on the likelihood that investors can sell an issue at or near its value. The primary measure of liquidity is the spread between the bid price and the ask price quoted by a dealer. The wider the dealer spread, the more the liquidity risk. Liquidity risk is not so important for an investor who plans to hold the bond until the maturity date.

PORTFOLIO RISK CHARACTERISTICS

When securities are combined in a portfolio, the risk characteristics of the portfolio will differ from those of the individual securities that constitute the portfolio. Risk can be decomposed into systematic risk and unsystematic risk. For fixed income securities, systematic risk arises from the influence of overall changes in interest rates, affecting both capital changes as well as reinvestment return. Because a change in interest rates can affect returns on all bonds, systematic risk is a pervasive characteristic of bond investing. While stocks are also exposed to systematic risk, the effects of overall market conditions are less pervasive in this case because corporate equities are far more heterogeneous than bonds. Thus stocks have much more risk specific to the individual security (unsystematic risk).

Specific or Unsystematic Risk

If interest rates do not change, and the security is held to maturity, the only source of risk in nominal terms is that of default. In this sense, then, the importance of unsystematic risk vis-á-vis systematic risk is much less for fixed income securities than for stocks. Through diversification of issuers and classes of fixed income securities, unsystematic risk can be minimized.

Another manifestation of specific risk is in the yield spread relationship that may pertain between securities. For example, a corporate bond that appears to be similar in all respects to another corporate bond but is selling at a higher yield reflects an issuing sector difference of some kind—typically in quality grade—that has gone undetected by the rating agencies. The variation in yield spread resulting from quality grade adjustments is an additional source of unsystematic risk.

By staying with high-quality securities, the risk of default or unsystematic risk can be essentially eliminated under all but the most drastic economic circumstances. For example, Treasury securities can be considered default-free. A portfolio of Treasury securities can therefore be considered as having only systematic risk and subject only to price and return variation arising out of changes in interest rates.

Market or Systematic Risk

A central issue is how one controls market or systematic risk, which is the dominant influence on marginal return, positive or negative, that is implied by a bond's current yield-to-maturity. Traditionally, systematic risk has been controlled by varying effective maturities (more accurately, durations, as discussed in the next chapter) over time. In effect, diversifying maturities provides one way to control systematic risk. Maximum systematic risk exposure as measured in terms of standard deviation of return, given a specified interest rate change, is achieved with the longest maturity (duration) portfolio. Conversely, the minimum exposure to systematic risk is achieved by a short maturity (duration) portfolio. This holds assuming there is an equal basis point move across all maturities, i.e., a parallel shift in the yield curve. If there is a nonparallel change in rates, then a closer evaluation of risk and return impact is necessary. Return simulation analysis, described in Chapter 7, is a useful tool in this case.

Another way to control systematic risk is to adopt investment strategies that seek to match maturity or duration of the securities (assets) with the investment need (liabilities) of the portfolio. By virtue of the size and certainty of cash flows, it is possible to minimize the adverse effects of systematic risk via immunization strategies, as described in Chapter 9.

To summarize, because investors who are very concerned with systematic risk can effectively immunize their bond portfolios, the only risk that remains is unsystematic risk, which can be essentially eliminated by diversifying the portfolio across a spectrum of high-quality bond issues.

Measuring Risk

As we explain in Chapter 11, suitable risk measures for asset allocation purposes are standard deviation and covariance of returns. In the context of fixed income securities, these are directly related to the volatility of interest rates. As the magnitude of interest rate change increases, so will the standard deviation of fixed income returns. Because systematic risk is attributable to changes in interest rates, this implies a need to evaluate the standard deviation of interest rate changes.

In recent years we have seen an increase in the standard deviation of bond returns, which reflects a sharp change in the riskiness of fixed income securities. If this trend indicates a long term rather than a cyclical change in the risk characteristics of these securities, investors will have to reassess the role of bonds in the investment universe. The traditional role of bonds as a "safe" asset, with low price volatility and predictable cash flow, has been clouded by recent experience. Abrupt changes in the characteristics of a class of securities like bonds, however, are difficult to forecast with implicit or explicit models.

But even though return and risk are not static phenomena, it is of some comfort to know that time has a way of smoothing out the peaks and valleys in bond market prices and returns. Risk, in particular, has a tendency to increase more slowly than return increases as the investor's time horizon is extended. Hence for investors with relatively long future time horizons, portfolio strategies allow and even encourage the inclusion of higher-return, higher-risk assets such as long-maturity bonds.

SUMMARY

In this chapter we have described the various sources of return and risk. Yield measures offer little insight into the potential return from holding a bond to its maturity or over shorter holding periods. The major source of return for a short holding period is the capital appreciation or depreciation resulting from a change in the level of interest rates. For longer holding periods, reinvestment return replaces return from capital gain or loss as the dominant factor. The potential return from holding a bond over some investment horizon can be measured by the total return.

The risks associated with investing in fixed income securities include interest-rate risk, reinvestment risk, call risk (prepayment risk in the case of mortgage-backed securities), yield-curve risk, volatility risk, default risk, exchange-rate risk, inflation risk, and liquidity risk. In the next chapter we explain how to quantify two of these risks, interest-rate risk and yield curve risk.

Understanding the risk and return characteristics of fixed income securities and portfolios that include these securities allows implementation of alternative strategies making use of these features.

Chapter 3

Measuring Interest-Rate Risk and Yield-Curve Risk

As we explained in the previous chapter, two major sources of risk are interest-rate risk and yield-curve risk. To effectively employ fixed income portfolio active strategies and to control these risks, it is necessary for a portfolio manager to be able to quantify them. In this chapter, we provide measures of interest-rate risk and yield-curve risk.

PRICE VOLATILITY CHARACTERISTICS OF OPTION-FREE BONDS

A fundamental principle of an option-free bond (that is, a bond that does not have any embedded options) is that the price of the bond changes in the opposite direction from a change in the bond's yield. Exhibit 3.1 illustrates this property for four hypothetical bonds, where the bond prices are shown assuming a par value of $100.

When the price/yield relationship for any option-free bond is graphed, it exhibits the shape shown in Exhibit 3.2. Notice that as the yield rises, the price of the option-free bond declines. However, this relationship is not linear (that is, it is not a straight line). The shape of the price/yield relationship for any option-free bond is referred to as

Exhibit 3.1

Price/Yield Relationship for Four Hypothetical Bonds

Coupon	6.00%	6.00%	9.00%	9.00%
Maturity	5	20	5	20
Yield				
4.00%	108.9826	127.3555	122.4565	168.3887
5.00	104.3760	112.5514	117.5041	150.2056
5.50	102.1600	106.0195	115.1201	142.1367
5.90	100.4276	101.1651	113.2556	136.1193
5.99	100.0427	100.1157	112.8412	134.8159
6.00	100.0000	100.0000	112.7953	134.6722
6.01	99.9574	99.8845	112.7494	134.5287
6.10	99.5746	98.8535	112.3373	133.2472
6.50	97.8944	94.4479	110.5280	127.7605
7.00	95.8417	89.3225	108.3166	121.3551
8.00	91.8891	80.2072	104.0554	109.8964

convex. The price/yield relationship that we have discussed refers to an instantaneous change in the yield.

Properties of Option-Free Bonds

Exhibit 3.3 shows the percentage price changes for the four hypothetical bonds in Exhibit 3.1 for various changes in the yield, assuming that the initial yield for all six bonds is 6%. An examination of Exhibit 3.3 reveals several properties of the price volatility of an option-free bond.

Property 1: Although the prices of all option-free bonds move in the opposite direction from the change in yield, the percentage price change is not the same for all bonds.

Property 2: For very small changes in yield, the percentage price change for a given bond is roughly the same, whether the yield increases or decreases.

Exhibit 3.2

Price/Yield Relationship

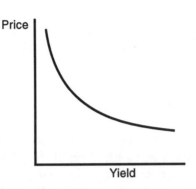

Property 3: For large changes in yield, the percentage price change is not the same for an increase in yield as it is for a decrease in yield.

Property 4: For a given change in basis points, the percentage price increase is greater than the percentage price decrease.

The implication of Property 4 is that if an investor is long a bond, the price appreciation that will be realized if the yield drops is more than the capital loss that will be realized if the yield rises by the same number of basis points. For an investor short a bond, the reverse is true: The potential capital loss is greater than the potential capital gain if the yield changes by a given number of basis points.

The reason for these four properties of bond price volatility lies in the convex shape of the price/yield relationship. We explore this in more detail later in the chapter.

Characteristics of a Bond That Affect Its Price Volatility

Two characteristics of an option-free bond determine its price volatility: coupon and term-to-maturity.

Characteristic 1: For a given term-to-maturity and initial yield, the lower the coupon rate, the greater the price volatility of a bond.

Characteristic 2: For a given coupon rate and initial yield, the longer the term-to-maturity, the greater the price volatility.

These properties can be verified by examining Exhibit 3.3.

An implication of the second characteristic is that investors who want to increase a portfolio's price volatility because they expect interest rates to fall, all other factors being constant, should hold bonds with long maturities. To reduce a portfolio's price volatility in anticipation of a rise in interest rates, bonds with shorter-term maturities should be held.

The Effects of Yield-to-Maturity

We cannot ignore the fact that credit considerations cause different bonds to trade at different yields, even if they have the same coupon and maturity. How, then, holding other factors constant, does the yield to maturity affect a bond's price volatility? As it turns out, the higher the yield to maturity that a bond trades at, the lower the price volatility.

To see this, we can compare a 6% 20-year bond initially selling at a yield of 6%, and a 6% 20-year bond initially selling at a yield of 10%.

Exhibit 3.3

Instantaneous Percentage Price Change for Four Hypothetical Bonds

Initial yield for all four bonds is 6%

	Percent price change			
New yield	*6%/5-year*	*6%/20-year*	*9%/5-year*	*9%/20-year*
4.00%	8.98%	27.36%	8.57%	25.04%
5.00	4.38	12.55	4.17	11.53
5.50	2.16	6.02	2.06	5.54
5.90	.43	1.17	.41	1.07
5.99	.04	.12	.04	.11
6.01	−.04	−.12	−.04	−.11
6.10	−.43	−1.15	−.41	−1.06
6.50	−2.11	−5.55	−2.01	−5.13
7.00	−4.16	−10.68	−3.97	−9.89
8.00	−8.11	−19.79	−7.75	−18.40

The former is initially at a price of 100, and the latter carries a price of 65.68. Now, if the yields on both bonds increase by 100 basis points, the first bond trades down by 10.68 points (10.68%). After the assumed increase in yield, the second bond will trade at a price of 59.88, for a price decline of only 5.80 (or 8.83%). Thus, we see that a bond that trades at a lower yield is more volatile in both percentage price changes and absolute price changes, as long as the other bond characteristics are the same.

An implication of this effect is that, for a given change in yields, price volatility is greater when yield levels in the market are low, and price volatility is lower when yield levels are high.

MEASURING INTEREST-RATE RISK

Now we know that coupon and maturity affect a bond's price volatility when yield changes, and that the level of interest rates affects price volatility. What is needed is a measure that encompasses these three factors that affect a bond's price volatility when yields change.

To derive such a measure, we must first express the price of a bond mathematically as follows:[1]

(1)
$$P = \frac{C}{(1+y)^1} + \frac{C}{(1+y)^2} + \cdots + \frac{C+M}{(1+y)^n}$$

where P = price
C = semiannual coupon interest (in $)
y = one-half the yield to maturity
M = maturity value (in $)
n = number of semiannual periods (number of years × 2)

We will refer to equation (1) as the "price equation."

To determine the approximate change in price for a small change in yield, the first derivative of equation (1) can be computed:

(2)
$$\frac{dP}{dy} = \frac{(-1)C}{(1+y)^2} + \frac{(-2)C}{(1+y)^3} + \cdots + \frac{(-n)(C+M)}{(1+y)^{n+1}}$$

---

1 Equation (1) assumes that the next coupon payment is exactly six months from now, and that there is no accrued interest.

Rearranging equation (2), we obtain:

(3) $$\frac{dP}{dy} = -\frac{1}{(1+y)}\left[\frac{1\,C}{(1+y)^1} + \frac{2\,C}{(1+y)^2} + \cdots + \frac{n\,(C+M)}{(1+y)^n}\right]$$

The term in brackets is the weighted average term-to-maturity of the cash flows from the bond, where the weights are the present value of the cash flow.

Equation (3) indicates the approximate dollar price change for a small change in yield. Dividing both sides of equation (3) by P gives the approximate percentage price change:

(4) $$\frac{dP}{dy}\frac{1}{P} = -\frac{1}{(1+y)}\frac{1}{P}\left[\frac{1\,C}{(1+y)^1} + \frac{2\,C}{(1+y)^2} + \cdots + \frac{n\,(C+M)}{(1+y)^n}\right]$$

The expression in the brackets divided by the price (or here multiplied by the reciprocal of the price) is commonly referred to as *Macaulay duration*.[2] That is

$$\text{Macaulay duration} = \frac{\dfrac{1\,C}{(1+y)^1} + \dfrac{2\,C}{(1+y)^2} + \cdots + \dfrac{n\,(C+M)}{(1+y)^n}}{P}$$

Substituting Macaulay duration into equation (4) for the approximate percentage price change gives:

(5) $$\frac{dP}{dy}\frac{1}{P} = -\frac{1}{(1+y)}\,\text{Macaulay duration}$$

Investors commonly refer to the ratio of Macaulay duration to $(1+y)$ as *modified duration*; that is:

(6) $$\text{Modified duration} = \frac{\text{Macaulay duration}}{(1+y)}$$

Substituting equation (6) into equation (5) gives:

---

2 Frederick Macaulay, *Some Theoretical Problems Suggested by the Movement of Interest Rates, Bond Yields, and Stock Prices in the U.S. Since 1856* (New York: National Bureau of Economic Research, 1938).

(7) $$\frac{dP}{dy}\frac{1}{P} = -\text{Modified duration}$$

Equation (7) states that modified duration is related to the approximate percentage change in price for a given change in yield. Because for all option-free bonds modified duration is positive, equation (7) states that there is an inverse relationship between modified duration and the approximate percentage change in price for a given yield change. This is to be expected from the fundamental principle that bond prices move in the opposite direction of interest rates.

Exhibit 3.4 shows the computation of the Macaulay duration and modified duration for a 9% five-year coupon bond. The duration computed in the exhibit is in terms of duration per period. Consequently, the duration is in half-years because the cash flows of the bond occur every six months. To adjust the durations to an annual figure, the duration must be divided by 2, as shown at the bottom of Exhibit 3.4.

In general, if the cash flows occur m times per year, the durations are adjusted by dividing by m. That is:

$$\text{Duration in years} = \frac{\text{Duration in m periods per year}}{m}$$

Properties of Duration

The modified duration and Macaulay duration of a coupon bond are less than the bond's maturity. The Macaulay duration of a zero coupon bond is equal to its maturity; a zero coupon bond's modified duration, however, is less than its maturity. Also, the lower the coupon, generally the greater the modified and Macaulay duration of the bond.[3]

There is a consistency between the properties of bond price volatility we showed earlier and the properties of modified duration. As explained earlier, if all other factors are constant, the longer the maturity, the greater the price volatility. A property of modified duration is that when all other factors are constant, the longer the maturity, the greater the modified duration. We also showed that the lower the coupon rate, all other factors being constant, the greater the bond price volatility. As we have just seen, generally the lower the coupon rate, the greater the modified duration. Therefore, the greater the modified

---

3 This property does not hold for long-maturity deep-discount bonds.

Exhibit 3.4

Calculation of Duration for a 9% 5-Year Bond Selling to Yield 6%

Coupon	9.00%
Maturity	5.00
Yield	6.00%

Period	Cash flow	PV at 3%	PV x t
1	$ 4.50	4.3689	4.3689
2	4.50	4.2417	8.4834
3	4.50	4.1181	12.3544
4	4.50	3.9982	15.9928
5	4.50	3.8817	19.4087
6	4.50	3.7687	22.6121
7	4.50	3.6589	25.6124
8	4.50	3.5523	28.4187
9	4.50	3.4489	31.0399
10	104.50	77.7578	777.5781
	Total	112.7953	945.8694

$$\text{Macaulay duration (in half years)} = \frac{945.8694}{112.7953} = 8.39$$

$$\text{Macaulay duration (in years)} = \frac{8.39}{2} = 4.19$$

$$\text{Modified duration} = \frac{4.19}{1.03} = 4.07$$

---

duration, the greater the price volatility. Finally, as we noted earlier, another factor that will influence the price volatility is the yield-to-maturity. All other factors constant, the higher the yield level, the lower the price volatility. This is also a property of duration.

Thus, duration (whether Macaulay or modified) is a proxy measure for the interest-rate risk exposure of a bond or a portfolio of bonds.

Using Duration to Approximate Price Change

If we multiply both sides of equation (7) by the change in the required yield (dy), we have the relationship:

$$(8) \qquad \frac{dP}{P} = -\text{Modified duration} \times dy$$

Rather than using dP and dy, we can denote small changes by the Greek letter delta, Δ:

$$(9) \qquad \frac{\Delta P}{P} = -\text{Modified duration} \times \Delta y$$

Equation (9) can be used to approximate the percentage price change for a given change in required yield.

To illustrate how to use equation (9), consider the 9% 20-year bond selling at 134.6722 to yield 6%. The Macaulay duration for this bond is 10.98 years. Modified duration is 10.66:

$$\text{Modified duration} = \frac{10.98}{(1 + .06/2)} = 10.66$$

If yields increase instantaneously from 6.00% to 6.10%, a yield change (Δy) in decimal form of +.0010, equation (9) indicates that the percentage price change is

$$-10.66 \times (+.0010) = -.01066 = -1.066\%$$

Notice from the second panel of Exhibit 3.3 that the actual percentage price change is –1.06%. Similarly, if yields decrease instantaneously from 6.00% to 5.90% (a 10-basis point decrease), equation (9) indicates that the percentage change in price would be +1.066%. From the second panel of Exhibit 3.3, the actual percentage price change would be +1.07%. This example illustrates that for small changes in yield, duration does an excellent job of approximating the percentage price change.

Instead of a small change in yield, let's assume that yields increase by 200 basis points, from 6% to 8% ($\Delta y = +.02$). The percentage change in price using equation (9) is:

$$-10.66 \times (+.02) = -.2132 = -21.32\%$$

How good is this approximation? As can be seen from the second panel of Exhibit 3.3, the actual percentage change in price is only –18.40%. Moreover, if the yield decreases by 200 basis points from 6% to 4%, the approximate percentage price change based on duration would be +21.32%, compared to an actual percentage price change of +25.04%. Thus, not only is the approximation off, but we can see that duration estimates a symmetric percentage change in price. As we pointed out earlier in this chapter, symmetry is not a property of the price/yield relationship for option-free bonds.

Exhibit 3.5 shows the approximate percentage change in price for various changes in yield for all four bonds estimated using duration. Notice that for a 100-basis point change in yield, equation (9) tells us that the percentage price change will be equal to the bond's modified duration. *Consequently, a useful working definition of modified duration is that it is the approximate percentage change in price for a 100-basis point change in yield*. Thus a bond with a modified duration of 5 will change by approximately 5% for a 100-basis point change in yield. This defini-

---

Exhibit 3.5

Estimated Percentage Price Change Based on Duration

Initial yield = 6%

New yield	6%/5-year	6%/20-year	9%/5-year	9%/20-year
4.00%	8.54%	23.12%	8.14%	21.32%
5.00	4.27	11.56	4.07	10.66
5.50	2.14	5.78	2.04	5.33
5.90	.43	1.16	.41	1.07
5.99	.04	.12	.04	.11
6.01	−.04	−.12	−.04	−.11
6.10	−.43	−1.16	−.41	−1.07
6.50	−2.14	−5.78	−2.04	−5.33
7.00	−4.27	−11.56	−4.07	−10.66
8.00	−8.54	−23.12	−8.14	−21.32

---

tion is only an approximation because, as explained earlier, for large yield changes modified duration does not do as good of a job in estimating the percentage price change.

Modified duration is a proxy for the percentage change in price. Portfolio managers also like to know the dollar price volatility of a bond. Of course, equation (2) can be used to compute the dollar price volatility. Alternatively, multiplying both sides of equation (9) by P gives:

(10) $\Delta P = -\,\text{Modified duration} \times \Delta y \times P$

The product of modified duration and the price is called *dollar duration*. That is:

(11) $\text{Dollar duration} = (\text{Modified duration}) \times P$

Thus, equation (10) can be rewritten as:

(12) $\Delta P = -\,\text{Dollar duration} \times \Delta y$

For small changes in the yield, equation (12) does a good job in estimating the change in price. When there are large movements in the yield, dollar duration or modified duration are not adequate to approximate the price reaction. Duration will overestimate the price change when the yield rises, thereby underestimating the new price. When the yield falls, duration will underestimate the price change and thereby underestimate the new price.

Convexity

Duration does a good job of estimating the actual price change only for small changes in yield. It does not capture the effect of the convexity of a bond on its price performance when yields change by more than a small amount. The duration measure can be supplemented with an additional measure to capture the curvature or convexity of a bond.

In Exhibit 3.6, a tangent line is drawn to the price/yield relationship at yield y*. The tangent shows the rate of change of price with respect to a change in interest rates at that point (yield level). The slope of the tangent line is closely related to the dollar duration. Consequently, for a given starting price, the tangent (which tells the rate of absolute price

Exhibit 3.6

Price/Yield Relationship with Tangent Line

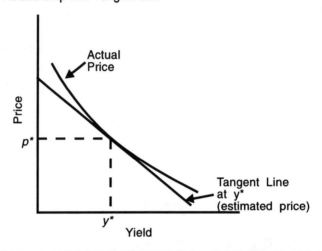

changes) is closely related to the duration of the bond (which tells about
the rate of percentage of price changes). The steeper the tangent line,
the greater the duration; the flatter the tangent line, the less the duration.

Thus, for a given starting price, the tangent line and the duration
can be used interchangeably and can be thought of as one and the same
method of estimating the rate of price changes. Notice what happens
to duration (steepness of the tangent line) as yield changes: As yield
increases (decreases), duration decreases (increases). This property
holds for all option-free bonds as we noted earlier.

If we draw a vertical line from any yield (on the horizontal axis), as
in Exhibit 3.7, the distance between the horizontal axis and the tangent
line represents the price approximated by using duration starting with
the initial yield y*. The approximation will always understate the actual
price. This agrees with what we demonstrated earlier about the relationship between duration (and the tangent line) and the approximate
price change. When yields decrease, the estimated price change will be
less than the actual price change, so the actual price will be under-es-
timated. On the other hand, when yields increase, the estimated price
change will be greater than the actual price change, resulting in an
underestimate of the actual price. For small changes in yield, the

Exhibit 3.7

Price/Yield Showing Estimation Error

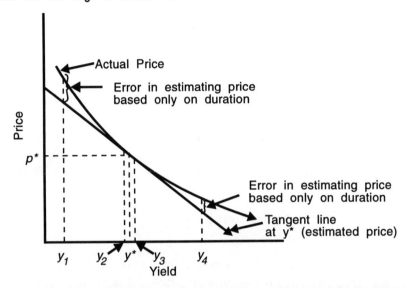

tangent line and duration do a good job in estimating the actual price, but the farther away from the initial yield y*, the worse the approximation. It should be apparent that the accuracy of the approximation depends on the convexity of the price/yield relationship for the bond.

Measuring Convexity: Duration (modified or dollar), attempts to estimate a convex relationship with a straight line (the tangent line). Is it possible to specify a mathematical relationship that provides a better approximation to the price of the bond if the required yield changes? We can use the first two terms of a Taylor series to approximate the price change as follows:[4]

$$(13) \qquad dP = \frac{dP}{dy} dy + \frac{1}{2} \frac{d^2P}{dy^2} (dy)^2 + \text{Error}$$

where $\dfrac{d^2P}{dy^2}$ = the second derivative of the price equation

---

4 A Taylor series can be used to approximate a mathematical function. Here, the mathematical function to be approximated is the price function.

Dividing both sides of equation (13) by P to get the percentage price change gives:

(14) $$\frac{dP}{P} = \frac{dP}{dy}\frac{1}{P}dy + \frac{1}{2}\frac{d^2P}{dy^2}\frac{1}{P}(dy)^2 + \frac{Error}{P}$$

The first term on the right-hand side of equation (14) is the first approximation and is the approximation based on duration.

The second term on the right-hand side of equation (14) includes the second derivative of equation (1). It is the second derivative that is used as a proxy measure for the convexity of the price/yield relationship. Market participants refer to the product of one-half and the second derivative of price as the *dollar convexity* of the bond. That is:

(15) $$\text{Dollar convexity} = \frac{1}{2}\frac{d^2P}{dy^2}$$

The product of the dollar convexity and the square of the change in the required yield indicates the estimated price change due to convexity. That is, the approximate change in price due to convexity is:

(16) $$dP = \text{Dollar convexity} \times (dy)^2$$

The dollar convexity divided by price is a measure of the percentage change in the price of the bond due to convexity, and is referred to simply as *convexity*. That is:

(17) $$\text{Convexity} = \frac{1}{2}\frac{d^2P}{dy^2}\frac{1}{P}$$

Substituting the second derivative of the price equation into equation (17) and rearranging terms, we obtain:

(18)
$$\text{Convexity} = \frac{1}{2}\frac{1}{(1+y)^2}\frac{1}{P}\left[\frac{1\,(2)\,C}{(1+y)^1} + \frac{2\,(3)\,C}{(1+y)^2} + \cdots + \frac{n(n+1)\,(C+M)}{(1+y)^n}\right]$$

The percentage price change due to convexity is:

$$(19) \qquad \frac{dP}{P} = (\text{Convexity})\,(dy)^2$$

Exhibit 3.8 shows how to calculate the convexity of the 9% five-year bond selling to yield 6%. The convexity measure is in terms of periods squared. To convert the convexity measures to an annual figure, equation (18) must be divided by 4 (which is 2 squared). In general, if the cash flows occur m times per year, convexity is adjusted to an annual figure as follows:

Exhibit 3.8

Calculation of Duration for a 9% 5-Year Bond Selling to Yield 6%

Coupon	9.00%
Maturity	5.00
Yield	6.00%

Period	Cash flow	PV at 3%	PV × t × (t+1)
1	$ 4.50	4.3689	8.7379
2	4.50	4.2417	25.4501
3	4.50	4.1181	49.4176
4	4.50	3.9982	79.9638
5	4.50	3.8817	116.4522
6	4.50	3.7687	158.2845
7	4.50	3.6589	204.8991
8	4.50	3.5523	255.7686
9	4.50	3.4489	310.3988
10	104.50	77.7578	8553.3596
	Total	112.7953	9762.7321
			20.3960
			40.792

$$\text{Convexity (in half years)} = \frac{9{,}762.7321}{2\,(1.03)^2\,112.7953} = 40.792$$

Convexity (in years) = 40.792 over 4 = 10.198

$$\text{Convexity in years} = \frac{\text{Convexity in m periods per year}}{m^2}$$

The convexity measure is measuring the rate of change of dollar duration as yields change. For all option-free bonds, duration increases as yields decline. This is a positive attribute of an option-free bond, because as yields decline, price appreciation accelerates. When yield increases, the duration for all option-free bonds will decrease. Once again, this is a positive attribute because as yields decline, this feature will mitigate the rate of the price depreciation. This is the reason why the percentage price change is greater when yields decline compared to when they increase by the same number of basis points. Thus, an option-free bond is said to have *positive convexity*.

Approximating Percentage Price Change Due to Convexity: The approximate percentage change estimated by convexity can be obtained from equation (19).[5] Replacing dP and dy with ΔP and Δy, we can rewrite equation (19) as:

(20) $$\frac{\Delta P}{P} = (\text{Convexity}) \times (\Delta y)^2$$

For example, for the 9% coupon bond maturing in 20 years, the approximate percentage price change due to convexity if the yield increases from 6% to 8% (+.02 yield change) is

$$82.053 \times (0.02)^2 = .0328 = 3.28\%$$

If the yield decreases from 6% to 4% (–.02 yield change) the approximate percentage price change due to convexity would also be 3.28%.

Using Duration and Convexity

The approximate total percentage price change based on both duration and convexity is found by simply adding the two estimates. That is:

Estimated percentage price change =
– Modified duration × Yield change
+ Convexity × (Yield change)^2

---

5   Some dealer firms such as Goldman Sachs refer to this percentage price change as the "convexity gain."

For example, if yields change from 6% to 8%, the estimated percentage price change would be:

Duration =	−21.32%
Convexity =	+ 3.28%
Total =	−18.04%

The actual percentage price change is −18.40%.

For a decrease of 200 basis points, from 6% to 8%, the approximate percentage price change would be as follows:

Duration =	+21.32%
Convexity =	+ 3.28%
Total =	+24.60%

The actual percentage price change is +25.04%.

YIELD-CURVE RISK

In the pricing equation, equation (1), we assumed that all cash flows are discounted at the same discount rate, y. But as we emphasize throughout this book, each cash flow should be discounted at a unique discount rate. Thus, the correct specification of the pricing equation is:

$$(21) \qquad P = \frac{C}{(1+y_1)^1} + \frac{C}{(1+y_2)^2} + \cdots + \frac{C+M}{(1+y_n)^n}$$

In the derivation that led to the modified duration as a measure of interest-rate risk, the first derivative with respect to yield is calculated. In equation (21), there is not one yield but a structure of yields (y_1, y_2, ..., y_n). Thus, the assumption in deriving interest-rate risk earlier is that the structure of interest rates is flat (that is, the yields for all maturities are equal) and when they do shift, the shift is a parallel one.

This assumption is commonly referred to as the "parallel yield curve shift assumption." The problem is that yield curves typically do not shift in a parallel fashion. Despite the unreality of this assumption, the impact of a nonparallel shift in the yield curve is not critical for many option-free bonds. This is not true, however, for a portfolio of bonds.

The duration of a portfolio is calculated as the weighted average duration of the portfolio. But how do we interpret the portfolio duration? It is the approximate percentage change in the portfolio when yield changes. But what yield change? If the portfolio consists of bonds across the maturity spectrum, which yield is assumed to have changed? The answer is that it is assumed that the yields for all maturities change by the same number of basis points. When they do not, two portfolios with the same duration can perform quite differently, depending on the composition of the portfolio and how the yield curve shifts.

Several methods have been suggested to measure the exposure of a portfolio to yield curve shifts.[6] One recent development in this area is known as *functional duration*. Functional duration is defined as the price sensitivity of a bond to a particular rate change, with all other rates being held constant. The t-year functional duration is the price sensitivity to a standard shift in term structure. The standard shift is represented by a triangle type shift in the term structure centered at t-year. One vertex of the triangle starts from $t - k$ year, and the other vertex ends at $t + h$ year.

The new price of the bond with a standard shift in term structure becomes

$$(22) \quad P_t' = \frac{C}{(1 + y_1)^1} + \cdots + \frac{C}{(1 + y_{t-k})^{t-k}} + \sum_{i=1}^{k} \frac{C}{(1 + y_{t-k+i} + \frac{i \cdot \Delta y}{k})^{t-k+i}}$$

$$+ \sum_{i=1}^{h} \frac{C}{(1 + y_{t+i} + \frac{(h-i) \cdot \Delta y}{h})^{t+i}} + \cdots + \frac{C + M}{(1 + y_n)^n}$$

where   C   = the semiannual coupon payment

      y_t = the spot rate for period t

---

6   See, for example, Thomas E. Klaffky, Y.Y. Ma, and Ardavan Nozari, "Managing Yield Curve Exposure: Introducing Reshaping Durations," *Journal of Fixed Income* (December 1992), pp. 5–15; Robert R. Reitano, "Non-Parallel Yield Curve Shifts and Immunization," *Journal of Portfolio Management* (Spring 1992), pp. 36–43; Thomas Y. Ho, "Key Rate Durations: Measures of Interest Rate Risks," *Journal of Fixed Income* (September 1992), pp. 29–44; and Brian D. Johnson and Kenneth R. Meyer, "Managing Yield Curve Risk in an Index Environment," *Financial Analysts Journal* (November/December 1989), pp. 51–59.

Δy = the change in spot rate for period t
M = the par value

Functional duration is measured by a formula that is the partial elasticity of price with respect to a standard shift in term structure:

$$\frac{P_t' - P}{\Delta y} \cdot \frac{1}{P}$$

In this formula P_t' and P denote the new and initial prices of the bond, which can be estimated by equations (22) and (21).

If we select (m + 1) key rates including 0-year, the sum of these (m + 1) component functional durations is exactly equal to the duration. That is,

(23)
$$\frac{\Delta P}{\Delta y} \frac{1}{P} = \sum_{t=0}^{m} \frac{P_t' - P}{\Delta y} \cdot \frac{1}{P}$$

The functional duration of a bond can be illustrated using an example. Suppose there is a bond with an 8% coupon that matures in three years. The current price of the bond is 102.6643. Suppose the initial term structure is a flat 7%. What is the price sensitivity of a bond if the two-year (four-period) rate makes a standard triangular shift as follows: the two-year (four-period) rate shifts by 100 basis points, the 1.5-year (three-period) and the 2.5-year (five-period) rate shift by 50 basis points, and all other rates remain the same. The answer to this question is the two-year functional duration of the bond.

The new price of the bond can be found using equation (22) as follows:

$$\frac{4}{(1+.035)^1} + \frac{4}{(1+.035)^2} + \frac{4}{(1+.0375)^3} + \frac{4}{(1+.040)^4} + \frac{4}{(1+.0375)^5}$$
$$+ \frac{1.04}{(1+.035)^6} = 102.5313$$

The new price of the bond becomes 102.5315. Thus the price of this bond decreases by .13%, and the functional duration of this bond for the two-year rate is .13. We can get the functional durations for three-year, one-year, and 0-year by the same method. They are 2.388, .069, and .009, respectively. The sum of these four component functional durations is 2.596. The duration of the bond is also 2.596.

Exhibit 3.9 shows the four standard shifts in term structure assumed in this example: one for the 0-year, one-year, two-year, and three-year key rates, respectively. Note that we can get a parallel shift in term structure if we add these four standard shifts together.

Duration measures the sensitivity of a bond's price to a parallel shift in the term structure curve. Functional duration measures the sensitivity of a bond price to a shift in a particular rate, the terms of which are normally defined by the terms of Treasury benchmark issues. An advantage of using the functional duration is its ability to meet any type of term structure shift, because any given term structure shift can be approximated by a linear combination of the triangular-shaped standard shifts. Therefore, the functional durations-matching strategy can outperform the simple duration-matching strategy in index tracking or immunization discussed in Chapters 8 and 9.

Exhibit 3.9

Four Standard Shifts in Term Structure of Interest Rates

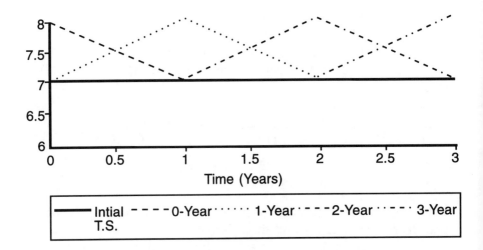

INTEREST-RATE RISK FOR BONDS WITH EMBEDDED OPTIONS

The calculation of both modified and Macaulay duration assumes that when yields change, the cash flows of a bond will *not* change. This is an unrealistic assumption for callable and putable bonds. In the case of a callable bond, a decline in the market yield below or near the coupon rate will reduce the price appreciation. This is because investors will be reluctant to pay the theoretical price based on the cash flows for a callable bond, because if the bond is called the investor will receive only the cash flow up to the call date and the call price at this date.

For example, consider a 9% 20-year bond. Suppose that this bond is callable two years from now at 105. If yields were to decline from 9% to 6%, the price of this bond if it is option-free would increase from 100 to 134.6722. Because the bond is callable, however, investors would not be willing to pay 134.6722 if the bond could be called in two years at 105. Macaulay duration or modified duration does not take any embedded option into account.

Exhibit 3.10 shows the price/yield relationship for both a noncallable bond and the same bond if it is callable. The convex curve a-a' is the price/yield relationship for the noncallable (option-free) bond. The unusual shaped curve denoted a-b is the price/yield relationship for the callable bond.

There is a reason for the shape of the price/yield relationship for the callable bond. When the prevailing market yield for comparable bonds is much higher than the coupon rate on the bond, it is unlikely that the issuer will call the bond. In option terminology, the call option is deep out-of-the-money. As the bond is unlikely to be called when it is deep out-of-the-money, a callable bond will have roughly the same price/yield relationship as a noncallable bond. Even when the option is near-the-money (the coupon rate is near the market yield), investors will not pay the same price for the bond if it is callable because there is still the chance the market yield may drop further, making it beneficial for the issuer to call the bond.

As yields in the market decline, the likelihood increases that the issuer will benefit from calling the bond. We may not know the exact yield level at which investors begin to view the issue likely to be called, but we do know that there is some level. In Exhibit 3.10, at yield levels below y*, the price/yield relationship for the callable bond departs significantly from the price/yield relationship for the noncallable

Exhibit 3.10

Noncallable and Callabale Bond Price/Yield Relationship

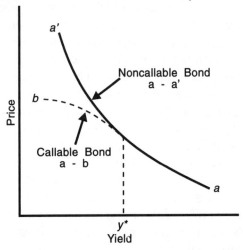

bond. Consequently, for a range of yields below y*, there is significant price compression—that is, there is limited price appreciation as yields decline. This characteristic is referred to as *negative convexity*.

DURATION AND CONVEXITY FOR ANY BOND

Market participants often create confusion about the main purpose of duration by referring to it as some measure of the weighted average life of a bond. This description comes from Macaulay's original use of duration. If you rely on this interpretation of duration, it will be difficult for you to understand why a coupon bond with a maturity of 20 years can have a duration greater than 20 years. For example, there are certain collateralized mortgage obligation (CMO) bond classes that have a duration greater than the underlying mortgage loans. That is, a CMO bond class can have a duration of 50, while the underlying mortgage loans have a maturity of 30 years. How can this happen?

The answer is that duration is the approximate percentage change in price for a small change in interest rates. In fact, a good way to keep in mind the workings of duration is that it is the approximate percentage change in price for a 100-basis point change in interest rates. Thus, subject to the drawbacks we have discussed, a bond or a portfolio with a duration of 4 should be interpreted as indicating that the price of the bond or portfolio will change by approximately 4% for a 100-basis point change in yield.

Certain CMO bond classes are leveraged instruments whose price sensitivity or duration, as a result, is a multiple of the underlying mortgage loans from which they are created. Thus, a CMO bond class with a duration of 50 does not mean the class has some type of weighted average life of 50 years. Instead, it means that for a 100-basis point change in yield that bond's price will change by roughly 50%.

We interpret the duration of a call (or put) option in the same way. A one-year call option can have a duration of 20. This is confusing to someone who interprets duration as some measure of the life of an option. What that statement means in fact is that if yields change by 100 basis points for the bond underlying the call option, the value of the call option will change by approximately 20%.

Once we understand that duration is related to percentage price change, none of the formulas given above is needed to calculate the approximate duration of a bond, or any other more complex derivative security or option. All we are interested in is the percentage price change of a bond when interest rates change by a small amount. This can be found quite easily by a three-step procedure.

1. Increase the yield on the bond by a small number of basis points, and determine the new price at this higher yield level. We denote this new price by P_+ and the new yield level as y_+.

2. Decrease the yield on the bond by the same number of basis points, and calculate the new price. We will denote this new price by P_- and the new yield level as y_-.

3. Letting P_0 be the initial price, duration can be approximated according to the formula:

$$\text{Approximate duration} = \frac{P_- - P_+}{P_0\,(y_+ - y_-)}$$

What the formula is measuring is the average percentage price change (relative to the initial price) per 1-basis point change in yield.

To see how good this approximation is, let's apply it to the 9% coupon 20-year bond trading at 6%. The initial price (P_0) is 134.6722. The steps are:

1. Increase the yield on the bond by 20 basis points from 6% to 6.2%. Thus, y_+ is .062. The new price (P_+) is 131.8439.

2. Decrease the yield on the bond by 20 basis points from 6% to 5.8%. Thus y_- is .058. The new price (P_-) is 137.5888.

3. Since the initial price, P_0, is 134.6722, the duration can be approximated as follows:

$$\text{Approximate duration} = \frac{137.5888 - 131.8439}{134.6722\,(.062 - .058)} = 10.66$$

How good is the approximation? The modified duration as calculated by equation (4) is 10.66. Thus, the approximation formula does an excellent job.

An investor interested in the duration of an option can use the same formula. However, to use the formula, it is necessary to have an option pricing model to get the new prices.

Similarly, the convexity of any bond can be approximated using the formula:

$$\text{Approximate convexity} = \frac{P_+ + P_- - 2\,P_0}{P_0\,[\,.5\,(y_+ - y_-)\,]^2}$$

The approximation formulas for duration and convexity are useful in estimating duration and convexity not only for an option-free bond, but also for a bond with an embedded option. This is accomplished by estimating what the theoretical price of a bond with an embedded option will be after allowing for the fact that the expected cash flows can change when yields change. Thus the prices P_+ and P_- are theoretical prices. We explain in Section II of this book how to obtain these theoretical values.

In general, we refer to "duration" as the sensitivity of a bond's price to yield changes. Modified duration measures price responsiveness assuming that changes in yield do not change the cash flows. This measure is appropriate for option-free bonds and bonds with embedded options where the embedded option is deep out-of-the-money (that is, when the market yield is substantially higher than the coupon rate on the callable bond). In contrast, *effective duration* assumes that changes in yield can affect cash flows and takes this into account.

The distinction between modified duration and effective duration is shown in Exhibit 3.11. The terms effective duration, option-adjusted duration, or simple adjusted duration are often used interchangeably.

SUMMARY

In this chapter, we provide measures of interest-rate risk and yield-curve risk. Duration is a measure of interest-rate risk. It does a good job of estimating the price sensitivity of a bond to small changes in yield. Duration is a linear approximation to the price/yield relationship. The convexity measure—the second term of the Taylor series—is needed to provide a more accurate measure of the price sensitivity of a bond to any change in yield.

Modified duration assumes that yield changes do not affect cash flow and therefore may be an unsuitable measure of interest-rate risk for bonds with embedded options. Effective duration allows for the cash flow to change when yield changes and therefore should be used for bonds with embedded options.

Exhibit 3.11

Modified Duration versus Effective Duration

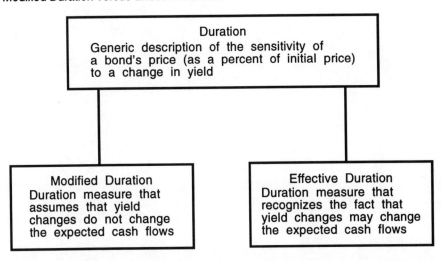

Duration does not capture the effect of nonparallel shifts in the yield curve. Functional duration can capture any type of shifts in the term structure, whether the term structure becomes steeper or flatter. Therefore, it can measure the sensitivity of price to term structure shifts more accurately, and is a better risk control tool than simple duration.

Section II

Techniques for Valuing Fixed Income Securities

Chapter 4

Bond Valuation and Term Structure Analysis

The value of any fixed income security is the present value of the expected cash flow. The cash flow is simply the dollars that are expected to be received: the sum of interest and principal repayment. Thus, the valuation of any fixed income security requires two steps: (1) estimating the cash flow, and (2) discounting each cash flow at an appropriate rate.

The traditional or conventional bond valuation process for an option-free bond (i.e., a bond with no options) is to discount *all* cash flows at the yield offered on a Treasury security with the same maturity plus an appropriate risk premium. The problem with this valuation approach even for an option-free bond is that the rate used to discount the cash flows of a coupon bond would be the same as that used to discount the cash flow of a zero coupon bond with the same maturity. Such a comparison makes little sense because the cash flow characteristics of the two are different. Because of this drawback, it is best to think of any bond as a package of cash flows, with each individual cash flow viewed as nothing more than a zero coupon instrument with the same maturity date as the date that the cash flow will be received. In these circumstances, each cash flow or zero coupon instrument is discounted at the rate that would be offered on a zero coupon Treasury instrument with a maturity equal to the maturity of the individual cash flow plus an appropriate risk premium. Thus, instead of one discount rate, we use multiple discount rates.

In our explanation of the bond valuation process, our focus is on the appropriate rate at which to discount each cash flow. To do this, we introduce the term structure of interest rates, which provides a characterization of interest rates as a function of maturity. Term structure analysis plays a prominent role in many of the fixed income management strategies that we discuss because of its role in pricing. It serves as a basis for the active management strategies described in Chapter 7, the return enhancement passive strategy described in Chapter 8, and portfolio performance evaluation described in Chapter 12. Our analysis of the traditional term structure includes discussion of the volatility of interest rates.

TERM STRUCTURE ANALYSIS

Spot Rates

The *spot interest rate* (or simply *spot rate*) of a given maturity is defined as the yield on a pure discount bond of that maturity. The spot rates are the discount rates determining the present value of a single payment at a given time in the future. Spot rates as a function of maturity are referred to as the *term structure* of interest rates.

Spot rates are not directly observable, since there are few pure discount bonds that have maturities beyond one year. Spot rates have to be estimated from the yields on actual securities by means of a term structure model. Each actual coupon bond can be considered a package of discount bonds, namely, one for each of the coupon payments and one for the principal payment. The price of each component discount bond is equal to the amount of the payment discounted by the spot rate of the maturity corresponding to this payment. The price of the coupon bond is then the sum of the prices of these component discount bonds.

The yield-to-maturity on a coupon bond is the internal rate of return of the bond payments, or the discount rate that would make the present value of the payments the same as the bond price. The yield, then, can be viewed as a mixture of spot rates of various maturities. To calculate the yield, each bond payment is discounted by the same rate, rather than by the spot rate corresponding to the maturity of that payment. Decomposing the actual yields on coupon bonds into the spot rates is the principal task of a term structure model.

Forward Rates

Spot rates describe the term structure by specifying the current interest rate of any given maturity. The implications of the current spot rates for future rates can be described in terms of *forward rates*. Forward rates are the one-period future reinvestment rates implied by the current term structure of spot rates.

Mathematically, if R_1, R_2, R_3 ... are the current spot rates, the forward rate F_t for period t is given by the equation

$$(1) \qquad 1 + F_t = \frac{(1 + R_t)^t}{(1 + R_{t-1})^{t-1}} \qquad t = 1, 2, 3, \cdots$$

This equation means that the forward rate for a given period in the future is the marginal rate of return from making an investment in a discount bond for one more period. By definition, the forward rate for the first period is equal to the one-period spot rate, $F_1 = R_1$.

The relationship of spot and forward rates described by equation (1) can also be stated:

$$(2) \qquad (1 + R_t)^t = (1 + F_1)(1 + F_2) \cdots (1 + F_t)$$

This equation shows that spot rates are obtained by compounding the forward rates over the term of the spot rate. Thus, the forward rate F_t can be interpreted as the interest rate over the period from $t - 1$ to t that is implicit in the current structure of spot rates.

Just as the forward rates are determined by the spot rates using equation (1), the spot rates can be obtained from the forward rates by equation (2). Thus, either the spot rates or the forward rates can be taken as alternative forms of describing the term structure. The choice depends on which of the two equivalent characterizations is more convenient for the particular purpose. Spot rates describe interest rates over periods from the current date to a given future date. Forward rates describe interest rates over one-period intervals in the future.

Discount Function

There is a third way of characterizing the term structure, namely, by means of the discount function. The discount function specifies the present value of a single payment in the future. It is thus the price of a pure discount riskless bond of a given maturity. The discount function D_t is related to the spot rate by the equation

(3) $$D_t = \frac{1}{(1 + R_t)^t}$$

and to the forward rates by the equation

(4) $$D_t = \frac{1}{(1 + F_1)(1 + F_2) \cdots (1 + F_t)}$$

The discount function D_t considered in continuous time t is a smooth curve decreasing from the starting value $D_0 = 1$ for $t = 0$ (since the value of one dollar now is one dollar) to zero for longer and longer maturities. It typically has an exponential shape.

While the discount function is usually more difficult to interpret as a description of the structure of interest rates than either the spot rates or the forward rates, it is useful in estimation of the term structure from bond prices. The reason is that bond prices can be expressed in a very simple way in terms of the discount function; that is, as the sum of the payments multiplied by their present value. In terms of the spot or forward rates, bond prices are a more complicated (nonlinear) function of the values of the rates to be estimated.

Market-Implicit Forecasts

The concept of forward rates is closely related to that of *market-implicit forecasts*. The market-implicit forecast $M_{t,s}$ of a rate of maturity s as of a given future date t is the rate that would equate the total return from an investment at the spot rate R_t for t periods reinvested at the rate $M_{t,s}$ for additional s periods, with the straight investment for $t + s$ periods at the current spot rate R_{t+s}. Mathematically, this can be written as:

(5) $$(1 + R_t)^t (1 + M_{t,s})^s = (1 + R_{t+s})^{t+s}$$

The market-implicit forecasts can be viewed as a forecast of future spot rates by the aggregate of market participants. Suppose that the current one-year rate is 6%, and that there is a general agreement among investors that the one-year rate a year from now will be 7.8%. Then the current two-year spot rate will be 6.9%, because

$$(1 + .06)(1 + .078) = (1 + .069)^2$$

The two-year rate would be set in such a way that the two-year security return matches the return of rolling over a one-year security for two years. There may not be such a general agreement as to the future rate, and in any case the forecast would not be directly observable. Knowing the current one-year and two-year spot rates, however, enables us to determine the future rate for the second year that would make the two-year bond equivalent in terms of total return to a rollover of a one-year bond. This rate is the market-implicit forecast.

The definition of the market-implicit forecasts as given by equation (5) may be clearer if stated in terms of the forward rates, as in the equation:

(6) $$(1 + M_{t,s})^s = (1 + F_{t+1})(1 + F_{t+2}) \ldots (1 + F_{t+s})$$

Specifically, the market-implicit forecast of the one-period rate is equal to the forward rate for that period,

$$M_{t,1} = F_{t+1}$$

From equation (6) you can see that the market-implicit forecast is obtained by compounding the forward rates over the period starting at the date of the forecasting horizon and extending for an interval corresponding to the term of the forecasted rate. In other words, the market-implicit forecast corresponds to the scenario of no change in the forward rates. The current spot rates then change by rolling along the forward rate series.

One last thing to mention about the market-implicit forecasts is that because it is a forecast of the future spot rates, we can also infer from it the corresponding forecast of yields, discount functions, and all other characterizations of the future term structure. The current and future term structures have the forward rates as the one common denominator, which makes the forward rates the basic building blocks of the structure of interest rates.

TERM STRUCTURE MODELING

The objective in empirical estimation of the term structure is to fit a spot rate curve (or any other equivalent description of the term structure, such as the discount function) that (1) fits the data sufficiently well, and (2) is a sufficiently smooth function. The second requirement, being less quantifiable than the first, is less often stated. It is nevertheless at least as important as the first, particularly because it is possible to achieve an arbitrary good (or even perfect) fit if the empirical model is given enough degrees of freedom, with the consequence that the resulting term structure makes little sense.[1]

A commonly used procedure to estimate the term structure is a simple "bootstrapping" technique. This is a nonstatistical technique that uses only on-the-run Treasury securities. For example, consider a hypothetical on-the-run yield curve, assuming for simplicity annual-pay full-coupon par bonds:

Maturity	Yield to maturity	Market value
1 year	3.50%	100
2 years	4.00%	100
3 years	4.50%	100

The one-year spot rate is the same as the yield-to-maturity, 3.5%. The two-year spot rate is found as follows. Since the coupon rate for the two-year Treasury is 4%, the cash flow per $100 par value (again, assuming annual-pay) is $4 one year from now and $104 two years from now. The theoretical price for this bond is the present value of the two cash flows discounted at the corresponding spot rates; that is:

$$\frac{4}{(1.035)} + \frac{104}{(1 + R_2)^2}$$

Notice that the first cash flow is discounted at the one-year spot rate and the second cash flow is discounted at the unknown two-year spot rate (R_2). By equating the theoretical price to the observed (market)

---

1 For a discussion of this point, see Terence C. Langetieg and Stephen J. Smoot, "An Appraisal of Alternative Spline Methodologies for Estimating the Term Structure of Interest Rates," working paper, University of Southern California, December 1981.

price of $100, and then solving for R_2, a value of 4.01% for the two-year spot rate is obtained.

Similarly, the three-year spot rate can be obtained by using the three-year bond's cash flows ($4.50 in year 1, $4.50 in year 2, and $104.50 in year 3) and discounting the cash flows by the appropriate spot rate; that is:

$$\frac{4.50}{(1.035)} + \frac{4.50}{(1+.041)^2} + \frac{104.50}{(1+R_3)^3}$$

By equating the theoretical price to the observed (market) price of $100 and then solving for R_3, a value of 4.541% for the three-year spot rate is obtained.

While the bootstrapping approach is used as a quick approximation, it fails to satisfy the objectives mentioned earlier. Moreover, it fails to recognize the information in Treasury prices other than the on-the-run issues.

Several statistical methodologies have been proposed to estimate the term structure of interest rates.[2] The statistical methodology developed by Vasicek and Fong is used in the applications throughout this book.[3] The methodology is explained in Appendix A.

This approach can be termed an exponential spline fitting. The methodology has been applied to historical price data on U.S. Treasury securities with satisfactory results, and it produces forward rates that are a smooth continuous function of time. The model has desirable asymptotic properties for long maturities, and exhibits both enough flexibility to fit a wide variety of shapes of the term structure and enough robustness to produce stable forward rate curves. An adjustment for the effect of taxes and for call features on U.S. Treasury bonds is included.

The term structure model was used to analyze the term structure for Treasury issues on November 30, 1990. There were a total of 234 bonds analyzed, but only 218 used because there were 16 outliers. The coefficient of determination for the estimated model was 99.91% and

---

2   Willard F. Carleton and Ian Cooper, "Estimation and Uses of the Term Structure of Interest Rates," *Journal of Finance* (September 1976), pp. 1067–1083; J. Huston McCulloch, "Measuring the Term Structure of Interest Rates," *Journal of Business* (January 1971), pp. 19–31; and McCulloch, "The Tax Adjusted Yield Curve," *Journal of Finance* (June 1975), pp. 811–830.

3   Oldrich A. Vasicek and H. Gifford Fong, "Term Structure Modeling Using Exponential Splines," *Journal of Finance* (May 1982), pp. 339–348.

the residual standard error of price was $ .338. Exhibit 4.1 shows the yield for the actual prices on November 30, 1990, and the yield for the fitted prices. Exhibits 4.2, 4.3, and 4.4 show the estimated discount function, spot rates, and one-month forward rates, respectively.

VOLATILITY AS A DETERMINANT
OF RISK AND RETURN

The volatility of interest rates is not a constant quantity. It changes through time. In some periods the bond market is very volatile, with interest rates changing drastically from day to day or from hour to hour. At other times, the fixed income markets are fairly quiet, with only gradual changes in interest rates. Typically, rates are more volatile when their level is high; there is less volatility in periods of generally low interest rates. The level of rates alone, however, does not explain the difference in volatility.

Volatility is the degree to which interest rates fluctuate from period to period. Specifically, we define volatility as the variance (or its square root, the standard deviation) of the changes in the short interest rate, expressed on an annualized basis.

Volatility is one of the elements making up the price, and hence return, of fixed income securities. Indeed, inspection of the literature on the behavior of the term structure of interest rates shows the presence of a volatility parameter in the bond pricing formula.

Term Structure Models Incorporating
the Dynamics of the Short Rate

Models of the term structure are formulated in terms of how they describe the dynamics of the short rate; that is, they specify how the short rate changes for small changes in the underlying variables that affect its value. The short rate is a *random* or *stochastic variable* because its value over time changes in an uncertain way.

A random variable can be classified as either a *continuous variable* or a *discrete variable*. A continuous variable is one that has no break. For example, consider the random variable of interest, the short rate. Suppose that the short rate can be between 0% and 25% and that it can take on any value within the range of probable outcomes. Thus, in moving from, say, 3% to 4%, the short rate can take on a value of

Exhibit 4.1

Actual and Fitted Yields (%)

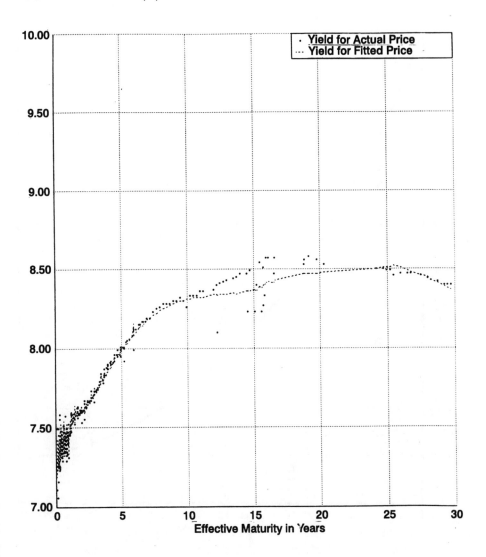

U.S. Treasury issues, 11-30-90

Exhibit 4.2

Discount Function—U.S. Treasury Issues, 11-30-90

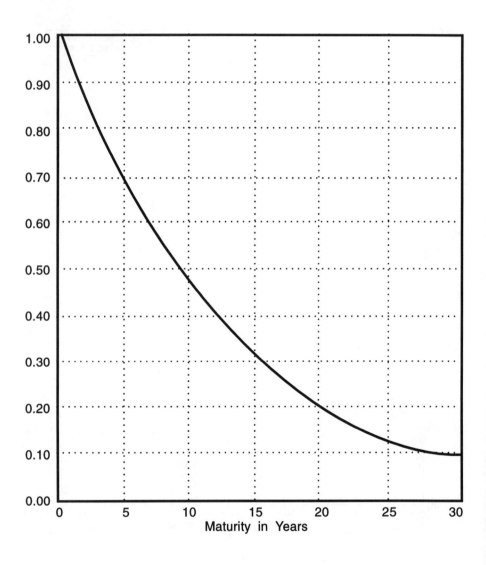

Exhibit 4.3

Spot Rates (%)

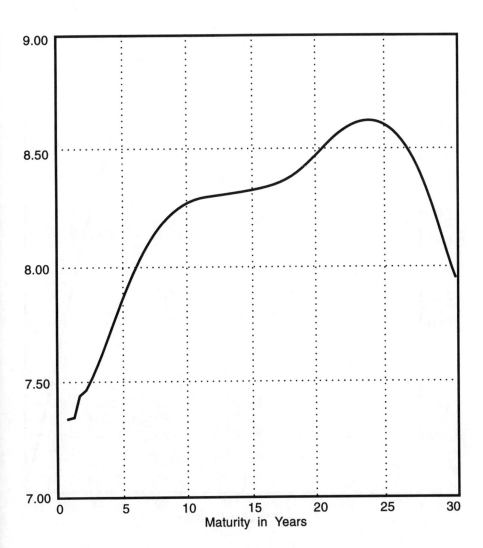

Maturity in Years

U.S. Treasury issues, 11-30-90

Exhibit 4.4

One-Month Forward Rates

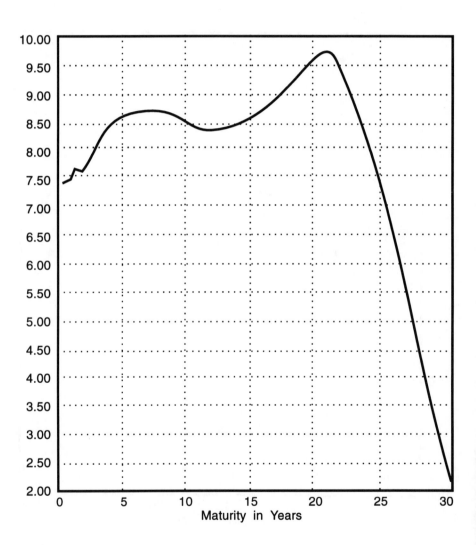

U.S. Treasury issues, 11-30-90

3.79217%. A discrete variable, by contrast, has breaks or jumps. For example, if in moving from 3% to 4% the short rate is restricted to taking on only values in 20-basis point increments (i.e., 3.2%, 3.4%, 3.6%, and 3.8%), it would be classified as a discrete variable. In the development of the models in this chapter and the next two, we shall assume that the random variables are continuous.

While the value of the short rate at some future time is uncertain, the pattern by which it changes over time can be assumed. In statistical terminology, this pattern or behavior is called a *stochastic process* or *probability distribution*. Thus, when we say that it is necessary to describe the dynamics of the short rate, we mean that it is necessary to specify the stochastic process that describes the movement of the short rate.

Stochastic processes can be classified according to when the value of the random variable can change. When the value of the random variable can change only at any fixed points in time, the stochastic process that describes the random process is called a *discrete-time stochastic process*. If, however, the random variable can change at any point in time (no matter how small the time interval), the stochastic process is called a *continuous-time stochastic process*.

In the models that we describe in this and the next chapter, we assume a continuous-time stochastic process; that is, we assume continuous trading. By assuming that the random variable is continuous and that the stochastic process is a continuous-time stochastic process, we allow the use of calculus to derive important results.

A simple stochastic process for describing the dynamics of the short rate is a *standard Wiener process*. It is expressed in equation form as:

$$(7) \qquad\qquad dr = b\, dt + \sigma\, dx$$

where dr = change in the short rate
       b   = expected direction of rate change
       dt = length of time interval
       σ = standard deviation of changes in the short rate
       dx = random process

Equation (7) states that the change in the short rate (dr) over a very small interval of time (dt) depends on the expected direction of the change in the short rate (b) and a random process (dx). The expected direction of the change in rate (b) is called the *drift rate*. The random nature of the change in the short rate comes from the random variable x in equation (7).

In a standard Wiener process it is assumed that the random variable x over a very small time interval is normally distributed with a mean of zero and a standard deviation of one.[4] The change in the short rate will then be proportional to the value for the random variable, the proportionality depending on the standard deviation of the changes in the short rate (σ). It is also assumed that changes in the short rate for any two different short intervals of time are independent.

Given these assumptions, two properties of the standard Wiener process follow. First, the expected value of the change in the short rate is equal to the drift rate (b). If the drift rate is assumed to be equal to zero, this means that the expected value of the change in the short rate is zero, and therefore the expected value for the short rate is its current value. The second property is that the variance of the change in the short rate over some interval of T is equal to T, and its standard deviation is the square root of T.

A special case of the standard Wiener process is to assume that both the drift rate and the standard deviation of the change in the short rate are a function of (i.e., depend on) the level of the short rate and time. This is expressed as follows:

$$(8) \qquad dr = b(r,t)\,dt + \sigma\,(r,t)\,dx$$

where all the symbols are the same as in equation (7). The notation $b(r,t)$ means that the drift rate depends on the short rate r and time t. Similarly, $\sigma\,(r,t)$ means that the standard deviation of the change in the short rate depends on the short rate and time. This special case of the standard Wiener process as formulated in equation (8) is called an *Ito process*.

Specification of the Drift Rate: In the Ito process to describe changes in the short rate over time, we assume that the drift rate is specified in a particular manner. Specifically, the drift rate is assumed to follow a *mean-reversion process* as described below:

$$b(r,t) = \alpha(\bar{r} - r)$$

---

4   Statistically, this means that x is drawn from a standardized normal distribution.

where α = the speed of adjustment
$\bar{r}$ = the long-run stable mean of the short rate

The mean-reverting process in the drift term drives the short rate to converge toward its long-run stable mean with the appropriate speed of adjustment (α).

Alternative Specifications of Volatility: There are three models suggested in the literature to describe the dynamics of the short rate. While these models differ in specification of the random component, the variance of some function of the short rate [$\sigma(r,t)$] is assumed to be a constant, and this constant then enters into the corresponding pricing equation. These three models are:

Vasicek specification:[5] $\sigma(r,t) = \sigma$
Cox-Ingersoll-Ross specification:[6] $\sigma(r,t) = \sigma\sqrt{r}$
Dothan specification:[7] $\sigma(r,t) = \sigma r$

The specification that we use throughout this book is the one specified by Cox, Ingersoll, and Ross (CIR). The square-root specification in the stochastic term shows that negative interest rates are precluded, and the variance of the process increases with the short rate. For the drift rate, we will assume it is mean-reverting as described earlier. Thus, the stochastic process that we assume for the short rate is:

(9) $$dr = \alpha(\bar{r} - r)\,dt + \sigma\sqrt{r}\,dx$$

This model is sometimes referred to as the *mean-reverting square-root diffusion process*. This assumed stochastic process of the short rate has been shown to be a reasonable approximation of interest rate behavior.

---

5 Oldrich A. Vasicek, "An Equilibrium Characterization of the Term Structure," *Journal of Financial Economics* (1977), pp. 177–188.

6 John C. Cox, Jonathan E. Ingersoll, Jr., and Stephen A. Ross, "A Theory of the Term Structure of Interest Rates," *Econometrica* (1985), pp. 385–407.

7 L. U. Dothan, "On the Term Structure of Interest Rates," *Journal of Financial Economics* (1978), pp. 385–407.

Why Bond Prices Should Depend on Interest Rate Volatility

It is not difficult to understand why bond prices should depend on interest rate volatility. Securities are not priced in a vacuum; rather, they are priced against investment alternatives. One possible alternative to a term bond is rolling over a short instrument for the same time span.

The rate of return R_{roll} on such a rollover strategy is given by

$$1 + R_{roll} = [(1 + r_1)(1 + r_2) \ldots (1 + r_n)]^{1/n}$$

where $r_1, r_2, \ldots, r_n$ are the holding-period rates of return on the short instrument. The rollover strategy rate of return is the geometric average of the rates of return realized on the short instrument.

It is known that the geometric average never exceeds the arithmetic average (which is the expected short rate level). Moreover, the difference is small if there is little fluctuation in the short rates $r_1, r_2, \ldots, r_n$ and large if there is a lot of variability. Consequently, the return on the rollover strategy is inversely related to the variability of the short rate.

The return on the term bond must be in an equilibrium relationship with the return on the rollover strategy. The term bond yield will be low when the volatility of the short rate is high, and high if the volatility is low. The bond price is thus an increasing function of volatility.

If the price of straight default-free bonds depends on volatility, the same is true with equal force for callable bonds, mortgage-backed securities, futures contracts, and other instruments with embedded options. All option pricing results, starting with the well-known Black-Scholes formula, show strong dependence of the option price on the variance of the underlying process. The available theories of the term structure of interest rates all show the presence of a volatility parameter in the bond pricing formula.[8]

The practical impact of these considerations is that if volatility increases unexpectedly, the price of a fixed income instrument with a positive volatility exposure will instantly increase for a capital gain. An

---

8 See, for example, Vasicek, "An Equilibrium Characterization of the Term Structure"; Cox, Ingersoll, and Ross, "A Theory of the Term Structure of Interest Rates"; Dothan, "On the Term Structure of Interest Rates"; D. Heath, R. Jarrow, and A. Morton, "Bond Pricing and the Term Structure of Interest Rates: A New Methodology," working paper, Cornell University, 1988; and Michael J. Brennan and Eduardo S. Schwartz, "A Continuous Time Approach to the Pricing of Bonds," *Journal of Banking and Finance* (1979), pp. 133–155.

unexpected decrease in the interest rate volatility will generate a capital loss. If the volatility exposure of an investor's portfolio differs from that of a bond index or other benchmark of performance, the capital gains or losses will not match those of the benchmark, and may result in substandard performance. Like changes in the interest rate level, a change in volatility of rates is a source of risk and return.

Note that it is not possible to obtain a meaningful volatility exposure measure from a term structure model in which volatility is a deterministic parameter, rather than a stochastic factor. Varying the parameter to determine the price sensitivity would violate the assumptions of the model that the parameter is constant, and would therefore invalidate its conclusions.

A STOCHASTIC VOLATILITY TERM STRUCTURE

In one term structure theory, the stochastic factors are the short rate and its instantaneous variance.[9] The exposure of security prices to each of the factors is determined, resulting in identification of duration and the volatility exposure as the dual measures of risk and return. In later chapters we show the implications of this theory and discuss its applications.

Incorporating Volatility into the Term Structure

We know that term structure theory is concerned with the characterization of the behavior of interest rates. Its starting point is to identify those quantities that are the stochastic (random) factors that explain the movement of interest rates. The stochastic processes that govern the behavior of the factors need then to be specified in a formulation that is a reasonable approximation of their actual behavior. The next step in the development of a term structure theory consists of deriving an equilibrium condition that precludes the possibility of riskless arbitrage, and specifying the nature of the risk premiums associated with these factors.

This typically results in a partial differential equation for the bond price. For the theory to be practical, it is desirable that a closed-form

---

9 This model was first introduced by H. Gifford Fong and Oldrich A. Vasicek, "Interest-Rate Volatility as a Stochastic Factor," Gifford Fong Associates, February 1991.

solution be achievable. The exposure of the bond price to the stochastic factors can then be evaluated, allowing quantification of the risk measures. Finally, the pricing should be extended to more complex instruments, such as interest rate-contingent claims.

The stochastic volatility term structure (SVTS) describes the behavior of the short rate r by a diffusion process

(10) $dr = \alpha\,(\bar{r} - r)\,dt + \sqrt{v}\;dx$

where dr = change in the short rate
       α = speed of reversion to the mean r
       $\bar{r}$ = long-term mean of the short rate
       dt = change in time
       v   = instantaneous variance (volatility)
       dx = random element

This equation describes the short rate as a continuous process with a tendency to revert to a long-term mean value. The strength of this tendency is proportional to its current deviation from the mean. Thus, high rates have a tendency to come down, while low rates tend to go up. Extremely high or extremely low rates have a stronger tendency to move toward the average value than moderately high or moderately low rates.

In all cases, however, there is a random component associated with the change in interest rates, which can make high rates go even higher or low rates go even lower. The magnitude of this random component is described by its variance $v = \sigma^2$.

If the variance v is a constant, as previous models have assumed, a one-factor (short rate) description of the term structure can be derived. In the SVTS specification, the variance (volatility) v is a second stochastic factor, described by the equation:

(11) $dv = \gamma\,(\bar{v} - v)\,dt + \xi\,\sqrt{v}\;dy$

where dv = change in volatility
       γ = speed of reversion to mean $\bar{v}$
       $\bar{v}$ = long-term average volatility
       dt = change in time
       $\xi^2 v$ = instantaneous variance
       dy = random element

Similar in form to the short rate equation (10), the volatility equation (11) also has a mean-reverting tendency with strength proportional to the current deviation from the mean level. Unlike the equation for the short rate, however, the random component has a variance proportional to the current level of volatility. This means that very quiet markets, while likely to become more volatile in time, typically will not do so abruptly; very unstable markets are likely to calm down suddenly, or to become even more volatile.

In addition, the random element dx of the short rate and the random element dy of the volatility can be correlated with a correlation coefficient ρ. Thus, increasing levels of rates are typically accompanied by an increase in their volatility and vice versa, as indeed happens in reality.

Under this two-factor description of the term structure, the price P = P(t,r,v) of a zero coupon bond with term t is subject to the equation

$$(12) \qquad \frac{dP}{P} = \mu\,dt - \phi\,dx + \psi\,dy$$

where μ = expected return of the bond
  dt = change in time
  ϕ = component of the return variance due to rate change
  dx = random process for the rate change
  ψ = component of the return variance due to volatility change
  dy = random process for the volatility change

In words, the price change of a bond is a function of the nominal expected return of the bond less a component attributable to the rate change plus a component attributable to the volatility change.

Applying an arbitrage argument to the equation for price leads to the equilibrium condition

$$(13) \qquad \mu = r + q\,\phi + p\,\psi$$

where μ = expected return
  r = short rate
  q = market price of risk attributable to interest rate changes
  ϕ = component of the return variance attributable to rate changes

p   = market price of risk attributable to volatility changes
ψ   = component of the return variance attributable to
      volatility changes

This equation states that the expected return on the term bond is equal to the short rate plus two risk premiums corresponding to the two sources of uncertainty. The market prices of risk q and p are assumed to be proportional to the risk level $\sigma = \sqrt{v}$.

Equations (10) through (13) are the basic elements determining the SVTS. They are used to construct a partial differential equation that determines the price of the bond.

The solution of the partial differential equation has the form:

(14) $P(t,r,v) = \exp\left[-rD(t) + vF(t) + G(t)\right]$

where $P(t,r,v)$ = price of a zero coupon bond with term t, given the current values r for the rate level, and v for the volatility level.

The quantities $D(t)$, $F(t)$, and $G(t)$ in equation (14) are functions of the term t alone. They are obtained as the solutions of ordinary differential equations to which the partial differential equation reduces.

In particular, the function $D(t)$ is given by

(15) $D(t) = (1 - e^{-\alpha t})/\alpha$

The functions $F(t)$ and $G(t)$ are given by more complicated (but closed-form) expressions. The exact formulas are not produced here.[10]

We should point out that the form of the bond pricing equation (14) as well as specification of the functions D, F, and G are deduced from the condition of market efficiency, rather than simply declared. This provides a theoretically consistent framework that goes beyond the intuitive description that is commonly the first and only step in many term structure formulations.

The term structure of interest rates is determined from the pricing equation (14). If we define $R(t,r,v)$ as the spot rate of term t, then

(16) $R(t,r,v) = rD(t)/t - vF(t)/t - G(t)/t$

---

10 The functions $F(t)$ and $G(t)$ involve confluent hypergeometric functions. The exact formulas can be found in Fong and Vasicek, "Interest-Rate Volatility as a Stochastic Factor."

Equation (16) describes the behavior of interest rates as a function of the term and the development in time of the two stochastic factors r and v. The resulting spot rate curves can be monotonic or have one or two humps.

Exhibits 4.5, 4.6, and 4.7 depict the shapes of the spot rate curves for several values of the parameters. Note in particular in Exhibit 4.7 that the SVTS allows for the possibility of different yield curves when both the short and the long ends of the curves are fixed, which cannot happen in a single-factor model.

Volatility Exposure Measure

As we explained in the previous chapter, exposure measures for factors that affect price must be developed. Since volatility is a factor affecting price, we seek to derive such a measure.

From the form of the solution for the bond price in equation (14) we note that

$$(17) \qquad D(t) = -\frac{1}{P}\frac{\partial P}{\partial r}$$

Exhibit 4.5

Term Structure of Interest Rates for Different Values of the Short Rate

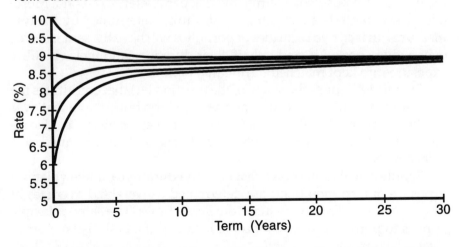

Exhibit 4.6

Term Structure of Interest Rates for Different Values of Risk Premium

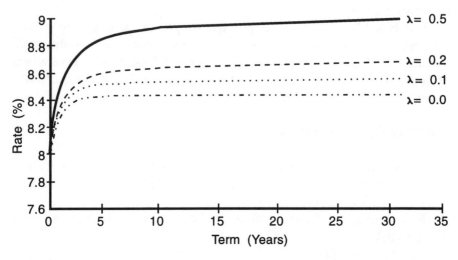

$$F(t) = -\frac{1}{P}\frac{\partial P}{\partial v} \tag{18}$$

The quantities D and F are thus the rate exposure (i.e., duration) and the exposure to volatility, respectively. Together, the duration and the volatility exposure constitute the risk parameters of a bond. Moreover, the expected rate of return is also fully determined by the two measures. In fact, two securities or portfolios will have the same returns over a given period if, and only if, their durations and their volatility exposures are kept matched during that period.

Exhibit 4.8 depicts the shape of the function F(t) that constitutes the measure of volatility exposure for a zero coupon bond. Note that over most of its range it is a concave function, unlike, for instance, Macaulay's duration or convexity (which are linear and convex quadratic, respectively).

Simple calculation shows that both the duration and the volatility exposure of a coupon bond are determined as weighted averages of those corresponding to the individual cash flows. The same principle applies to portfolios of fixed income instruments: Both risk measures

Exhibit 4.7

Term Structure of Interest Rates for Different Values of Current Volatility

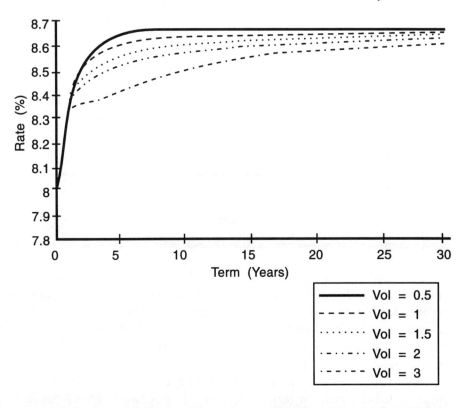

combine linearly as a function of the market value of the portfolio components.

SUMMARY

This chapter explains the bond valuation process. The process involves the estimation of a bond's cash flow and the discounting of each cash flow at an appropriate rate. Determination of the appropriate default-free rates that should be used to discount cash flows is the focus of the chapter.

Exhibit 4.8

Volatility Exposure

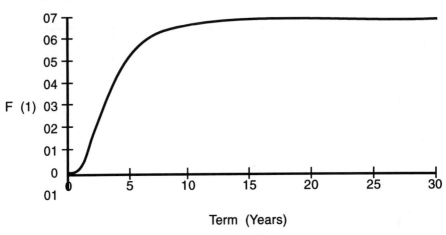

Term (Years)

The spot rate of a given maturity is defined as the yield on a zero coupon bond of that maturity. The term structure of interest rates is represented by the relationship between spot rates and maturity. It is the spot rates that should be used to discount default-free cash flows. While not directly observable, spot rates can be estimated from the yields on actual securities by using a term structure model.

Forward rates are one-period future reinvestment rates that are implied by the current term structure of spot rates. Spot rates and forward rates are related. Specifically, spot rates are obtained by compounding the forward rates over the term of the spot rate. The concept of forward rates is closely related to that of market-implicit forecasts, which can be viewed as a forecast of future spot rates by the aggregate of market participants.

Another way of characterizing the term structure is through the discount function. It specifies the present value of a single payment in the future, and is therefore the price of a pure discount riskless bond of a given maturity.

A commonly used procedure to estimate the term structure is a simple "bootstrapping" technique. This is a nonstatistical technique that uses only on-the-run Treasury securities. Several statistical methodologies have been proposed to estimate the term structure of interest rates from all Treasury securities.

Models of the term structure are formulated in terms of how they specify the short rate changes for small changes in the underlying variables that affect its value. While the value of the short rate at some future time is uncertain, the stochastic process by which it changes over time can be assumed. Volatility is defined as the variance (or the standard deviation) of the changes in the short interest rate, expressed on an annualized basis. The three models suggested in the literature to describe the dynamics of the short rate that we review in this chapter are one-factor models.

While these three models differ in their specification of the random component, the variance of some function of the short rate is assumed to be a constant. In contrast, the stochastic volatility term structure assumes that the variance of the short rate is a second stochastic factor.

Chapter 5
Contingent Claims Analysis

Interest rate-contingent claims are fixed-income securities whose cash flows are conditional on the interest rate environment because of some option features. Perhaps the best-known example of a security subject to contingent claims is a callable bond. Neither the timing nor the amount of interest and principal payments on a callable bond is known with certainty because the bond can be called (paid off) at the issuer's option at any time (after some protection period). If interest rates drop by some amount, it is to the issuer's advantage to pay bondholders off and refinance the debt at lower rates. This option always works against the investor, so a callable bond will sell at lower prices than an otherwise equivalent noncallable bond. Correctly pricing contingent claim securities is one of the goals of *contingent claims analysis.*

A callable bond has a different response to interest rate changes than an equivalent noncallable bond. The response of a fixed-income security to rate changes is customarily described in terms of its duration, which measures price elasticity with respect to yield. Callable bonds typically have a shorter duration than noncallable bonds. As interest rates decline, the duration of callable bonds may also decline (even during the protection period) as the probability of future calls increases. The rate of change in duration per change in yields is measured by the security's convexity. Evaluation of duration and convexity are further goals of the analysis of contingent claims.

Securities other than callable bonds may be subject to contingent claims. Corporate bonds with sinking fund provisions, for example, often allow the issuer to accelerate repayment of the debt. Extendable and retractable bonds give bondholders an option (so they sell at a price premium); other bonds carry an option to reinvest the coupon at a fixed price. Mortgage-backed securities (passthroughs, collateralized mortgage obligations, and stripped mortgage-backed securities) are prime examples of contingent claims: As rates decline, holders of the underlying mortgages are likely to prepay, altering the expected cash flows.

The liabilities of a pension plan or an insurance company can similarly behave like contingent claims. For instance, single-premium deferred annuities typically provide options to withdraw funds or to invest additional funds at guaranteed rates. In the case of whole life policies, an option allows the policyholder to borrow against the policy at a specified interest rate. Depending on future interest rates, these options may or may not be exercised. If the insurance company tries to match its assets to its liabilities, it must have a means of evaluating the contingent features in both.

The purpose of this chapter is to explain contingent claims valuation analysis. The framework is then applied to the valuation of callable corporate bonds. In the next chapter, the same model is applied to the valuation of mortgage-backed securities.

ASSUMPTIONS IN CONTINGENT CLAIMS MODELS

The proper analysis of contingent claims must recognize the stochastic, or probabilistic, nature of the contingencies. A traditional way of dealing with callable bonds, however, has been to apply the yield-to-worst approach. This involves calculating the yield to each call date as well as to maturity, and taking as the effective maturity the date for which the yield is the lowest. This approach is appropriate only if interest rates never change. In the real world, where future rates are uncertain, it produces patently incorrect answers.

A fairly simple way of characterizing the behavior of interest rates is to assume as in the previous chapter that the term structure of rates is driven by a single factor, which can be assumed to be the instantaneous spot rate (a very short rate). This spot rate moves over time to keep pulling the short rate toward its long-term mean; a stochastic element causes it to fluctuate around the mean level. This is the mean-reverting square root diffusion process given by equation (9) in Chapter 4.

Once the parameters of the process governing the short rate are specified, the behavior of interest rates of all maturities follows from a term structure equation describing market equilibrium. This description of the term structure of interest rates also governs the pricing of noncontingent fixed income securities, such as noncallable bonds. If the market is efficient in the sense that it is impossible to realize arbitrage profits with no investment and no risk, the pricing of contingent claims must be related to the pricing of noncontingent claims. To derive this relationship in the form of a contingent claim model, we make three explicit assumptions:

1. The value of the security depends only on current and future interest rates.

2. The interest rate structure is described by a stochastic process driven by the short rate.

3. No profitable riskless arbitrage is possible.

These assumptions allow development of a model that can be used for valuation of contingent claims and for determining their risk characteristics, most importantly the duration and convexity.

THE VALUATION MODEL

In an efficient market, the value of a security is determined by the factors that influence its behavior. Any interest rate-dependent security, including contingent claims, can be valued by an equation that relates the value of that security to interest rates. The valuation equation is:

(1) $$\frac{\delta P}{\delta t} + [\alpha(\bar{r} - r) - q\,r]\frac{\delta P}{\delta r} + \frac{1}{2}\sigma^2\,r\,\frac{\delta^2 V}{\delta r^2} + C - r\,P = 0$$

where $P = P(r,t)$, the value of the security as a function of interest rates and time; r is the short rate; α and σ^2 are the speed of adjustment and variance, respectively, of the short rate; q is the market price of risk (the expected excess return on any security divided by its systematic risk); and C is the coupon rate on the security.

The parameters α, $\bar{r}$, and σ^2 come from the stochastic process of interest rates described in the previous chapter. The market risk parameter q is a utility-dependent measure from the general equilibrium characteristics with the assumption of a logarithmic utility function as specified in Cox, Ingersoll, and Ross.[1] The cash flow term, C, may characterize the specific types of interest rate-dependent securities. For instance, when C is zero, P is the price of pure discount bonds; when C is the coupon rate, P is the price of regular coupon bonds.

Equation (1) is a partial differential equation of second order in two variables: the short rate and time. The short rate drives the term structure development, and time characterizes the maturing of the security. The equation indicates that a portfolio of discount bonds that is constructed to be perfectly, instantaneously correlated with the security and to have the same risk will also have the same expected return. In other words, the market price of risk is the same for all securities. This is the essence of efficient market pricing.

A partial differential equation must be further specified for a solution. To obtain the solution for a particular contingent claim, three characteristics of the security must be specified:

1. The cash flows.

2. The boundary conditions.

3. The embedded options.

The cash flow specification simply describes the contractual payments on the security, possibly as a function of the state of the security. For example, the cash flows on a callable bond are equal to the coupon payments for as long as the bond has not been called, and zero after the bond has been called.

The boundary conditions specify the value of the security at maturity and at extreme rate levels. For a callable bond, the value at maturity is the face amount, and its value for infinitely high interest rates is zero.

---

1   John C. Cox, Jonathan E. Ingersoll, Jr., and Stephen A. Ross, "A Theory of the Term Structure of Interest Rates," _Econometrica_ (1985), pp. 385–407.

The option functions express the relationship of the value of the security at any date at which an option may be executed to its value immediately following option exercise. For a callable bond, this is the smaller of the call price at any call date and the value of the bond if it is not called.

For callable bonds, these three characteristics are often easy to specify. Once they are specified, contingent claims analysis becomes a mathematical problem: Solve the partial differential equation subject to these particular conditions. The solution is the security value as a function of rates. Duration and convexity can then be calculated from the first and second derivatives of that function with respect to rates.

It is rarely possible to solve the equation in a closed analytical form. The famous Black and Scholes option pricing model for stock calls and puts is one instance where there is an analytical solution.[2] The formula comes from a partial differential equation similar to the valuation equation. The difference is that the Black-Scholes equation and its corresponding boundary conditions are much simpler because the governing stochastic process is more tractable.

Specifically, in the case of a fixed income security, price cannot exceed the undiscounted value of the cash flows, or negative interest rates would be realized. In the Black-Scholes model, the source of the random element is the value of the stock, which follows a logarithmic random walk, a relatively simple process. The valuation of interest rate-dependent claims requires dealing with interest rate behavior, which is more complicated. Finally, equity options are much more simple than callable securities, where it is necessary to deal with a whole series of call dates and prices.

The valuation equation may be solved numerically using the finite difference method. To do that, a grid is set up of the two state variables (namely, time and rate), and the differentials are replaced by a set of linear equations. These equations are solved iteratively, starting with the boundary conditions and exercising the option at each available time.[3]

---

2 Fischer Black and Myron Scholes, "The Pricing of Options and Corporate Liabilities," *Journal of Political Economy* (1973), pp. 637–654.

3 For a discussion of finite difference methods, see Michael J. Brennan and Eduardo S. Schwartz, "Finite Difference Methods and Jump Processes Arising in the Pricing of Contingent Claims: A Synthesis," *Journal of Financial and Quantitative Analysis* (September 1978), pp. 642–674; and George Courtadon, "A More Accurate Finite Difference Approximation for the Valuation of Options," *Journal of Financial and Quantitative Analysis* (December 1982),pp. 697–705.

An Interpretation

While the mathematics looks complicated, the idea is simple. We can illustrate it using callable bonds.

Consider a callable bond at maturity. The value of the bond at that time is simply the principal plus the last coupon payment (remember that the value of the bond includes accrued interest). This is independent of the interest rates then prevailing. Now consider the bond just before maturity. As a function of rates then in effect, the value of the bond would be the maturity value discounted by each level of the short rate. If such a value is higher than the price at which the bond can be called, however, the issuer would call the bond and pay only the call price plus the accrued interest. We therefore need to truncate the value (as a function of rates) by the call price to arrive at the value of the bond just prior to maturity.

Now let us move another short period back in time (two short intervals prior to maturity). We know what the bond would be worth a short while later as a function of interest rates then. Depending on rates now, and knowing how rates can move over the next short interval, we can value the bond as a function of current rates. This valuation involves determining the expected value at the next period (expected values are affected by convexities, so these have to be considered), and discounting it to the present by rates that include a risk premium. This risk premium depends on the risk of the bond, which must therefore be simultaneously evaluated. This will then give us the value of the bond at that time if not called, expressed as a function of interest rates. Again, this value is overridden whenever it is higher than the call price.

Solving the equation with its boundary and option conditions is the same as repeating this process from the maturity date backward to the present. At each particular time, the value of the bond immediately afterward is already known (as a function of interest rates). The value at each earlier time is then obtained by (1) evaluating the expected value resulting from rate movements (including the convexity effect, which corresponds to the second derivative in the equation), (2) discounting at each rate level together with the risk premium, (3) adding cash flows on payment dates, and (4) executing the option (that is, truncating the bond value at the then-applicable call price). When this process gets us to the actual current date, we have arrived at the value of the callable bond. The first and second derivatives of that value as a function of rates then provide the duration and convexity. This will accomplish the goals of the analysis.

Implementation

This methodology is implemented using a computer program that solves the valuation equation by numerical methods. Depending on the type of the contingent claim to be valued, the cash flows, the boundary conditions, and the option functions supplied. It is also necessary to specify the parameters of the interest rate structure, including the market price of risk.

There are several practical considerations to observe in order to reach a solution with sufficient accuracy. Some are purely technical, such as transforming the interest rate variable to reduce the infinite range to finite intervals. Others are more fundamental. It is useful, for instance, to value an appropriate noncontingent security together with the contingent claim and derive the value of the option as the difference. That is, the value of the embedded call is expressed as the difference between the value of the callable bond and a noncallable equivalent. This will make the solution less dependent on the assumed interest rate structure.

In the case of mortgage-backed securities, valuation must take into account the behavioral aspects of mortgage prepayments. Unless these are included in the statement of the problem, an options model will assume that mortgages are always prepaid whenever the borrower can refinance at a lower rate. In fact, some people prepay their mortgages even if current rates are high (when they move, for example), while others fail to prepay even when rates drop below their current interest rate. These conditions can be accommodated by incorporating empirically estimated prepayment patterns in addition to the strictly rational option pricing as explained in the next chapter.

While valuation necessitates a careful analysis of the particular class of contingent securities, the general methodology is extremely powerful. With proper application, it allows meaningful valuation of interest rate-contingent claims.

VALUING CALLABLE CORPORATE BONDS

Now let's apply the contingent claim valuation framework to the valuation of callable corporate bonds. The factors that affect the value of corporate bonds are (1) the structure of the cash flows, and (2) the risk-adjusted term structure of interest rates. By the structure of the cash flows we mean the coupon, the maturity, any sinking fund provisions and whether those provisions are mandatory or optional, and any embedded options such as a call or a put. By the risk-adjusted term structure of interest rates we mean the default-free term structure and the credit spread.

Decomposing a Callable Corporate Bond's Value

The value of a callable corporate bond can be decomposed as follows:

$$(2) \qquad\qquad P_{CB} = P_{NCE} - V - W$$

where P_{CB} = the value of a callable corporate bond
P_{NCE} = the value of a default-free noncallable equivalent bond
V = the value of the embedded call option
W = the value of credit risk

Thus, there are three components that must be valued to determine the value of a callable corporate bond: (1) the value of a default-free noncallable equivalent bond, (2) the value of the embedded call option, and (3) the value of credit risk.

The first component can be calculated by the traditional model, which calculates the sum of the present values of the noncallable bond cash flows discounted by the default-free spot rates estimated by the term structure model.

The value of the embedded call option is equal to the price of the noncallable equivalent bond less the price of the callable bond. The prices of both the noncallable equivalent bond and the callable bond are estimated by the contingent claims model.

The advantage of equation (2) in valuing a callable bond is as follows. The traditional model is very powerful in projecting the price of a noncallable bond, while the contingent claims model is better able to predict the value of the embedded call option than the traditional model. Equation (2) combines the best of both the traditional model and the contingent claims model.

The value of credit risk is measured by the difference between the value of the default-free noncallable equivalent bond and the value of the noncallable equivalent bond. The value of the former is simply the sum of the present values of the cash flows discounted by the default-free term structure. The value of the latter is the sum of the present values of the cash flows discounted by the credit-adjusted theoretical term structure. The credit-adjusted theoretical term structure is constructed by adding the credit spread, which compensates for the credit risk, to the theoretical term structure. The theoretical term structure commonly used is derived using the Cox, Ingersoll, and Ross model explained in the previous chapter.

The question is the credit spread to use. For unseasoned issues, the appropriate choice is the new issue spread from dealers. For seasoned issues, a market-implied credit spread is used.

The procedure for estimating the market-implied credit spread is as follows: (1) select a corporate bond index such as Lehman Brothers Corporate Bond Index; (2) group the bonds according to the sector/quality classifications; (3) determine the credit spread for each bond (explained in the next section); and (4) then find the average credit spread for each sector/quality. This average credit spread is the market-implied credit spread.

The Option-Adjusted Spread

Contingent claims analysis can also be cast in terms of yields rather than value. For a noncallable bond, the credit risk yield premium is simply the difference between the actual yield on the bond and a Treasury equivalent yield. For a callable bond, the credit risk yield premium, also called the option-adjusted spread, is the difference between a noncallable equivalent yield and the Treasury yield.

Estimating the option-adjusted spread takes two steps: (1) find the internal spread; and (2) transform the internal spread into the yield spread.

First we find the value of the internal spread, s, that makes the theoretical price of the bond equal to the market price of the bond:

$$(3) \qquad P_A = {}_{TM(t,s)}P_{NCE} - \left[{}_{CCM(t,s)}P_{NCE} - {}_{CCM(t,s)}P_{CALL} \right]$$

where P_A = the market price of the bond
     $_{TM(t,s)}P_{NCE}$ = the price of a noncallable equivalent bond
                   estimated by the traditional model
     $_{CCM(t,s)}P_{NCE}$ = the price of a noncallable equivalent bond
                   estimated by the contingent claims model
     $_{CCM(t,s)}P_{CALL}$ = the price of a callable bond estimated by the
                   contingent claims model
     s   = the internal spread

To determine the internal spread, s, we shift both observed and theoretical spot rate curves in a parallel fashion until the theoretical price is equal to the market price. This requires an iterative process until the condition is satisfied.

The second step is to transform the internal spread into the yield spread. Given the internal spread, the price of the noncallable equivalent bond, $_{TM(t,s)}P_{NCE}$, is known. The price of the default-free noncallable equivalent bond, $_{TM(t,0)}P_{NCE}$, is also known. Then, assuming a semiannual coupon-paying bond, we find the yields that correspond to these two prices by the equation:

$$(4) \quad P = \frac{C}{(1+y)^1} + \frac{C}{(1+y)^2} + \frac{C}{(1+y)^3} + \cdots + \frac{C+M}{(1+y)^n}$$

where P = the price of the bond
       C = the semiannual coupon payment
       y = yield of the bond divided by 2
       M = the par value
       n = number of coupon payments

Substituting $_{TM(t,s)}P_{NCE}$ and $_{TM(t,0)}P_{NCE}$ for P in equation (4), we find the yield for the noncallable equivalent bond, y_s, and the yield for the default-free noncallable equivalent bond, y_{df}. The option-adjusted spread is the difference between these two yields, $y_s - y_{df}$.

Note that for a callable corporate bond, the option-adjusted spread includes both a call risk premium and a credit risk spread. For a noncallable corporate bond, the option-adjusted spread is simply equal to the credit risk spread.

Exhibit 5.1 shows the relationship between the price of the bond and the option-adjusted spread. In Exhibit 5.1, the value of credit risk is measured by the difference between $_{TM(t,0)}P_{NCE}$ and $_{TM(t,s)}P_{NCE}$. The

Exhibit 5.1

Option-Adjusted Spread

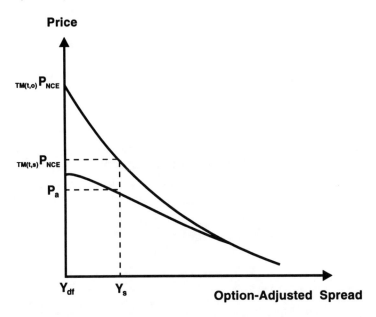

value of the embedded call option is measured by the difference between $_{TM(t,s)}P_{NCE}$ and P_A.

Effective Duration and Convexity

We noted earlier some drawbacks of the standard duration and convexity measure. One drawback is that it assumes that cash flows are not affected by the level of interest rates. Certainly this is an unrealistic assumption for securities with embedded options, except for deep out-of-the-money options. The solution is to estimate *effective* duration by allowing the cash flow to change when interest rates are shifted up or down in a parallel fashion by a small number of basis points, and then calculating the percentage change in price.

In the case of callable corporate bonds, the effective duration and convexity can be calculated by moving the credit-adjusted spot curve up and down by a small number of basis points, then determining the change in the present value of the callable cash flows.

APPLICATIONS

Contingent claims analysis has several applications. First, it provides for better control of the effective duration and convexity than the traditional modified duration, which does not recognize the interest rate-dependent nature of the cash flows. Evidence of this advantage will be seen in the immunization, dedication, and indexing strategies that we discuss in later chapters, as well as in performance evaluation. Second, the identification of mispriced securities with embedded options (rich/cheap analysis) requires a contingent claims framework. Finally, in the case of private placements, a valuation model is needed to ensure that the lender is properly compensated for the risks of holding a callable corporate issue. The contingent claims model can be used to determine how changing the call structure (such as the protection period and the call price) and changing the coupon rate influence the bond value.

Chapter 6

Valuation of Mortgage-Backed Securities

In the previous chapter, we focused on the application of contingent claims theory to the valuation of corporate bonds. In this chapter we look at how this theory can be applied to the valuation of mortgage-backed securities (passthroughs, stripped mortgage-backed securities, and collateralized mortgage obligations). The major difficulty in pricing mortgage-backed securities is the uncertainty of cash flows, because mortgagors can prepay their loans at any time before maturity without a prepayment penalty. The mortgage-backed security investor would then receive the scheduled payment, which consists of the coupon interest and the principal amortization, plus any additional prepayment of principal in the pool. Fortunately, principal prepayment behaviors are not purely random. Prepayments tend to increase, and the duration of the mortgage-backed security tends to shorten, when interest rates are falling. Thus, actual prepayment is dependent on interest rates. Prepayment systematically lowers return and increases investor risk, which ultimately affects the security's value.

The main issue in pricing mortgage-backed securities, therefore, is how to treat the uncertain cash flows and how to express the premium that an investor should demand as fair compensation for the extra risk from the unscheduled prepayments. This chapter describes a framework for valuing mortgage-backed securities that is based on contingent claims pricing theory. We begin with an overview of mortgages and mortgage-backed securities.

MORTGAGES

A mortgage is a loan secured by some specified real estate collateral that obliges the borrower to make a predetermined series of payments. The mortgage gives the lender *(mortgagee)* the right, if the borrower (the *mortgager*) defaults (i.e., fails to make the contracted payments), to "foreclose" on the loan and seize the property in order to ensure that the debt is paid off. The interest rate on the mortgage loan is called the *mortgage rate.* A loan based on the credit of the borrower and on the collateral for the mortgage is said to be a *conventional mortgage.* The lender also may take out mortgage insurance to guarantee the fulfillment of the borrower's obligations.

The types of real estate properties that can be mortgaged are divided into two broad categories: residential and nonresidential properties. The first category includes houses, condominiums, cooperatives, and apartments. Residential real estate can be subdivided into single-family (one- to four-family) structures and multi-family structures (apartment buildings in which more than four families reside). Nonresidential property includes commercial and farm properties. Our focus in this chapter is on residential mortgage loans.

A borrower can select from many types of mortgage loans. These include level-payment fixed-rate fully amortized mortgages, adjustable-rate mortgages, graduated-payment mortgages, growing equity mortgages, balloon mortgages, two-step mortgages, fixed-rate tiered payment mortgages, and fixed/adjustable-rate mortgage hybrids. Below we describe just the first two mortgage designs in order to demonstrate the basic principles that will be encountered in a pool of mortgages.[1]

Level-Payment Fixed-Rate Mortgage

The basic idea behind the design of the level-payment fixed-rate mortgage, or simply level-payment mortgage, is that the borrower pays interest and repays principal in equal installments over an agreed-upon period of time, called the maturity or term of the mortgage. Thus at the end of the term, the loan has been fully amortized.

---

1 The other mortgage designs are discussed in Frank J. Fabozzi and Lynn Edens, "Mortgages," Chapter 23 in Frank J. Fabozzi and T. Dessa Fabozzi (eds.), *The Handbook of Fixed Income Securities* (Burr Ridge, IL: Irwin Professional Publishing, 1994).

For a level-payment mortgage, each monthly mortgage payment is due on the first of each month and consists of: (1) interest of 1/12th of the fixed annual mortgage rate times the amount of the outstanding mortgage balance at the beginning of the previous month, and (2) a repayment of a portion of the outstanding mortgage balance (principal). The difference between the monthly mortgage payment and the portion of the payment that represents interest equals the amount that is applied to reduce the outstanding mortgage balance. The monthly mortgage payment is designed so that after the last scheduled payment is made, the amount of the outstanding mortgage balance is zero (i.e., the mortgage is fully repaid).

The portion of the monthly mortgage payment applied to interest declines each month, and the portion applied to reducing the mortgage balance increases. The reason for this is that as the mortgage balance is reduced with each monthly mortgage payment, the interest on the mortgage balance declines. Because the monthly mortgage payment is fixed, an increasingly larger portion of the monthly payment is applied to reduce the principal in each subsequent month.

Adjustable-Rate Mortgage

An adjustable-rate mortgage (ARM) is a loan whose mortgage rate is reset periodically in accordance with some reference rate.

ARMs typically have reset periods of one month, six months, one year, or five years. The mortgage rate at the reset date is equal to a reference rate plus a spread. The monthly mortgage payments, and hence the investor's cash flow, are affected by other specifications in the form of (1) periodic and (2) lifetime rate caps and floors. Rate caps limit the amount by which the mortgage rate may increase or decrease at the reset date. The rate cap is expressed in percentage points. The most common rate cap on annual reset loans is 2%. ARMs have an upper limit on the mortgage rate that can be charged over the life of the loan. This lifetime loan cap is expressed in terms of the initial rate, and the most common lifetime cap is 5% to 6%. For example, if the initial mortgage rate is 7% and the lifetime cap is 5%, the maximum mortgage rate that the lender can charge over the life of the loan is 12%. Many ARMs also have a lower limit on the mortgage rate that can be charged over the life of the loan.

The presence of a periodic cap means that the investor has effectively given the homeowner the right to borrow funds at a below-market interest rate. Thus, the investor has sold the homeowner an option on an interest rate. In fact, since the cap goes into effect each year, the investor has sold not one option but a package of options to the homeowner. The lifetime cap can also be looked at as an option: a homeowner's effective option on an interest rate. In the case of a lifetime floor, the homeowner is compensating the investor for the possibility that the interest rate might fall below the floor. In this case, the homeowner has sold the investor an option. From the investor's perspective, an ARM with a lifetime cap and floor is equivalent to a "collar"—a maximum interest rate and a minimum interest rate. This, then, is equivalent to selling an option (the cap) at one interest rate and buying an option (the floor) at a lower interest rate.

Some ARMs can be converted into fixed-rate mortgages. These are called *convertible ARMs*. There are also fixed-rate mortgages that allow reduction in mortgage rate if rates fall by some predetermined level.

Mortgage Servicing

Unlike other fixed income instruments such as Treasury bonds or corporate bonds, every mortgage loan must be serviced. An investor who acquires a mortgage may service the mortgage or sell the right to service the mortgage. In the first case, the investor's cash flow is the entire cash flow from the mortgage. In the second case, it is the cash flow net of the servicing fee. The monthly cash flow from a mortgage loan, regardless of the mortgage design, can therefore be decomposed into three parts: (1) the servicing fee; (2) the interest payment net of the servicing fee; and (3) the scheduled principal repayment.

Prepayments and Cash Flow Uncertainty

The assumption is that the homeowner will not pay any portion of the mortgage balance off prior to the scheduled due date. But homeowners do pay off all or part of their mortgage balances prior to the maturity date. Payments made in excess of the scheduled principal repayments are called *prepayments*. The effect of prepayments is that the cash flow from a mortgage is not known with certainty. By "uncertainty," then, we mean that both the amount and the timing of the cash flow are uncertain. This is true for all mortgage loans. We discuss the reasons for prepayments and how to treat them later in this chapter.

MORTGAGE-BACKED SECURITIES

There are three types of mortgage-backed securities: passthrough securities, stripped mortgage-backed securities, and collateralized mortgage obligations.

Passthrough Securities

A mortgage passthrough security, or simply a passthrough, is created when one or more mortgage holders form a pool of mortgages and sell shares or participation certificates in the pool. Mortgage loans that are included in a pool to create a passthrough are said to be *securitized*. The process of creating a passthrough is referred to as *securitization*.

Cash Flow Characteristics: The aggregate monthly cash flow for a pool of mortgages consists of three components: (1) interest; (2) scheduled principal repayment; and (3) prepayments (that is, payments in excess of the regularly scheduled principal repayment).

Payments are made to security holders each month. The monthly cash flow for a passthrough is less than the monthly cash flow of the underlying mortgages by an amount equal to servicing and other fees. The other fees are those charged by the issuer or guarantor of the passthrough for guaranteeing the issue. The coupon rate on a passthrough, called the *passthrough coupon rate,* is less than the mortgage rate on the underlying pool of mortgage loans by an amount equal to the servicing and guaranteeing fees.

Because of prepayments, an investor in a passthrough is always exposed to prepayment risk. This risk can never be eliminated. The expectation is that while the investor in an individual loan may find it quite difficult to predict the prepayment behavior of the borrower, the same is not true for a pool consisting of a large number of mortgages. Rather, the historical experience of a pool of mortgages allows the investor to project the prepayment behavior better.

Types of Passthroughs: Passthroughs can be classified as either agency passthroughs or private label (or conventional) passthroughs. The former include passthroughs issued or guaranteed by one of three government agencies: the Government National Mortgage Association ("Ginnie Mae"), the Federal Home Loan Mortgage Corporation ("Freddie Mac"), and the Federal National Mortgage Association ("Fannie Mae"). More than 95% of passthroughs issued are agency pass-throughs.

Ginnie Mae is a part of the Department of Housing and Urban Development. The security guaranteed by Ginnie Mae is called a *mortgage-backed security* (MBS) and carries the full faith and credit of the U.S. government. Only mortgage loans insured or guaranteed by either the Federal Housing Administration, the Veterans Administration, or the Farmers Home Administration can be included in a mortgage pool guaranteed by Ginnie Mae.

Freddie Mac and Fannie Mae are government-sponsored enter-prises. A guarantee of these two entities is not a guarantee of the U.S. government, but rather, an implicit guarantee. The passthroughs is-sued by Freddie Mac are called *participation certificates* (PCs). Those issued by Fannie Mae are *mortgage-backed securities* (MBS).

Private label passthrough securities are issued by thrifts, commer-cial banks, and private conduits. These passthroughs are rated by commercial rating agencies such as Moody's and Standard & Poor's. Credit enhancements are needed to obtain a desired investment grade. Credit enhancement may be external enhancements such as corporate guarantees, letters of credit, or mortgage insurance, or internal en-hancements creating two classes of security holders, senior and subor-dinated interests.

Stripped Mortgage-Backed Securities

A passthrough divides the cash flow from the underlying pool of mortgages on a pro rata basis to the security holders. A stripped mortgage-backed security is created by altering the distribution of principal and interest from a pro rata distribution to an *unequal* distri-bution. For example, one class may be entitled to receive all of the principal and the other class all of the interest.

There are two types of stripped MBS: (1) synthetic-coupon passthroughs and (2) interest-only/principal-only securities. The first generation of stripped mortgage-backed securities were the synthetic-coupon passthroughs. This is because the unequal distribution of coupon and principal resulted in a synthetic coupon rate that is differ-ent from that of the underlying collateral. In early 1987, stripped MBS began to be issued in which all of the interest is allocated to one class (the interest-only or IO class) and all of the principal to the other class (the principal-only or PO class). The IO class receives no principal payments.

Of course, since the securities are backed by a pool of mortgages, investors in stripped mortgage-backed securities are exposed to prepayment risk. The value of POs and IOs is highly sensitive to expected prepayments. The owner of a PO benefits from fast prepayments and is hurt by slow prepayments. The opposite is true for an investor in an IO. Moreover, while the owner of a PO is assured of receiving the stated principal, the owner of an IO cannot be assured of recovering the amount invested in the security.

Collateralized Mortgage Obligations

From an asset/liability perspective, fixed-rate passthroughs are an unattractive investment for many institutional investors because of prepayment risk. More specifically, certain institutional investors are concerned that a passthrough's life will extend, while others are concerned that its life will contract.

As an example of the former, consider depository institutions. These institutions raise funds on a short-term basis, either through the issuance of certificates of deposit or short-term money market obligations. If they invest the proceeds in a fixed-rate passthrough, they will be mismatched because a passthrough is a long-term security. More specifically, the concern of a depository institution is that the passthrough's average life will become even longer than the liabilities. This would occur if rates in the mortgage market rise and prepayments slow down. Under this scenario, the institution would be locked into a security paying a below-market interest rate and forced to borrow funds at a higher rate. This form of prepayment risk is called *extension risk*. It is so named because the average life of the passthrough would extend.

Now consider a pension fund with a predetermined set of long-term liabilities that must be paid. Purchase of a passthrough exposes these institutional investors to the risk that prepayments will speed up; as a result, the passthrough's maturity will shorten considerably. Prepayments will speed up if interest rates decline, thereby forcing reinvestment of the principal received at a lower interest rate. In this case, the pension fund is exposed to the risk that the average life of the passthrough will contract. This form of prepayment risk is called *contraction risk*.

Thus some institutional investors are concerned with extension risk and others with contraction risk when they invest in a passthrough. Fortunately, it is possible, by redirecting cash flows from a passthrough to different bond classes, to redistribute prepayment risk to investors who want to reduce their exposure to one of these two types of prepayment risk. Because the total prepayment risk of a passthrough is not changed by altering the cash flows in this way, other investors must be willing to accept the unwanted prepayment risk.

The collateralized mortgage obligation (CMO) structure was developed to broaden the appeal of mortgage-backed products to traditional fixed income investors. A CMO is a security backed by either (1) a pool of passthroughs, (2) principal-only mortgage-backed securities, or (3) a pool of mortgage loans that have not been securitized. CMOs are structured so that there are several classes of bond holders with varying maturities. The different bond classes are also called *tranches*. The principal payments from the underlying collateral are used to retire the bonds according to a set of rules specified in the prospectus. There are also rules for the distribution of the net interest (i.e., interest after servicing and other fees). The rules for distribution of the principal and interest can be simple (as in the earlier deals) or quite complex (as in more recent deals).

Exhibit 6.1 shows how a simple CMO structure can be created from a pool of mortgages that have been securitized. Exhibit 6.2 provides generic characteristics of some CMO classes.

CONVENTIONAL VALUATION MODELS

The conventional valuation models of mortgage-backed securities focus on the prepayment model. The prepayment model simply adjusts the projected cash flows of the mortgage-backed security by some predetermined formula. Therefore, once a specific prepayment model is adopted, its cash flows are assumed to be certain. In this case, the price of the mortgage-backed security is the present value of the projected cash flows discounted by appropriate rates. Alternatively, given the market price of a mortgage-backed security and the assumed cash flow, a yield can be calculated. This yield is commonly referred to as the *cash flow yield*. The cash flow yield is then compared to a comparable Treasury security, meaning a Treasury with the same

Exhibit 6.1

Creation of a Simple CMO Structure

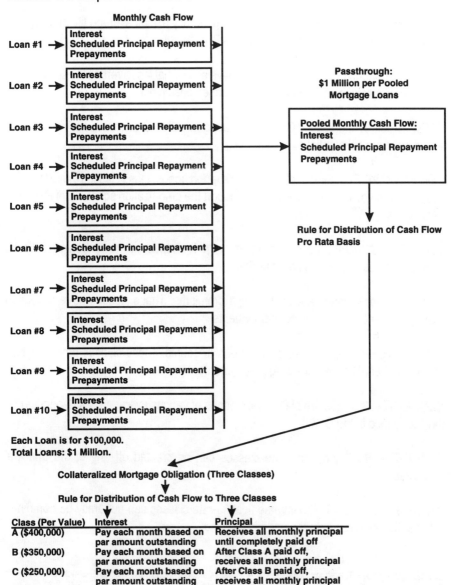

Each Loan is for $100,000.
Total Loans: $1 Million.

Collateralized Mortgage Obligation (Three Classes)

Rule for Distribution of Cash Flow to Three Classes

Class (Per Value)	Interest	Principal
A ($400,000)	Pay each month based on par amount outstanding	Receives all monthly principal until completely paid off
B ($350,000)	Pay each month based on par amount outstanding	After Class A paid off, receives all monthly principal
C ($250,000)	Pay each month based on par amount outstanding	After Class B paid off, receives all monthly principal

Source: Frank J. Fabozzi, Chuck Ramsey, and Frank Ramirez, *Collateralized Mortgage Obligations: Structures and Analysis* (Buckingham, PA: Frank J. Fabozzi Associates, 1994), p. 6.

Exhibit 6.2

Generic Characteristics of Some CMO Classes

PAC Is: Planned Amortization Class bonds generally exhibit average life stability and call and extension risk protection inside the PAC bands.

PAC IIs: Second-tier PAC bonds typically have somewhat less average life stability with correspondingly less call protection and more extension risk.

TACs: Targeted Amortization Class bonds are generally call-protected above the target speed but have substantial extension risk.

COMPANIONS: Sometimes referred to as support bonds, these classes exhibit volatile average lives and have cash flows that support the amortization schedule of PAC and TAC bonds.

Z BONDS (ACCRUAL): These are long average-life bonds with no up-front cash flows. Interest accrues to this class over its life.

IOs: Interest-only bonds are sold at high premiums. These classes have a bearish profile and benefit from slowing prepayments.

POs: Principal-only bonds are sold at deep discounts. These classes have a bullish profile and benefit from increasing prepayments.

SEQUENTIALS: These are plain vanilla bonds of various average lives depending on their sequence in the CMO.

FLOATERS: Floating-coupon rate classes can be created off any of the principal structures.

INVERSE FLOATERS: The inverse floating-rate classes can generally be combined with the floater to recreate the underlying bond.

Source: David T. Yuen, T. Anthony Coffey, Roger A. Bayston, and Shannon R. Owens, "CMO Structure Analysis," in Frank J. Fabozzi (ed.), *CMO Portfolio Management* (Summit, NJ: Frank J. Fabozzi Associates, 1994), p. 39.

average life or duration.[2] The average life, duration, and convexity of the mortgage-backed security are computed based on the assumed pattern of cash flows.

Prepayment Benchmark Conventions

Estimating the cash flow from a passthrough requires making an assumption about future prepayments. The rate at which prepayments are assumed to be made is called the *prepayment speed*, or simply *speed*. Historically, several conventions have been used as a benchmark for prepayment rates: (1) a 12-year life assumption; (2) Federal Housing Administration (FHA) experience; (3) the constant prepayment rate; and (4) the Public Securities Association (PSA) prepayment benchmark. While the first two conventions are no longer used, we discuss them because of their historical significance.

In the earliest stages of the passthrough market's development, cash flows were calculated assuming no prepayments for the first 12 years, after which all the mortgages in the pool would prepay. This naive "12-year life assumption" was then replaced by the "FHA prepayment experience" approach, where the prepayment experience for 30-year mortgages derived from an FHA table on mortgage survivals was the most commonly used benchmark. It calls for the projection of the cash flow for a mortgage pool on the assumption that the prepayment rate will be the same as the FHA experience or some multiple of FHA experience (faster or slower than FHA experience).

Despite this method's past popularity, prepayments in FHA experience are not necessarily indicative of the prepayment rate for a particular pool, mainly because FHA prepayments are for mortgages originated over various types of interest rate periods. Because prepayment rates are tied to interest rate cycles, an average prepayment rate over various cycles is not very useful in estimating prepayments. Moreover, new FHA tables are published periodically, causing confusion about which FHA table prepayments should be based on. Because

---

2 The average life of a mortgage-backed security is the weighted average time to receipt of principal payments (scheduled payments and projected prepayments). The formula for the average life (in years) is:

$$\frac{1\,(Principal_1) + 2\,(Principal_2) + \ldots + T\,(Principal_T)}{12\,(Total\ principal\ received)}$$

where $Principal_t$ is the projected principal in month t, and T is the number of months.

estimated prepayments using FHA experience may be misleading, the resulting cash flow is not meaningful for valuing passthroughs.

Another benchmark for projecting prepayments for a passthrough assumes that some fraction of the remaining principal of the underlying mortgages at the beginning of the year will prepay each year. This fraction is called the *constant prepayment rate (CPR)*. For example, a CPR of 6% for a newly originated passthrough means that if the mortgage balance of the underlying loans is $100 million, approximately $6 million will prepay in the first year. In the second year, the remaining mortgage balance would be about $94 million, and 6%, or approximately $5.64 million, will prepay. The CPR assumed for a pool depends on the characteristics of the pool (including its historical prepayment experience) and the current and expected future economic environment. The advantage of this approach is its simplicity. What's more, changes in economic conditions that impact prepayment rates or changes in the historical prepayment pattern of a pool can be analyzed quickly.

The problem with the CPR is that prepayments will be the highest in the earlier years since the mortgage balance is the largest during those years. Yet historically, the amount prepaid is lowest right after a mortgage is originated. The current market convention, the Public Securities Association (PSA) prepayment benchmark, takes this into consideration. The basic PSA model assumes that prepayment rates are low for newly originated mortgages and then will speed up as the mortgages become seasoned.

The PSA standard benchmark is expressed as a monthly series of annual CPRs. It assumes for 30-year mortgages: (1) a CPR of .2% for the first month, increased by .2% per month for the next 30 months until it reaches a CPR of 6%, and (2) a 6% CPR for the remaining years. This benchmark is referred to as "100% PSA" or simply "100 PSA." Slower or faster speeds are then referred to as some percentage of PSA. For example, 50 PSA means one-half the CPR of the PSA benchmark prepayment rate; 165 PSA means 1.65 times the CPR of the PSA benchmark prepayment rate; 300 PSA means three times the CPR of the benchmark prepayment rate.

Drawbacks of the Conventional Valuation Analysis

There are several drawbacks of the conventional valuation analysis either to price mortgage-backed securities or to measure relative value by calculating the yield spread between a mortgage-backed security and a comparable Treasury security. The first drawback is that the yield is not a proper measure for either the mortgage-backed security investigated or the comparable Treasury because the calculation does not take into consideration the term structure of interest rates. More specifically, the proper valuation of any security should be based on the Treasury spot rates.

The second drawback is that the Treasury security is option-free, while a mortgage-backed security has embedded options. That is, the value of a mortgage-backed security should reflect the option granted to homeowners. Changes in mortgage rates will affect future prepayments because they will change the refinancing opportunities available to homeowners. Consequently, the future cash flow will change as interest rates change. Conventional analysis assumes that interest rates remain the same in the future; hence, the cash flow yield measure is sometimes referred to as the *static* cash flow yield. Since future cash flow depends on future interest rates, the expected volatility of interest rates will be an important determinant of the cash flow. This should not be surprising, because a mortgage-backed security is a security with an embedded option, and the value of an option is affected by volatility.

Finally, the PSA prepayment benchmark used now is simply a market convention. It is a product of a study by the Public Securities Association of FHA prepayment data. Data that the PSA committee examined seemed to suggest that mortgages become "seasoned" (i.e., prepayment rates tend to level off) after 30 months, and the CPR tended to be 6%. So how did the PSA come up with the CPRs used for months 1 through 29? Not on the basis of empirical evidence, in fact. Instead, the PSA assumes a linear increase from month 1 to month 30, so that at month 30 the CPR is 6%. Moreover, the same benchmark or seasoning process is used in quoting passthroughs regardless of the underlying pool of mortgages—30- and 15-year loans, fixed- and adjustable-rate loans, and conventional and VA/FHA-insured loans—despite the fact that the data used to construct the PSA model are for 30-year, fixed-rate FHA mortgage loans. One study of fixed-rate passthroughs, for example, finds that the seasoning process takes considerably longer than 30 months.[3] How much longer depends on the type of underlying mort-

---

3 David Jacob, Clark McGranery, Sean Gallop, and Lynn Tong, "The Seasoning of
   Prepayment Speeds and Its Effect on the Average Lives and Values of MBS," in
   Frank J. Fabozzi, (ed.) *The Handbook of Mortgage-Backed Securities*, 3rd. ed. (Chicago:

gage loans. Freddie Mac and Fannie Mae passthroughs (which are backed by conventional mortgage loans) take longer to season than Ginnie Mae passthroughs (which are backed by FHA/VA-insured mortgage loans). Sufficient historical information is not available on the prepayment experience of balloon mortgages, yet the practice is to use the PSA benchmark.

Consequently, to value mortgage-backed securities properly, we must consider in any analysis: (1) the term structure of interest rates; (2) the option-like character of these securities; and (3) a prepayment model that reflects the economic and noneconomic decisions of home-owners as to whether to prepay a mortgage. Such a model is described in the remainder of this chapter.

CONTINGENT CLAIMS APPROACH

The contingent claims pricing theory described in the previous chapter can be applied to the valuation models of mortgage-backed securities. Under this approach, a mortgage-backed security can be viewed as a composite security having two parts. One component is a mortgage-backed security without prepayments such that the coupon interest and the scheduled principal amortization are known with certainty for the life of the security. This component can be thought of as the "noncallable equivalent mortgage-backed security." The other is a call option on the noncallable mortgage-backed security with a strike price equal to par. That is, the mortgagors have the right to prepay at any time prior to maturity. Therefore, the option pricing model, which is a special case of contingent claims pricing theory, can be used in the valuation process if it can be modified to value the call option inherent in the mortgage-backed security.

This type of approach to the valuation of mortgage-backed securities has been attempted in the academic literature. By incorporating the unique characteristics of Ginnie Mae passthrough securities, Dunn and McConnell[4] and Schwartz and Torous[5] have developed a valuation model of these securities based on the generic model for pricing interest

Probus Publishing, 1992).

4 Kenneth B. Dunn and John J. McConnell, "Valuation of GNMA Mortgage-Backed Securities," *Journal of Finance* (June 1981), pp. 599–616.

5 Eduardo S. Schwartz and Walter N. Torous, "Prepayment and the Valuation of Mortgage-Backed Securities," *Journal of Finance* (June 1989), pp. 376–392.

rate contingent claims developed by Brennan and Schwartz[6] and Cox, Ingersoll, and Ross.[7]

Because the contingent claims approach described in the previous chapter is a continuous time, dynamic, uncertainty model that is based on a general equilibrium theory of the term structure of interest rates, it has not only the theoretical rigor but also the practical flexibility to handle complicated, uncertain cash flows related to the mortgagor's prepayment option. This section develops a framework for valuing mortgage-backed securities by using this contingent claims theory.

Prepayment Rate

The unique characteristics of a mortgage-backed security are reflected in the boundary conditions of the pricing equation to be described in the next subsection and the cash flow terms. The solution for the mortgage-backed security price is subject to the appropriate boundary conditions and the appropriate specification of the cash flow terms. Thus, we begin with the specification of the cash flow terms.

A cash flow from a mortgage-backed security is composed of interest payment, scheduled principal payment, and prepayment of principal. The former two are certain and can be derived by a mathematical specification, but the prepayment of principal is uncertain. The underlying factors that govern the uncertainty associated with prepayments can be decomposed into three factors.

The first factor is an economic factor. The prepayment decision can be regarded as an optimal stopping problem in the following sense. A mortgagor will refinance an existing mortgage when interest rates have fallen. Specifically, the mortgagor has an economic motivation to prepay if an existing loan can be refinanced at a lower contract interest rate. This kind of prepayment is sensitive to a change in interest rates and has a systematic effect on the value of a mortgage-backed security.

The second factor is associated with the path-dependency of the prepayment speed. Path-dependency effects explain the effects of past interest paths on future prepayment behavior. In general, if interest rates have been high compared to the current level, the propensity to refinance will be very high. If interest rates have been low compared

---

6 Michael J. Brennan and Eduardo S. Schwartz, "Savings Bonds, Retractable Bonds, and Callable Bonds," *Journal of Financial Economics* (August 1977), pp. 67–88.

7 John C. Cox, Jonathan E. Ingersoll, and Stephen A. Ross, "A Theory of Term Structure of Interest Rates," *Econometrica* (March 1985), pp. 385–407.

to the current level, those mortgagors likely to refinance the loan have already refinanced, leaving the current pool. The prepayment may occur at a reduced speed even if the current interest rate is low. This phenomenon is called the "burnout" effect.

The third factor represents noneconomic factors. The economic motivation described above is not the only reason to prepay a mortgage. Noneconomic factors such as job transfer, change in family size, and retirement may cause someone to prepay an existing mortgage. This kind of prepayment, however, is insensitive to interest rates. The mortgagor is forced by noneconomic factors to exercise the call option at par even though the present value of the underlying mortgage is less than the par amount. Some low-coupon mortgages are, therefore, prepaid though prepayment is not economically justified. The converse is that another interest rate-insensitive group of mortgagors may not refinance a high-coupon mortgage. Some in this group may not have enough cash to pay for refinancing costs, or may not qualify for a new mortgage because household income has fallen since the mortgage was first approved. Others may lack information about refinancing or may simply be lazy.

If only the first economic factor were of consequence, we could apply the contingent claims model assuming perfect exercise of the option when the market value of a loan exceeds its remaining principal balance plus refinancing costs. Yet, the prepayment decision depends on all three factors, not just the economic factor. Thus, the optimal stopping rule that applies to the valuation of a callable bond is not directly applicable to the valuation of a mortgage-backed security.

To consider the influences of path-dependency of prepayment rate and of noneconomic factors on the prepayment rate, we construct a prepayment function estimated by a statistical method to determine the future cash flow under an assumed interest rate scenario.

Empirical observation shows that prepayment behavior varies by the issuer, type, and coupon of the mortgage-backed security. It also differs by geographical region. In addition to these, prepayment behavior depends on the interest rate differential between the refinancing rate and the current mortgage rate, which is called the spread, age of the pool, and time of the year.

Thus, we construct a prepayment function that depends on the spread and the age of the pool. An illustration of the prepayment function for the 30-year fixed 8% FHLM pool is given in Exhibit 6.3. The prepayment function is shown as a surface, so we'll call it a *prepayment surface*. The prepayment surface is usually estimated monthly.

In Exhibit 6.3, the prepayment rate is measured in terms of PSA speed on the z-axis in the three-dimensional space. Both the spread and the age of the pool are measured on the x-axis and y-axis. Exhibit 6.3 shows that there always will be some prepayments because of home-owners' mobility even if the spread is positive. For example, for a three-year-old pool, the prepayment rate is 165 when the spread is a positive 300 basis points. As the spread becomes more negative, the economic incentive to refinance becomes stronger. For instance, pre-payment rates for a three-year-old pool have been observed to increase from 624 to 877 as the spread declines from –100 to –200 basis points. These observations show the presence of noneconomic factors and the normal relationship between the prepayment rate and the interest rate changes.

Exhibit 6.3

FHLMCP 8% Coupon

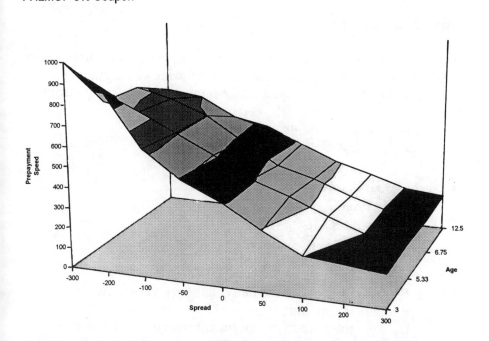

The "burnout" effect can be captured through a comparison of the prepayment schedules for different age levels of the pool. As an example, let's compare the prepayment schedules for 3.00-year and 6.75-year-old pools in Exhibit 6.3. For the 3.00-year-old pool, the prepayment rate has been observed to increase from 624 to 877 as the spread declines from –100 to –200 basis points. For the 6.75-year-old pool, the prepayment rate has been observed to increase from 601 to 675 as the spread declines from –100 to –200 basis points. This comparison shows that the lower the spread, the more significantly the refinancing incentive tends to be weakened as the age of the pool increases.

The "burnout" effect is reflected through the relationship between the prepayment rate and the previous path of the interest rate. This relationship can be quantified by the relationship between the prepayment rate and the relative proportion of the pool previously prepaid. Hence, in the valuation model, we assume that the prepayment rate is a function of the interest rate and the relative proportion of the pool prepaid.

The prepayment rate also can be adjusted using a dummy variable to reflect the seasonality effect; that is, more residential housing transactions take place during May through August.

The Valuation Model

For ease of exposition, we ignore the path-dependency of prepayment rate for the time being. Then the standard arbitrage argument yields the following differential equation for a mortgage-backed security

$$
(1) \quad \frac{\partial P}{\partial t} + \frac{\sigma^2}{2} \frac{\partial^2 P}{\partial r^2} + b \frac{\partial P}{\partial r} - rP - R(r)P + c + [1 - R(r)] = 0
$$

subject to boundary conditions

$$
(1a) \qquad\qquad\qquad P(r,T) = 0
$$

$$
(1b) \qquad\qquad\qquad P(\infty,t) = 0
$$

where $P(r,t)$ = the price of the mortgage-backed security
   r = the spread
   c = the coupon rate of the mortgage-backed security

b	= the instantaneous expected change of the interest rate
σ^2	= the instantaneous volatility of the interest rate
R(r)	= the principal payment rate
t	= the age of the mortgage
T	= the maturity date

Notice that this partial differential equation for the mortgage-backed security does not have the boundary condition that the market value of the mortgage should be less than the remaining principal balance plus the refinancing costs. This condition is embedded in the partial differential equation through the principal payment term, $-R(r)P$, which consists of both the scheduled payment and unscheduled prepayment. In addition, in the termination boundary condition (1a), the price of the mortgage-backed security becomes 0 at the time of maturity because there are no further cash flows to be received. Other than these differences, this partial differential equation is quite similar to that for a callable bond presented in the previous chapter, and, hence, can be solved by a finite difference method.

If we introduce the path-dependency of the prepayment rate, the prepayment rate becomes a function of the spread and the relative portion of the pool prepaid. Because the relative portion of the pool prepaid determines the pool factor, the path-dependency of the prepayment rate can be incorporated into the model through the pool factor. The pool factor becomes another state variable. Thus, we have two sets of partial differential equations: one for the price of the mortgage-backed security, the other for the pool factor. The property of path-dependency of the prepayment makes the solution process by finite difference method very complicated. Therefore, we rely on the Monte Carlo simulation method.

Monte Carlo Simulation and Quasi-Monte Carlo Simulation Method

The partial differential equation describing the value of a mortgage-backed security can be solved by the Monte Carlo simulation method because it can be written in stochastic integration form by taking an expectation over the possible interest rates

(2) $$P(r) = \hat{E} \int_0^T e^{-\int_0^t r_\tau d\tau + R(r,t)} [1 - R(r,t) + c] \, dt$$

where $\hat{E}$ is the expectation in a risk-neutral world and τ is the time such that $0 \leq \tau \leq t$.

To calculate the value of P(r) in equation (2), the Monte Carlo simulation method assumes a lot of paths according to the probability distribution of interest rates and then calculates the average price. In practice, this simulation is a very time-consuming process. An alternative method that assumes multiple paths of interest rates and calculates the average of the prices corresponding to each path is called the *quasi-Monte Carlo simulation*.

SUMMARY

The cash flow from a mortgage-backed security consists of the net interest, the scheduled principal payments, and prepayments. Investing in a mortgage involves uncertainty because the cash flow is not known for sure because of prepayments. This risk is referred to as prepayment risk. The investor in any mortgage-backed security (passthrough, collateralized mortgage obligation, and stripped mortgage-backed security) is exposed to prepayment risk.

The conventional valuation models for mortgage-backed securities assume that the cash flow is fixed, according to some prepayment model. The current practice is to use the Public Securities Association (PSA) prepayment benchmark, a series of constant prepayment rates, to obtain the cash flow. The PSA prepayment benchmark is a market convention that has many limitations in determining the value of a passthrough.

The proper way to value a mortgage-backed security is to use a contingent claims approach. Subtleties in the valuation of the mortgage-backed securities arise for several reasons. For mortgage-backed securities, the refinancing decision depends on the collective behavior of all the mortgagors in the pool. The collective behavior depends not only on the current level and previous path of interest rates but also on some noneconomic factors. In some cases the mortgagor may make a suboptimal refinancing decision. This is the reason why portfolio managers use the statistically estimated prepayment function to estimate future cash flow and effects of refinancing decisions.

The prepayment rate, considering its path-dependency, is represented as a function of the interest rate spread and the pool factor. Thus, the partial differential equation for the pricing depends on two state variables, one of them path-dependent. This property leads us to rely on Monte Carlo simulation instead of the finite difference method. In practice, we use a simple version of Monte Carlo simulation in which many possible scenarios of interest rate movement are postulated and the price of the mortgage-backed security is solved for each scenario to get the average price.

Section III

Portfolio Management Strategies

Chapter 7
Active Strategies

In the most general sense, active management is an approach that will achieve the maximum return for a given level of risk. That is, the emphasis is on return maximization—seeking the highest return possible while not exceeding some defined risk. Active strategies can be differentiated from passive strategies, as discussed in the next chapter, where risk aversion dominates and a less-than-maximum return objective is acceptable. When investment horizons are long or risk tolerances are high, active management is the preferred strategy. Many pension funds and some closed-end mutual funds embrace active management.

When the emphasis is on expected return, the role of expectations becomes key. More precisely, expectations are the prime driving force behind the return sought. The uncertainty associated with expectations becomes a source of risk in the active management process. How the portfolio manager best uses expectations in the face of uncertainty is the answer to risk-minimizing in the active strategy. Our focus in this chapter is on how a portfolio manager harnesses these expectations.

We assume that the manager has a set of expectations, however derived. The next step is to transform them effectively into managerial action. After reviewing a number of ways in which expectations may be formulated, we discuss some useful tools for implementing the expectations. Our assumption is that proper classification of expectations, with fortification by the appropriate techniques, tends to produce better decision making and, hence, better investment results.

OVERVIEW OF THE ACTIVE MANAGEMENT PROCESS

Exhibit 7.1 describes, in the most general sense, what the active management process is all about. Typically, the manager starts in the position at the left side of the exhibit: a portfolio plus a potential purchase list.

The process begins with the step identified next: return simulation. In this process the manager takes a set of expectations and expresses them as expected rates of return, or a bottom-line output. These expected rates of return capture all the expectations that go into the process, whether they are expectations about interest rate changes, yield curve changes, credit risk changes, or spread relationship changes. These are all expressed in an expected rate of return for both individual securities and the portfolio as a whole.

The results of return simulation lead directly to portfolio optimization, or suggestions for specific changes to the portfolio by integration of other appropriate portfolio policy considerations with the expected rates of return. In this way, specific client preferences, or a particular managerial style, can be incorporated into the optimization process.

The center vertical track of Exhibit 7.1 specifies the second step. Here we identify a benchmark portfolio, some "bogey" against which the manager will compare the portfolio. This could be any portfolio that the manager and the client decide is appropriate.

By subjecting the benchmark portfolio to the return simulation process, the manager again transforms expectations into expected rates of return. These expected rates of return are subjected to the same policy considerations applied to the actual portfolio for a portfolio optimization analysis. The manager then compares the actual portfolio and the benchmark, evaluates the differences, and determines the potential ability of the actual portfolio to outperform the bogey.

A third element of active management starts with a bogey universe, the column at the right in Exhibit 7.1. The basic difference between this track and the second step is that a bogey universe is likely to include many more securities than those in a benchmark portfolio. The manager might start with an index such as the Lehman Corporate Bond Index, which covers approximately 4,000 securities. While such a bogey may be appropriate, in order to subject it to the same kind of expectations transformation and optimization analysis as in the first

Exhibit 7.1

Active Management Framework

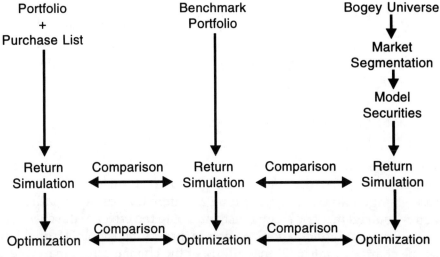

track, the manager must carry out interim analysis that turns a large universe into a manageable portfolio.

Starting with the 4,000 securities, the manager can apply *market segmentation*, which essentially decomposes the universe into sectors. A bogey portfolio would be selected for each sector to track a bond index that in effect replicates the return behavior of the larger universe. The manager then subjects the securities in the bogey portfolio to the return simulation process. This provides the manager with the transformation of expectations into expected rates of return. Finally, the manager subjects that set of expected rates of return to an optimization analysis.

Optimization allows cross-comparisons to see how the actual portfolio—before and after any portfolio changes that will be made—compares with a benchmark portfolio or, alternatively, with the bogey universe.

This is a simplified schematic way to represent active management. In fact, much of its essence is captured in the return simulation stage. Whatever techniques the portfolio manager selects, the important element is subjecting the technique to return simulation.

TECHNIQUES OF ACTIVE MANAGEMENT

Active strategies, which are dominated by interest rate anticipation and sector/security strategies, encompass a wide range of possibilities. Volatility in the bond market has stimulated the development of some active management techniques. We describe some of the interest rate anticipation strategies and sector/security strategies that a bond port-folio manager might use.

Interest Rate Anticipation Strategies

As we explained in Chapter 2, interest rate change is the dominant source of marginal total return—marginal in relation to the return if no rate change had occurred. As long as interest rates are volatile, an active management strategy must anticipate the effect of the changes.

Interest rate anticipation operates in three dimensions: (1) direction of the change in rates; (2) magnitude of the change across maturities; and (3) the timing of the change. If interest rates drop, the price of the bond will rise to reflect the new yield level; if rates increase, the price of the bond will decline. The increase or decrease is directly related to the security's duration. Therefore, the maturity should be lengthened and the coupon decreased—or, equivalently, duration should be in-creased—when rates are expected to drop. The opposite action should be taken when rates are expected to rise. Positioning of the portfolio on the maturity spectrum should be guided by the shape of the expected yield curve change. Finally, the timing of an interest rate change is a factor in evaluating the relative importance of rate change, coupon return, and reinvestment return. We discuss the timing question in more detail later in this section.

For our purposes here, we do not explore how the required interest rate forecast is generated. It is, at best, extremely difficult to forecast the future direction of interest rates, much less the magnitude of any change. In fact, some would assert that it is impossible. Our emphasis, however, is on how the portfolio manager can use a forecast once it is determined. We show first how to apply the forecasts of interest rate change to a portfolio to assess the impact and implications of the change.

Exhibit 7.2 summarizes inputs suitable for simulating the effect of interest rate change for the portfolio of 23 bonds shown in Exhibit 7.3.

We use a framework of one year for the illustration; the actual length would vary according to the portfolio manager's needs.

Three scenarios for interest rate change are shown: a bullish scenario, a market-implicit forecast scenario, and a bearish scenario. The market-implicit forecast is based on the term structure analysis described in Chapter 4 and in Technical Appendix A. These forecasts take the form of optimistic (declining rates), no change, and pessimistic (rising rates). The manager's own particular forecast, of course, is an alternative. In Exhibit 7.2 we assume each scenario has the same probability of coming to pass. Exhibit 7.2 shows the forecast spot rate for each scenario as well as the present spot rates.

Additional factors can be imposed to reflect the effect of quality, issuing, or coupon sectors that will modify the basic shift in the Treasury yield curves. A single A-rated bond, for example, may be expected to shift 10 percentage points less than the anticipated shift of a Treasury bond of the same maturity. That is, if the Treasury bond yield shifts 100 basis points, the modified shift for the single-A bond would be 90 basis points. The additional factors of issuing sector and coupon group could modify the primary shift further. All these factors can be termed *volatility factors*. They modify, on the margin, the anticipated change attributable to overall interest rates, allowing some fine-tuning of the anticipated reaction to interest rate changes according to the unique characteristics of the bond.[1]

Exhibit 7.4 shows the results of translating interest rate change into expected (composite) rates of return for the 23 bonds in the portfolio for each of the three scenarios. Exhibit 7.5 summarizes the portfolio return for each scenario and the composite return for the 23-issue portfolio in the return simulation.

Return simulation analysis of this sort can be extremely helpful in executing an effective active management strategy. The partitioning of expected interest rate changes into implied rates of return gives some

---

1 The volatility factor for an issuing sector can be estimated from historical data using a simple linear regression:

$$\Delta S_t = a + (1 + b) \Delta T_t + e_t$$

where ΔS_t = change in interest rate for the issuing sector in month t (in basis points)

   ΔT_t = change in interest rate for the Treasury issue in month t (in basis points)

   e_t = error term in month t

and a and b are the parameters of the model to be estimated. The parameter b is the issuing sector volatility, and the parameter a is the issuing sector spread change.

Exhibit 7.2

Assumptions for Three Scenarios for Bond Sensitivity Analysis (2/26/93)

Spot Rate Projection (%)

Maturity (years)		.25	.50	1.00	2.00	3.00	4.00	5.00	7.00	10.00	15.00	20.00	25.00	30.00
Beginning		2.970	3.096	3.335	3.845	4.420	4.921	5.320	5.886	6.395	6.835	7.301	7.750	7.231
Scenario 1	Up 100	3.970	4.096	4.335	4.845	5.420	5.921	6.320	6.886	7.395	7.835	8.301	8.750	8.231
Scenario 2	No change	2.970	3.096	3.335	3.845	4.420	4.921	5.320	5.886	6.395	6.835	7.301	7.750	7.231
Scenario 3	Down 100	1.970	2.096	2.335	2.845	3.420	3.921	4.320	4.886	5.395	5.835	6.301	6.750	6.231

Scenario Parameters

	Scenario probability (%)	Reinvestment rate (%) (Auto)	Payout rate (%)	Payout reinvestment (%)
Scenario 1	33.333	Automatic	.000	.000
Scenario 2	33.333	Automatic	.000	.000
Scenario 3	33.333	Automatic	.000	.000

Exhibit 7.3

Issues Used in Bond Sensitivity Analysis

Bd No.	Par value	% of Portfolio	CUSIP	Issuer	Sector	Qlality	Coupon	Stated mat. date	Effective mat. date	Price	Adj YTM	Adj dur.	Adj conv.	OAS
1	1,000.0	3.25	02635KAV	American Gen Fin Corp	CR	A1	8.500	06/15/99	03/23/98	108.836	7.03	4.02	.68	1.45
2	1,300.0	3.97	046003EB	Assoc Corp N.A.	CR	A1	6.750	10/15/99		101.290	6.51	5.15	.33	.83
3	1,500.0	5.12	071813AB	Baxter Intl Inc	IM	A3	9.500	06/15/08	08/24/03	114.139	8.25	6.42	.65	1.73
4	1,600.0	5.26	081721BS	Beneficial Corp	CR	A2	9.125	02/15/98		111.403	6.41	4.01	.20	1.19
5	1,000.0	3.23	125569CG	CIT Group Hldgs Inc	CR	A1	8.750	02/15/96		109.438	5.27	2.62	.09	.87
6	1,000.0	3.30	155658AA	GNMA Pool	GP	AGY	8.000	06/15/16	02/10/96	112.062	3.49	-.82	-.82	-1.56
7	1,000.0	3.41	190441AF	Coastal Corp	EG	BAA3	11.750	06/15/06	11/09/97	113.750	8.52	3.31	.00	2.49
8	2,000.0	7.00	209864AS	Consolidated Rail Corp	XR	A2	9.750	12/01/00		116.750	6.92	5.47	.39	1.07
9	1,000.0	3.07	3129969E	FH Gld 30	PH	AGY	7.000	02/01/21	11/27/98	103.895	5.98	3.87	-2.46	.25
10	3,500.0	11.84	313309AJ	Federal Express Corp	XP	BAA3	9.650	06/15/12		113.083	8.28	8.74	1.19	1.55
11	1,500.0	4.52	3133112D	Fed Farm Cr Bk	AG	AGY	6.100	05/01/95		100.469	5.86	1.98	.05	1.90
12	1,200.0	3.80	370424FM	General Mtrs Acep Cor	CR	BAA1	8.625	06/15/99	02/25/98	106.072	7.54	3.88	.22	1.96
13	1,250.0	3.84	411347AB	Hanson Overseas	YK	A1	7.375	01/15/03		103.826	6.84	6.90	.61	.67
14	1,000.0	3.35	423328AH	Heller Finl Inc	CR	A2	9.375	03/15/98		109.687	7.06	3.89	.19	1.82
15	1,500.0	4.70	44812CY	Household Fin Corp	CR	A3	8.400	08/03/94		105.973	4.07	1.35	.03	.44
16	1,200.0	3.86	450680CB	ITT Finl Corp	CR	A3	8.550	06/15/09	06/22/01	107.650	8.50	5.79	1.77	1.91
17	1,000.0	3.24	450680CN	ITT Finl Corp	CR	A3	9.250	07/15/01	09/11/99	109.052	7.36	4.76	.13	1.41
18	1,000.0	3.02	693160AA	Prudential Bache 92-A	A4	AAA	6.250	07/15/98	01/07/96	102.765	4.21	2.62	-.08	-.42
19	950.0	3.33	81371FAA	Secured Finance	CR	AAA	9.050	12/15/04		117.301	6.88	7.36	.74	.58
20	2,000.0	.86	912803AQ	US Strip Prin	TR	TSY	0.000	02/15/19		14.566	7.56	25.02	6.38	-.19
21	2,500.0	8.91	912810EG	US 8.750 08/14/20	TR	TSY	8.750	08/15/20		120.937	7.02	10.79	1.89	.01
22	1,250.0	4.23	941063AD	Waste Mgmt Inc	IM	A1	8.750	05/01/18	11/08/14	112.229	7.51	9.04	1.16	.50
23	1,000.0	2.89	96040 2AQ	Westinghouse Elec	IM	BA1	8.625	08/01/12		97.498	8.90	8.76	1.20	2.14

Exhibit 7.4

Individual Bond Summary

BEGINNING DATE: 02/26/93
ENDING DATE: 02/26/94

1. 02635KAV AMERICAN GEN FIN CORP 8.500 06/15/99 FI A1

	Par Value	Effective Maturity	Prob. WAL	Price	Adj YTM	Adj Dur.	Adj Conv.	OAS	Exercise Factor	Components of Total Return (%) Yield Curve	Time	Spread	Option	Interest	Coupon Rnv.	Mat/Called Rnv.	Principal Rnv.	Total Return
BEGINNING	1,000.00	03/23/98	5.07	108.836	7.03	4.02	.68	1.45										
SCENARIO 1	985.34	12/12/97	3.80	105.001	7.77	3.21	.45	1.45	0.01	-3.98	0.18	0.00	0.38	7.68	0.27	0.00	0.00	4.53
SCENARIO 2	998.83	08/20/98	4.48	108.466	6.77	3.70	.46	1.45	0.00	0.00	0.19	0.00	-0.52	7.69	0.24	0.00	0.00	7.59
SCENARIO 3	1,000.00	02/06/99	4.95	112.612	5.78	4.04	.38	1.45	0.00	4.25	0.19	0.00	-1.02	7.70	0.20	0.00	0.00	11.32
WTD AVE	994.72	07/24/98	4.41	108.693	6.77	3.65	.43	1.45	0.01	0.09	0.19	0.00	-0.39	7.69	0.24	0.00	0.00	7.81

2. 046003EB ASSOC CORP N.A. 6.750 10/15/99 FI A1

	Par Value	Effective Maturity	Prob. WAL	Price	Adj YTM	Adj Dur.	Adj Conv.	OAS	Exercise Factor	Components of Total Return (%) Yield Curve	Time	Spread	Option	Interest	Coupon Rnv	Mat/Called Rnv	Principal Rnv	Total Return
BEGINNING	1,300.00	10/15/99	6.64	101.290	6.51	5.15	.33	.83										
SCENARIO 1	1,300.00	10/15/99	5.64	97.666	7.26	4.48	.25	.83	0.00	-4.44	0.95	0.00	0.00	6.51	0.30	0.00	0.00	3.31
SCENARIO 2	1,300.00	10/15/99	5.64	102.271	6.26	4.53	.25	.83	0.00	0.00	0.95	0.00	0.00	6.51	0.26	0.00	0.00	7.71
SCENARIO 3	1,300.00	10/15/99	5.64	107.143	5.27	4.58	.26	.83	0.00	4.70	0.95	0.00	0.00	6.51	0.21	0.00	0.00	12.36
WTD AVE	1,300.00	10/15/99	5.64	102.360	6.26	4.53	.25	.83	0.00	0.09	0.95	0.00	0.00	6.51	0.26	0.00	0.00	7.79

3. 071813AB BAXTER INTL INC 9.500 06/15/08 IN A3

	Par Value	Effective Maturity	Prob. WAL	Price	Adj YTM	Adj Dur.	Adj Conv.	OAS	Exercise Factor	Components of Total Return (%) Yield Curve	Time	Spread	Option	Interest	Coupon Rnv	Mat/Called Rnv	Principal Rnv	Total Return
BEGINNING	1,500.00	08/24/03	10.49	114.139	8.25	6.42	.65	1.73										
SCENARIO 1	1,500.00	01/06/02	7.86	107.752	9.17	5.38	.45	1.73	0.00	-7.15	0.12	0.00	1.53	8.19	0.34	0.00	0.00	3.03
SCENARIO 2	1,500.00	04/06/04	10.11	113.750	8.19	6.37	1.02	1.73	0.00	0.00	0.12	0.00	-0.45	8.19	0.31	0.00	0.00	8.16
SCENARIO 3	1,500.00	01/11/06	11.87	121.383	7.21	7.24	1.09	1.73	0.00	8.00	0.12	0.00	-1.87	8.19	0.27	0.00	0.00	14.70
WTD AVE	1,500.00	02/07/04	9.95	114.295	8.19	6.33	.86	1.73	0.00	0.28	0.12	0.00	-0.27	8.19	0.31	0.00	0.00	8.63

4. 081721BS BENEFICIAL CORP 9.125 02/15/98 FI A2

	Par Value	Effective Maturity	Prob. WAL	Price	Adj YTM	Adj Dur.	Adj Conv.	OAS	Exercise Factor	Components of Total Return (%) Yield Curve	Time	Spread	Option	Interest	Coupon Rnv	Mat/Called Rnv	Principal Rnv	Total Return
BEGINNING	1,600.00	02/15/98	4.97	111.403	6.41	4.01	.20	1.19										
SCENARIO 1	1,600.00	02/15/98	3.97	107.078	7.05	3.31	.14	1.19	0.00	-3.25	-0.63	0.00	0.00	8.17	0.16	0.00	0.00	4.46
SCENARIO 2	1,600.00	02/15/98	3.97	110.703	6.05	3.34	.14	1.19	0.00	0.00	-0.63	0.00	0.00	8.17	0.14	0.00	0.00	7.68
SCENARIO 3	1,600.00	02/15/98	3.97	114.480	5.05	3.36	.14	1.19	0.00	3.38	-0.63	0.00	0.00	8.17	0.12	0.00	0.00	11.04
WTD AVE	1,600.00	02/15/98	3.97	110.753	6.05	3.34	.14	1.19	0.00	0.05	-0.63	0.00	0.00	8.17	0.14	0.00	0.00	7.73

Exhibit 7.4 (Continued)

5. 125569CG CIT GROUP HLDGS INC — 8.750 — 02/15/96 — FI — A1

	Par Value	Effective Maturity	Prob. WAL	Price	Adj YTM	Adj Dur	Adj Conv	OAS	Exercise Factor	Yield Curve	Time	Spread	Option	Interest	Coupon Rtn	Mat/Called Rtn	Principal Rtn	Total Return
BEGINNING	1,000.00	02/15/96	2.97	109.438	5.27	2.62	.09	87	0.00	0.00								
SCENARIO 1	1,000.00	02/15/96	1.97	105.528	5.74	1.80	.04	87	0.00	-1.76	-1.81	0.00	0.00	7.98	0.13	0.00	0.00	4.54
SCENARIO 2	1,000.00	02/15/96	1.97	107.453	4.74	1.81	.04	87	0.00	1.80	-1.81	0.00	0.00	7.98	0.11	0.00	0.00	6.27
SCENARIO 3	1,000.00	02/15/96	1.97	109.425	3.74	1.82	.04	87	0.00	1.80	-1.81	0.00	0.00	7.98	0.08	0.00	0.00	8.05
WTD AVE	1,000.00	02/15/96	1.97	107.469	4.74	1.81	.04	87	0.00	0.01	-1.81	0.00	0.00	7.98	0.11	0.00	0.00	6.29

6. 156568AA GNMA POOL — 8.000 — 06/15/16 — MS — AGY

	Par Value	Effective Maturity	Prob. WAL	Price	Adj YTM	Adj Dur	Adj Conv	OAS	Exercise Factor	Yield Curve	Time	Spread	Option	Interest	Coupon Rtn	Mat/Called Rtn	Principal Rtn	Total Return
BEGINNING	1,000.00	02/10/96	2.96	112.062	3.49	-.82	-.82	-1.56										
SCENARIO 1	768.88	05/11/98	4.21	111.194	4.88	1.63	-.92	-1.56	0.23	-5.19	0.06	0.00	4.54	6.34	0.19	-2.48	0.56	4.01
SCENARIO 2	688.78	02/07/97	2.95	112.596	3.54	-.86	-.83	-1.56	0.31	0.00	0.05	0.00	0.03	6.05	0.15	-3.34	0.64	3.57
SCENARIO 3	594.87	03/20/96	2.06	111.958	2.15	-1.50	-.47	-1.56	0.41	4.50	0.04	0.00	-4.60	5.69	0.11	-4.35	0.67	2.07
WTD AVE	684.18	03/24/97	3.07	111.782	3.52	-.25	-.74	-1.56	0.32	-0.23	0.05	0.00	-0.01	6.02	0.15	-3.39	0.62	3.22

7. 19044AF COASTAL CORP — 11.750 — 06/15/06 — EU — BAA3

	Par Value	Effective Maturity	Prob. WAL	Price	Adj YTM	Adj Dur	Adj Conv	OAS	Exercise Factor	Yield Curve	Time	Spread	Option	Interest	Coupon Rtn	Mat/Called Rtn	Principal Rtn	Total Return
BEGINNING	1,000.00	11/09/97	4.70	113.750	8.52	3.31	.00	2.49	0.00									
SCENARIO 1	1,000.00	05/14/98	4.22	108.329	9.39	2.81	-.29	2.49	0.00	-5.12	-0.80	0.00	1.25	10.12	0.44	0.00	0.00	5.89
SCENARIO 2	1,000.00	06/03/97	3.27	111.586	8.42	2.32	-.04	2.49	0.00	0.00	-0.80	0.00	-1.06	10.12	0.39	0.00	0.00	8.65
SCENARIO 3	1,000.00	10/13/96	2.63	114.381	7.44	1.97	-.01	2.49	0.00	5.54	-0.80	0.00	-4.19	10.12	0.34	0.00	0.00	11.01
WTD AVE	1,000.00	07/10/97	3.37	111.432	8.42	2.37	-.11	2.49	0.00	0.14	-0.80	0.00	-1.33	10.12	0.39	0.00	0.00	8.52

8. 209864AS CONSOLIDATED RAIL COR — 9.750 — 12/01/00 — XP — A2

	Par Value	Effective Maturity	Prob. WAL	Price	Adj YTM	Adj Dur	Adj Conv	OAS	Exercise Factor	Yield Curve	Time	Spread	Option	Interest	Coupon Rtn	Mat/Called Rtn	Principal Rtn	Total Return
BEGINNING	2,000.00	12/01/00	7.76	116.750	6.92	5.47	.39	1.07	0.00									
SCENARIO 1	2,000.00	12/01/00	6.76	110.455	7.73	4.89	.31	1.07	0.00	-4.76	-0.53	0.00	0.00	8.19	0.32	0.00	0.00	3.22
SCENARIO 2	2,000.00	12/01/00	6.76	116.123	6.74	4.96	.32	1.07	0.00	0.00	-0.53	0.00	0.00	8.19	0.27	0.00	0.00	7.94
SCENARIO 3	2,000.00	12/01/00	6.76	122.165	5.75	5.03	.32	1.07	0.00	5.07	-0.53	0.00	0.00	8.19	0.23	0.00	0.00	12.97
WTD AVE	2,000.00	12/01/00	6.76	116.248	6.74	4.96	.32	1.07	0.00	0.10	-0.53	0.00	0.00	8.19	0.27	0.00	0.00	8.04

Components of Total Return (%)

Exhibit 7.4 (Continued)

9. 3129969E   FH GLD 30   7.000   02/01/21   MS   AGY

	Par Value	Effective Maturity	Prob. WAL	Price	Adj YTM	Adj Dur	Adj Conv	OAS	Exercise Factor	Yield Curve	Time	Spread	Option	Interest	Coupon Rtn	Mat/Called Rtn	Principal Rtn	Total Return
														Components of Total Return (%)				
BEGINNING	1,000.00	11/27/98	5.76	103.895	5.98	3.87	-2.46	.25										
SCENARIO 1	894.66	04/07/02	8.11	97.778	7.30	5.54	-2.57	.25	.11	-4.96	.77	0.00	-1.05	6.37	.26	-.39	.37	1.36
SCENARIO 2	838.57	09/14/99	5.55	103.461	6.01	2.50	-2.62	.25	.16	0.00	.72	0.00	-1.07	6.18	.23	-.60	.50	5.95
SCENARIO 3	776.75	01/25/98	3.91	107.005	4.71	1.61	-.85	.25	.22	4.81	.67	0.00	-3.17	5.97	.19	-.83	.59	8.23
WTD AVE	836.66	01/05/00	5.86	102.748	6.01	3.22	-2.01	.25	.16	-.05	.72	0.00	-1.76	6.17	.23	-.61	.49	5.18

10. 313309AJ   FEDERAL EXPRESS CORP   9.650   06/15/12   XP   BAA3

	Par Value	Effective Maturity	Prob. WAL	Price	Adj YTM	Adj Dur	Adj Conv	OAS	Exercise Factor	Yield Curve	Time	Spread	Option	Interest	Coupon Rtn	Mat/Called Rtn	Principal Rtn	Total Return
														Components of Total Return (%)				
BEGINNING	3,500.00	06/15/12	19.30	113.083	8.28	8.74	1.19	1.55										
SCENARIO 1	3,500.00	06/15/12	18.30	104.038	9.19	8.20	1.06	1.55	0.00	-8.11	.24	0.00	0.00	8.39	.35	0.00	0.00	0.88
SCENARIO 2	3,500.00	06/15/12	18.30	113.364	8.22	8.60	1.14	1.55	0.00	0.00	.24	0.00	0.00	8.39	.32	0.00	0.00	8.95
SCENARIO 3	3,500.00	06/15/12	18.30	124.018	7.26	9.00	1.22	1.55	0.00	9.27	.24	0.00	0.00	8.39	.28	0.00	0.00	18.18
WTD AVE	3,500.00	06/15/12	18.30	113.807	8.22	8.60	1.14	1.55	0.00	.39	.24	0.00	0.00	8.39	.32	0.00	0.00	9.34

11. 3133112D   FED FARM CR BK   6.100   05/01/95   AG   AGY

	Par Value	Effective Maturity	Prob. WAL	Price	Adj YTM	Adj Dur	Adj Conv	OAS	Exercise Factor	Yield Curve	Time	Spread	Option	Interest	Coupon Rtn	Mat/Called Rtn	Principal Rtn	Total Return
														Components of Total Return (%)				
BEGINNING	1,500.00	05/01/95	2.18	100.469	5.86	1.98	.05	1.90										
SCENARIO 1	1,500.00	05/01/95	1.18	99.681	6.38	1.10	.02	1.90	0.00	-1.10	.33	0.00	0.00	5.96	.22	0.00	0.00	5.41
SCENARIO 2	1,500.00	05/01/95	1.18	100.809	5.38	1.11	.02	1.90	0.00	0.00	.33	0.00	0.00	5.96	.19	0.00	0.00	6.47
SCENARIO 3	1,500.00	05/01/95	1.18	101.956	4.38	1.11	.02	1.90	0.00	1.12	.33	0.00	0.00	5.96	.15	0.00	0.00	7.56
WTD AVE	1,500.00	05/01/95	1.18	100.815	5.38	1.11	.02	1.90	0.00	.01	.33	0.00	0.00	5.96	.19	0.00	0.00	6.48

12. 370424FM   GENERAL MTRS ACCEP C   8.625   06/15/99   FI   BAA1

	Par Value	Effective Maturity	Prob. WAL	Price	Adj YTM	Adj Dur	Adj Conv	OAS	Exercise Factor	Yield Curve	Time	Spread	Option	Interest	Coupon Rtn	Mat/Called Rtn	Principal Rtn	Total Return
														Components of Total Return (%)				
BEGINNING	1,200.00	02/25/98	5.00	106.072	7.54	3.88	.22	1.96										
SCENARIO 1	783.66	11/08/97	3.70	102.017	8.28	2.94	.15	1.96	.35	-2.64	.27	0.00	-.09	7.99	.30	0.00	0.00	5.83
SCENARIO 2	1,187.33	05/31/99	5.26	105.835	7.28	4.14	.20	1.96	.01	0.00	.41	0.00	-.63	8.00	.27	0.00	0.00	8.05
SCENARIO 3	1,200.00	06/14/99	5.30	110.410	6.28	4.21	.09	1.96	0.00	4.26	.42	0.00	-.65	8.01	.23	0.00	0.00	12.27
WTD AVE	1,057.00	11/27/98	4.76	106.087	7.28	3.76	.15	1.96	.12	.54	.37	0.00	-.46	8.00	.27	0.00	0.00	8.72

Exhibit 7.4 (Continued)

13. 41134TAB — HANSON OVERSEAS — 7.375 — 01/15/03 — FN — A1

	Par Value	Effective Maturity	Prob. WAL	Price	Adj YTM	Adj Dur	Adj Conv	OAS	Exercise Factor	Yield Curve	Time	Spread	Option	Interest	Coupon Rtn	Mat/Called Rtn	Principal Rtn	Total Return
BEGINNING	1,250.00	01/15/03	9.89	103.826	6.83	6.89	.61	67										
SCENARIO 1	1,250.00	01/15/03	8.89	97.880	7.71	6.30	.51	67	0.00	-6.17	0.49	0.00	0.00	7.05	0.20	0.00	0.00	1.57
SCENARIO 2	1,250.00	01/15/03	8.89	104.337	6.72	6.41	.52	67	0.00	0.00	0.49	0.00	0.00	7.05	0.18	0.00	0.00	7.71
SCENARIO 3	1,250.00	01/15/03	8.89	111.343	5.73	6.53	.54	67	0.00	6.69	0.49	0.00	0.00	7.05	0.15	0.00	0.00	14.38
WTD AVE	1,250.00	01/15/03	8.89	104.520	6.72	6.41	.52	67	0.00	0.17	0.49	0.00	0.00	7.05	0.18	0.00	0.00	7.88

14. 423328AH — HELLER FINL INC — 9.375 — 03/16/98 — FI — A2

	Par Value	Effective Maturity	Prob. WAL	Price	Adj YTM	Adj Dur	Adj Conv	OAS	Exercise Factor	Yield Curve	Time	Spread	Option	Interest	Coupon Rtn	Mat/Called Rtn	Principal Rtn	Total Return
BEGINNING	1,000.00	03/15/98	5.05	109.687	7.06	3.89	.19	1.82										
SCENARIO 1	1,000.00	03/15/98	4.05	105.699	7.71	3.22	.13	1.82	0.00	-3.17	-0.33	0.00	0.00	8.23	0.46	0.00	0.00	5.19
SCENARIO 2	1,000.00	03/15/98	4.05	109.311	6.71	3.25	.14	1.82	0.00	0.00	-0.33	0.00	0.00	8.23	0.40	0.00	0.00	8.30
SCENARIO 3	1,000.00	03/15/98	4.05	113.077	5.71	3.28	.14	1.82	0.00	3.31	-0.33	0.00	0.00	8.23	0.34	0.00	0.00	11.54
WTD AVE	1,000.00	03/15/98	4.05	109.362	6.71	3.25	.14	1.82	0.00	0.05	-0.33	0.00	0.00	8.23	0.40	0.00	0.00	8.34

15. 441812CY — HOUSEHOLD FIN CORP — 8.400 — 08/03/94 — FI — A3

	Par Value	Effective Maturity	Prob. WAL	Price	Adj YTM	Adj Dur	Adj Conv	OAS	Exercise Factor	Yield Curve	Time	Spread	Option	Interest	Coupon Rtn	Mat/Called Rtn	Principal Rtn	Total Return
BEGINNING	1,500.00	08/03/94	1.44	105.973	4.07	1.35	.03	44										
SCENARIO 1	1,500.00	08/03/94	0.44	101.628	4.57	.43	.00	44	0.00	-0.41	-3.67	0.00	0.00	7.89	0.11	0.00	0.00	3.92
SCENARIO 2	1,500.00	08/03/94	0.44	102.066	3.57	.43	.00	44	0.00	0.00	-3.67	0.00	0.00	7.89	0.09	0.00	0.00	4.31
SCENARIO 3	1,500.00	08/03/94	0.44	102.508	2.57	.43	.00	44	0.00	0.41	-3.67	0.00	0.00	7.89	0.06	0.00	0.00	4.70
WTD AVE	1,500.00	08/03/94	0.44	102.067	3.57	.43	.00	44	0.00	0.00	-3.67	0.00	0.00	7.89	0.09	0.00	0.00	4.31

16. 450680CB — ITT FINL CORP — 8.550 — 06/15/09 — FI — A3

	Par Value	Effective Maturity	Prob. WAL	Price	Adj YTM	Adj Dur	Adj Conv	OAS	Exercise Factor	Yield Curve	Time	Spread	Option	Interest	Coupon Rtn	Mat/Called Rtn	Principal Rtn	Total Return
BEGINNING	1,200.00	06/22/01	8.32	107.650	8.50	5.79	1.77	1.91										
SCENARIO 1	1,200.00	07/15/00	6.38	102.776	9.42	5.10	.36	1.91	0.00	-7.20	0.42	0.00	2.32	7.82	0.34	0.00	0.00	3.70
SCENARIO 2	1,200.00	11/20/01	7.73	107.784	8.44	5.81	1.58	1.91	0.00	0.00	0.42	0.00	-0.30	7.82	0.30	0.00	0.00	8.24
SCENARIO 3	1,200.00	06/30/04	10.34	114.095	7.47	6.93	2.11	1.91	0.00	8.11	0.42	0.00	-2.64	7.82	0.27	0.00	0.00	13.98
WTD AVE	1,200.00	04/22/02	8.15	108.218	8.44	5.94	1.35	1.91	0.00	0.30	0.42	0.00	-0.20	7.82	0.30	0.00	0.00	8.64

Note: Columns Yield Curve, Time, Spread, Option, Interest, Coupon Rtn, Mat/Called Rtn, and Principal Rtn are grouped under "Components of Total Return (%)".

Exhibit 7.4 (Continued)

17. 450680CN ITT FINL CORP 9.250 07/15/01 FI A3

	Par Value	Effective Maturity	Prob. WAL	Price	Adj YTM	Adj Dur	Adj Conv	OAS	Exercise Factor	Yield Curve	Time	Spread	Option	Interest	Components of Total Return (%) Coupon Rtn	Mat/Called Rtn	Principal Rtn	Total Return
BEGINNING	1,000.00	09/11/99	6.55	109.052	7.36	4.76	.13	1.41										
SCENARIO 1	1,000.00	12/31/99	5.84	103.791	8.19	4.22	.02	1.41	0.00	-5.28	-0.08	0.00	0.58	8.40	0.26	0.00	0.00	3.88
SCENARIO 2	1,000.00	07/05/99	5.36	108.448	7.20	3.98	-.03	1.41	0.00	0.00	-0.08	0.00	-0.47	8.40	0.22	0.00	0.00	8.08
SCENARIO 3	1,000.00	01/29/99	4.92	113.057	6.21	3.74	-.02	1.41	0.00	5.65	-0.08	0.00	-1.94	8.40	0.19	0.00	0.00	12.23
WTD AVE	1,000.00	07/12/99	5.38	108.432	7.20	3.98	-.01	1.41	0.00	0.12	-0.08	0.00	-0.61	8.40	0.22	0.00	0.00	8.06

18. 693160AA PRUDENTIAL BACHE 92-A 6.250 07/15/98 AB AAA

	Par Value	Effective Maturity	Prob. WAL	Price	Adj YTM	Adj Dur	Adj Conv	OAS	Exercise Factor	Yield Curve	Time	Spread	Option	Interest	Components of Total Return (%) Coupon Rtn	Mat/Called Rtn	Principal Rtn	Total Return
BEGINNING	1,000.00	01/07/96	2.87	102.765	4.21	2.62	-.08	-.42										
SCENARIO 1	870.65	04/18/96	2.14	102.796	4.92	1.94	-.06	-.42	0.13	-1.75	1.79	0.00	-0.02	3.32	0.05	-0.35	0.17	3.22
SCENARIO 2	869.85	04/09/96	2.12	104.818	3.92	1.88	-.60	-.42	0.13	0.00	1.79	0.00	-0.06	3.32	0.04	-0.35	0.14	4.88
SCENARIO 3	867.08	03/09/96	2.04	106.734	2.89	1.60	-.53	-.42	0.13	1.80	1.79	0.00	-0.24	3.32	0.03	-0.36	0.10	6.43
WTD AVE	869.19	04/01/96	2.10	104.783	3.91	1.81	-.39	-.42	0.13	0.02	1.79	0.00	-0.11	3.32	0.04	-0.35	0.14	4.84

19. 81371FAA SECURED FINANCE 9.050 12/15/04 FI AAA

	Par Value	Effective Maturity	Prob. WAL	Price	Adj YTM	Adj Dur	Adj Conv	OAS	Exercise Factor	Yield Curve	Time	Spread	Option	Interest	Components of Total Return (%) Coupon Rtn	Mat/Called Rtn	Principal Rtn	Total Return
BEGINNING	950.00	12/15/04	11.80	117.301	6.88	7.36	.74	58										
SCENARIO 1	950.00	12/15/04	10.80	109.081	7.79	6.81	.63	58	0.00	-6.62	-0.28	0.00	0.00	7.60	0.27	0.00	0.00	0.97
SCENARIO 2	950.00	12/15/04	10.80	116.967	6.80	6.80	.65	58	0.00	0.00	-0.28	0.00	0.00	7.60	0.24	0.00	0.00	7.55
SCENARIO 3	950.00	12/15/04	10.80	125.626	5.82	7.15	.68	58	0.00	7.27	-0.28	0.00	0.00	7.60	0.20	0.00	0.00	14.79
WTD AVE	950.00	12/15/04	10.80	117.224	6.80	6.98	.65	58	0.00	0.22	-0.28	0.00	0.00	7.60	0.24	0.00	0.00	7.77

20. 912803AQ US STRIP PRIN 0.000 02/15/19 TR TSY

	Par Value	Effective Maturity	Prob. WAL	Price	Adj YTM	Adj Dur	Adj Conv	OAS	Exercise Factor	Yield Curve	Time	Spread	Option	Interest	Components of Total Return (%) Coupon Rtn	Mat/Called Rtn	Principal Rtn	Total Return
BEGINNING	2,000.00	02/15/19	25.97	14.566	7.56	25.02	6.38	-.19										
SCENARIO 1	2,000.00	02/15/19	24.97	12.328	8.56	23.94	5.85	-.19	0.00	-22.96	7.60	0.00	0.00	0.00	0.00	0.00	0.00	-15.36
SCENARIO 2	2,000.00	02/15/19	24.97	15.673	7.56	24.06	5.90	-.19	0.00	0.00	7.60	0.00	0.00	0.00	0.00	0.00	0.00	7.60
SCENARIO 3	2,000.00	02/15/19	24.97	19.947	6.56	24.18	5.96	-.19	0.00	29.35	7.60	0.00	0.00	0.00	0.00	0.00	0.00	36.94
WTD AVE	2,000.00	02/15/19	24.97	15.983	7.56	24.06	5.91	-.19	0.00	2.13	7.60	0.00	0.00	0.00	0.00	0.00	0.00	9.73

Exhibit 7.4 (Concluded)

21. 912810EG — US 8.750 08/15/20 — 8.750 — 08/15/20 — TR — TSY

	Par Value	Effective Maturity	Prob. WAL	Price	Adj YTM	Adj Dur	Adj Conv	OAS	Exercise Factor	Components of Total Return (%)								
										Yield Curve	Time	Spread	Option	Interest	Coupon Rtrn	Mat/Called Rtrn	Principal Rtrn	Total Return
BEGINNING	2,500.00	08/15/20	27.47	120.937	7.02	10.79	1.89	.01	0.00									
SCENARIO 1	2,500.00	08/15/20	26.47	108.605	7.96	10.02	1.66	.01	0.00	-9.86	-0.32	0.00	0.00	7.22	0.16	0.00	0.00	-2.79
SCENARIO 2	2,500.00	08/15/20	26.47	120.550	7.03	10.68	1.84	.01	0.00	0.00	-0.32	0.00	0.00	7.22	0.14	0.00	0.00	7.05
SCENARIO 3	2,500.00	08/15/20	26.47	134.747	6.09	11.39	2.03	.01	0.00	11.71	-0.32	0.00	0.00	7.22	0.13	0.00	0.00	18.74
WTD AVE	2,500.00	08/15/20	26.47	121.301	7.03	10.70	1.84	.01	0.00	0.62	-0.32	0.00	0.00	7.22	0.14	0.00	0.00	7.66

22. 941063AD — WASTE MGMT INC — 8.750 — 05/01/18 — IN — A1

	Par Value	Effective Maturity	Prob. WAL	Price	Adj YTM	Adj Dur	Adj Conv	OAS	Exercise Factor	Components of Total Return (%)								
										Yield Curve	Time	Spread	Option	Interest	Coupon Rtrn	Mat/Called Rtrn	Principal Rtrn	Total Return
BEGINNING	1,250.00	11/08/14	21.70	112.229	7.51	9.04	1.16	.50	0.00									
SCENARIO 1	1,250.00	11/08/15	21.70	102.211	8.43	8.52	.85	.50	0.00	-9.32	0.06	0.00	0.55	7.61	0.38	0.00	0.00	-0.73
SCENARIO 2	1,250.00	10/12/14	20.63	112.081	7.49	8.72	1.07	.50	0.00	0.00	0.06	0.00	-0.19	7.61	0.33	0.00	0.00	7.81
SCENARIO 3	1,250.00	08/05/13	19.44	123.264	6.54	8.85	.96	.50	0.00	10.96	0.06	0.00	-1.42	7.61	0.29	0.00	0.00	17.49
WTD AVE	1,250.00	08/29/14	20.59	112.519	7.48	8.70	.96	.50	0.00	0.54	0.06	0.00	-0.35	7.61	0.33	0.00	0.00	8.19

23. 960402AQ — WESTINGHOUSE ELEC — 8.625 — 08/01/12 — IN — BA1

	Par Value	Effective Maturity	Prob. WAL	Price	Adj YTM	Adj Dur	Adj Conv	OAS	Exercise Factor	Components of Total Return (%)								
										Yield Curve	Time	Spread	Option	Interest	Coupon Rtrn	Mat/Called Rtrn	Principal Rtrn	Total Return
BEGINNING	1,000.00	08/01/12	19.43	97.498	8.90	8.76	1.20	2.14	0.00									
SCENARIO 1	1,000.00	08/01/12	18.43	90.017	9.80	8.25	1.07	2.14	0.00	-8.19	0.56	0.00	0.00	8.79	0.28	0.00	0.00	1.45
SCENARIO 2	1,000.00	08/01/12	18.43	98.052	8.84	8.64	1.15	2.14	0.00	0.00	0.56	0.00	0.00	8.79	0.25	0.00	0.00	9.61
SCENARIO 3	1,000.00	08/01/12	18.43	107.238	7.87	9.05	1.23	2.14	0.00	9.36	0.56	0.00	0.00	8.79	0.23	0.00	0.00	18.95
WTD AVE	1,000.00	08/01/12	18.43	98.436	8.84	8.65	1.15	2.14	0.00	0.39	0.56	0.00	0.00	8.79	0.25	0.00	0.00	10.00

Exhibit 7.5

Summary of Portfolio Return for Each Scenario and the Composite (2/26/93–2/26/94)

	Yield change impact	Time (roll) impact	Spread change impact	Option value	Earned interest	Coupon reinvestment	Matured/ Called	Mat/Called reinvestment	Total	Annual total
Scenario 1	–5.63	–.08	.00	.38	7.57	.26	–.10	.04	2.43	2.42
Scenario 2	.00	–.07	.00	–.17	7.55	.23	–.14	.04	7.44	7.31
Scenario 3	6.33	–.08	.00	–.78	7.54	.20	–.18	.04	13.07	12.67
Wtd. Avg.	.23	–.07	.00	–.19	7.55	.23	–.14	.04	7.65	7.47

insight into the sources and hence the causes of performance. Analysis that looks beyond the total portfolio return permits both the establishment and monitoring of policy.

That is, the return attributable to overall changes in interest rates should dominate the return from spread relationships, if the manager focuses on anticipation of interest rate changes. Conversely, a manager seeking to take advantage of spread relationships should have this component dominate.

Relative Return Analysis

Relative return analysis allows a manager to compare alternative securities systematically. It recognizes that choosing the highest expected return security may be inappropriate, either because it may not be the security with the highest realized return, or because its level of risk may be too high. The objective of relative return analysis is to identify the highest expected return security for a given level of risk.

This technique is illustrated in Exhibit 7.6 for the no-change case (scenario 2). Duration is on the horizontal axis, and the expected return is on the vertical axis. The plot points are individual securities (asterisks and bond identification numbers). If Exhibit 7.6 displayed a regression line, it would represent the average relationship between return and duration of the individual securities making up the portfolio. Taking the regression line as fair value, the bonds above the line are those with higher expected return per unit of duration than the average relationship; bonds below the line have less return per unit of duration. For example, the bond that optimizes total expected return and duration appears to be bond 7, which has a duration of about 2.32 years and a total return of about 8.65%.

Relative return analysis should be performed for each scenario. Exhibit 7.7 shows the results for the best-case scenario (scenario 3).

This kind of two-dimensional framework gives a manager some basic ability to differentiate the return characteristics of the securities in a portfolio. This form of analysis is similar to the security market line approach, a common practice in the analysis of equity securities.[2]

In the fixed income market, of course, there is no measure of risk comparable to the equity measure of market risk or beta. The duration

---

2 William F. Sharpe and Gordon J. Alexander, *Fundamentals of Investments* (Englewood Cliffs, NJ: Prentice-Hall, 1989), pp. 173–177.

142

Chapter 7

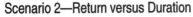

Exhibit 7.6

Scenario 2—Return versus Duration

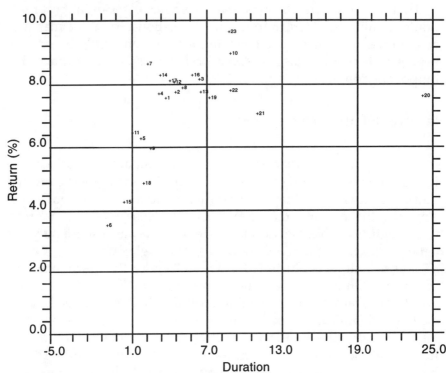

we use in the analysis is not necessarily a risk measure. It is a measure of volatility, which is a risk surrogate. Because duration, a measure of the length of the security, is a better measure, in many situations, than maturity, duration is a logical measure for differentiating securities.

Strategic Frontier Analysis: Strategic frontier analysis is a technique allowing evaluation of both the upside and the downside return characteristics of a security. It is a procedure for analyzing the return behavior of securities under alternative interest rate scenarios.

Exhibit 7.8 is a hypothetical example of strategic frontier analysis. Expected total return is shown on the vertical axis. This could be the total expected return of the most likely scenario of interest rate change, or perhaps the return of the most optimistic scenario of interest rate

Exhibit 7.7

Scenario 3—Return versus Duration

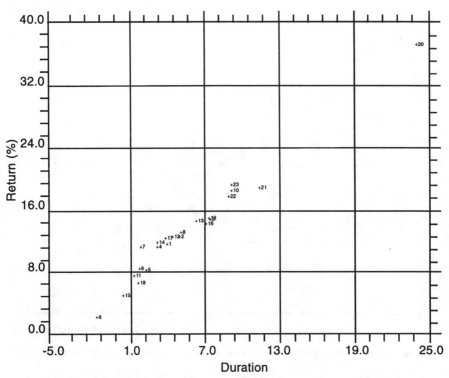

change. Worst-case total return is on the horizontal axis. The scenarios are those used in the return simulation process.

In Exhibit 7.8, the dots represent the individual security holdings in the portfolio we are analyzing as well as the securities on the potential purchase list. The intersection of the dashed lines indicates the portfolio average return; in this case a particular position is represented as average. Other positions are defined by their returns under either the optimistic scenario or the most likely scenario along one axis, and by returns from the worst case scenario along the other axis. Partitioning the diagram into four quadrants allows a manager to draw conclusions about the return behavior of the securities that fall into each of these quadrants.

Exhibit 7.8

Hypothetical Upside/Downside Trade-off

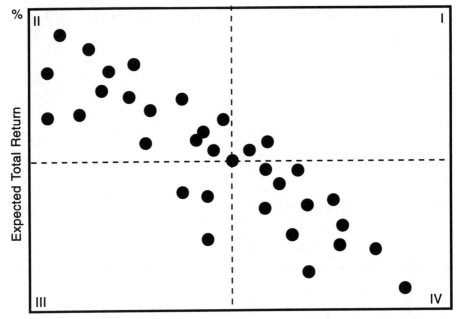

    Securities in quadrant II (upper left) might be considered *aggressive*
securities. They are aggressive in that, if the most likely scenario
prevails, a manager holding these securities would do extremely well.
If the worst-case scenario were to prevail, a manager would do relatively badly. So, a manager with strong convictions about the most
optimistic scenario would tend to choose securities from quadrant II.
    In quadrant IV are what might be considered *defensive* securities.
That is, if the worst-case scenario prevails, a manager would do relatively well. If the most likely scenario were to occur for these securities,
a manager would do relatively poorly. A manager wanting to take a
defensive posture would concentrate a portfolio in securities that fall
within quadrant IV.
    Quadrant III contains securities that are inferior because, whatever
the scenario outcome—either the most likely or worst case—these
securities would not perform as well as the portfolio average. Securities

falling into quadrant III represent potential sales from the existing portfolio because, by definition, they are no-win choices.

That leaves the securities falling in quadrant I. These are considered superior securities because, whatever the scenario outcome, these securities always outperform the portfolio, providing a no-loss result. Increases in holdings of the securities that fall in this quadrant would tend to move the portfolio results toward the upper right portion of the quadrant. That would enhance overall portfolio results, regardless of scenario outcome.

Exhibit 7.9 is another characterization of this type of trade-off analysis. It lays out a line we called a *strategic frontier*. This frontier essentially maps out the upper right region, where a manager can choose securities that would do the best job, depending on particular convictions. For example, a manager wanting maximum offense or

Exhibit 7.9

Strategic Frontier Analysis

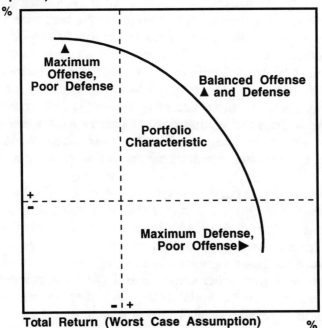

maximum aggressiveness, and willing to give up the defensive nature of some of the other securities, would choose securities along the strategic frontier mapped in or toward the upper left quadrant. A manager wishing a maximum defensive posture, and willing to live with the relatively poor returns if the most likely scenario prevails, would choose securities along the frontier in or toward the lower right quadrant. The ultimate objective, especially in the face of high uncertainty and no strong conviction about either scenario, would be to drive the portfolio into the upper right quadrant as far as possible.

For our sample portfolio of 23 bonds, Exhibit 7.10 plots the trade-off based on the total return for the best and worst case. Exhibit 7.11 lists the bonds and summarizes information for the securities in each quadrant. Exhibit 7.12 displays a plot of each bond's total return. The numbers 1 through 3 indicate the return for the scenarios and w indicates the composite return. Both the rank position of any one bond and its range of returns (generally analogous to variance) are seen at a glance. The return/risk characteristics of the portfolio composition are revealed by the overall wedge of the diagram.

Timing: Timing is an important factor in an active strategy. Over a given planning horizon, the manager must judge the best time to implement a strategy. When the yield curve is positively sloped, and if it is interpreted as a forecast of higher future interest rates, the strategy taken must be carefully timed. To benefit from an expected rate increase, a shortening of maturity (duration) is called for. Shortening maturity, however, means accepting a lower yield to maturity. Premature rate anticipation in these circumstances would result in a lower realized return for the period before rates actually increase; if the increase never materializes, significant return give-up may be experienced.

When the yield curve is negatively sloped, and rates are expected to decrease, timing again is important, because a premature lengthening of maturity will result in a lower yield to maturity with a much riskier longer-maturity (duration) portfolio. Effective timing of rate anticipation is thus a significant consideration.

Moreover, rate anticipation should not be considered complete after a decision on the initial timing. When to reverse or modify the strategy is always an issue. The return component interactions originally estimated are dynamic, and the manager must constantly balance anticipated capital changes against current yield and reinvestment

Exhibit 7.10

Strategic Frontier: Best Case versus Worst Case

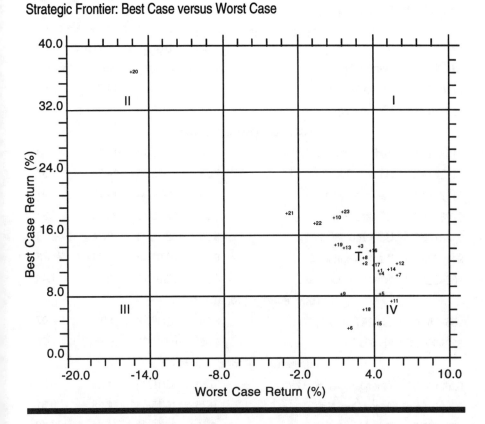

return effects. Successful rate anticipation is a "round-trip" action. That is, any rate anticipation efforts cannot be judged successful until the move taken in anticipation of any given rate increase (decrease) is reversed with a timely opposite move when rates are expected to decrease (increase). It should go without saying, however, that a manager's performance is judged most appropriately over an entire interest rate cycle and in the context of the entire portfolio rather than on individual transactions.

Another element to be analyzed is the effects of refunding terms. As interest rates rise, for example, prepayment rates of mortgage passthrough securities will decline, as homeowners tend to want to hold on to lower interest rate mortgages. If interest rates decline, homeowners have an incentive to refinance; hence, higher refunding

Exhibit 7.11

Bonds in Portfolios by Quadrant

Total return (%) for quadrant I

CUSIP	Description	Coupon rate (%)	Stated maturity	Best	Worst
071813AB	Baxter Intl Inc	9.50	06/15/08	14.70	3.03
450680CB	ITT Fin/Corp	8.55	06/15/09	13.98	3.70

Total return (%) for quadrant II

313309AJ	Federal Express Corp	9.65	06/15/12	18.18	.88
411347AB	Hanson Overseas	7.38	01/15.03	14.38	1.57
81371FAA	Secured Finance	9.05	12/15/04	14.79	.97
912803AQ	US Strip Prin	.00	02/15/19	36.94	−15.36
912810EG	US 8.750 08/15/20	8.75	08/15/20	18.74	−2.79
941063AD	Waste Mgmt Inc	8.75	05/01/18	17.49	− .73
960402AQ	Westinghouse Elec	8.63	08/01/12	18.95	1.45

Total return (%) for quadrant III

155658AA	GNMA Pool	8.00	06/15/16	4.01	2.07
3129969E	FH Gld 30	7.00	02/01/21	8.23	1.36

Total return (%) for quadrant IV

02635KAV	American Gen Fin Corp	8.50	06/15/99	11.32	4.53
046003EB	Assoc Corp N.a.	6.75	10/15/99	12.36	3.31
081721BS	Beneficial Corp	9.13	02/15/98	11.04	4.46
125569CG	CIT Group Hldgs Inc	8.75	02/15/96	8.05	4.54
190441AF	Coastal Corp	11.75	06/15/06	11.06	5.89
209864AS	Consolidated Rail Corp	9.75	12/01/00	12.97	3.22
3133112D	Fed Farm Cr Bk	6.10	05/01/95	7.56	5.41
370424FM	General Mtrs Accep Corp	8.63	06/15/99	12.27	5.83
423328AH	Heller Finl Inc	9.38	03/15/98	11.54	5.19
441812CY	Household Fin Corp	8.40	08/03/94	4.70	3.92
450680CN	ITT Finl Corp	9.25	07/15/01	12.23	3.88
693160AA	Prudential Bache 92-A	6.25	07/15/98	6.43	3.22

Exhibit 7.12

Ranking of Return

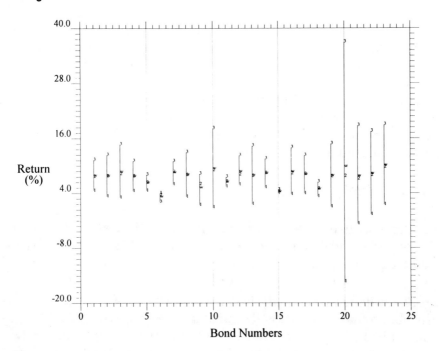

and shorter-lived passthroughs can be expected. Forearmed with knowledge of the anticipated average life of a passthrough security under various interest rate scenarios, the manager can decide whether to embrace or avoid these securities with their potentially altered average life.

As another example, bond call features tend to be unused if rates rise because the issuer has no need to retire or refinance bonds issued at rates lower than current rates. As a result, callability is not a concern for managers when scenarios call for rising rates. The opposite is true when rates are expected to fall; the issuer has an incentive to retire callable bonds to refinance at lower rates.

A variety of bond considerations can be addressed in return simulation analysis. The manager can then focus attention on the most important dimensions of direction, shape, and timing of interest rate change.

Interest rate forecasting in the United States is a good example of an activity emblematic of a highly efficient market. That is, wide distribution of information, low transactions costs, and the presence of many knowledgeable participants mean that it is hard to forecast the direction of rate changes consistently and correctly. This is not to say that some people are not accurate forecasters, but it does suggest that success is extremely difficult to achieve on a consistent basis. The rewards of being right are great, not only in terms of realized returns, but also in the amount of investment management business one can attract. The converse is also true.

Sector/Security Strategies

Another way to enhance returns relative to risk is to evaluate individual securities and subgroups of securities. This takes three basic forms: credit analysis, spread analysis, and valuation analysis.

Credit Analysis: Credit analysis is the assessment of default risk—the probability that the issuer will be unable to meet all contractual obligations fully and in a timely manner. Default risk is important for two reasons. The first is the chance of loss through an actual default. The second is the likelihood of adverse bond price changes precipitated by the increased probability of default. Typically this happens with downgrading of a bond's quality by the rating agencies, even though default may not take place.

Default risk has both systematic and unsystematic elements. For a variety of reasons, individual bond issuers may experience difficulty in meeting their obligations from time to time. If these are isolated acts of default, they may be diversified away or eliminated by effective credit analysis. More worrisome is the possibility of adverse general business conditions, such as occurred during the 1930s, the mid-1970s, and in the 1980s. Business cycles are associated with significant increases in defaults and widespread price declines due to concern over credit quality require more macro-oriented analysis.

Risk of default is often quantified by quality ratings provided by commercial rating companies. Historically, bond ratings have proved to be valid, but they are not foolproof indicators of default risk. Quality ratings appear to be closely related to the traditional measures of credit quality such as relative debt burden, earnings before interest and taxes, and variability in earnings streams. Yet many sophisticated, fixed income institutional investors do not rely exclusively on bond ratings; they also perform their own credit analysis.[3]

There are two motivations for credit analysis, both based on the assumption that yields in the marketplace are closely correlated to agency ratings, all other factors constant.

1. The analyst's assessment of credit quality may be more accurate or more timely than those of the rating agencies. In this case, the portfolio manager can achieve added yield at relatively small cost in terms of credit risk exposure, or can avoid paying in terms of reduced yield for nonexistent incremental quality.

2. Monitoring of ratings outstanding is believed to be one of the greatest difficulties facing the rating companies. A commercial rating company may have as many as 20,000 ratings outstanding. Delays inevitably occur for published reviews of ratings. With astute credit analysis, it may be possible to anticipate such upgrades or downgrades and profit from the yield and price changes which may ensue.

Spread Analysis: Spread analysis involves sector relationships. It may be possible to identify subclasses of fixed income securities that tend to behave similarly. Prices and yields on similar-grade bonds tend to move together, for example, as do yields on utility bonds. Such identifiable classes of securities are referred to as *sectors*. (In this sense, maturity ranges are also sectors, but the influence of maturity on total return is so dramatic that yield/maturity analysis is usually treated separately.) Relative prices or yields between one sector and another may change because of (1) altered perceptions of the creditworthiness of a sector or of the market's sensitivity to default risk; (2) changes in the market's valuation of some attribute or characteristic of the securities in the sector, such as a zero coupon feature; or (3) changes in supply and demand conditions.

Analysis of sector relationships coupled with appropriate management response can be rewarding in fixed income portfolio management. The objective, obviously, is to be invested in the sector or sectors

---

3   For a detailed discussion of credit analysis, see Jane Tripp Howe, "Credit Analysis for Corporate Bonds," Chapter 18 in Frank J. Fabozzi and T. Dessa Fabozzi (eds.), *The Handbook of Fixed Income Securities* (Homewood, IL: Business One-Irwin, 1994).

that will display the strongest relative price movements. In monitoring such sectoral relationships, it is customary to concentrate on spreads—i.e., the difference, usually measured in basis points, in yield between two sectors—among yield series that are broadly representative of the securities in the sector. A number of dealer firms maintain broadly representative historical yield series to help in identifying abnormal differences. These firms can perform specialized analyses such as measurement of the historical average, or the maximum or minimum spreads among sectors. Spread analysis, with consideration of other relevant factors, produces, in effect, a relative valuation of a sector's worth. If relative values diverge enough, investors can swap sectors so as to obtain the largest gain or smallest loss as sector yields return to more normal relationships.

Spread analysis, like credit analysis, offers significant potential for return enhancement. The drawbacks are that these strategies may require too many trades for the contribution to be meaningful, and that in fact overall changes in interest rates may dwarf their effects.

Valuation Analysis: The essence of bond valuation analysis is identifying the difference between the actual yield and the default-free yield, which constitutes the yield premium. To evaluate a corporate bond, the steps are to determine the yield premium on the bond; ascertain the components of that yield premium; define the normal values for that yield premium; and then compare the normalized value of that bond's yield with its actual yield. The difference is the bond's over- or undervaluation, depending on whether it is a negative or positive difference.

The yield premium is basically a compensation to the investor for a number of things such as default risk, issuer options, and any tax effects. So the problem in bond valuation is to attribute a value to each of these factors and any others that are significant.

The valuation framework described in Chapters 4, 5, and 6 is used to identify mispriced issues. A model provides a fitted value for each issue in a universe under investigation. The fitted value and the actual value can be given in terms of both price and yield. The difference between the actual value and the fitted value is the residual. Measured in terms of price (yield), a positive (negative) residual means that the issue is overvalued. A negative (positive) residual when price (yield) is used means that the issue is undervalued. T-statistics can be computed for each issue to determine whether the residual is statistically significant.

Bond valuation is also a useful tool in performance measurement, as discussed in Chapter 12.

PORTFOLIO OPTIMIZATION

Portfolio optimization can be thought of as a strategy for quantifying the optimal integration of risk and return expectations with desired portfolio objectives and policy. It may include either modification of an existing portfolio or creation of an entirely new one.

Portfolio optimization is the epitome of active portfolio management. The portfolio manager begins with a basic set of expectations in the form of expected rates of return, and structures a portfolio that meets the client's desired portfolio parameters. These parameters are a combination of the preferences and requirements of the client and the style and emphasis of the manager. Examples include minimum yield objectives, minimum and/or maximum concentration constraints, desired duration range or level, and minimum portfolio return requirements.

The objective of portfolio optimization is to maximize portfolio return for a given level of acceptable risk. The expected returns are straightforward; the estimate of risk is not. Two alternative portfolio optimization approaches differ primarily in their treatment of risk.

Variance/Covariance Approach

Both the variance/covariance approach and the traditional Markowitz formulation (discussed in Chapter 11) assist managers in making asset allocation decisions. For equity optimization, minimization of the standard deviation or variance of portfolio returns is the customary risk objective. The process involves creating a covariance matrix that, along with expectations of stock returns, is then optimized by a quadratic optimization program. The program embodies elements such as turnover, concentration, and dividend yield constraints to produce a minimum-risk portfolio for a given level of return. The problem is tractable since the creation of the covariance matrix can always resort to an estimate based upon historical return experience.

In bond analysis, however, no such convention is available. Because a fixed income security has a finite life, its covariance with other bonds changes with time, if for no other reason than shortening of the maturity of each bond with time. Moreover, with a given rate change, there can be yield curve shape changes as well as direction changes. Direction changes can alter, and in some cases reverse, the covariance relationships between securities. The problem thus becomes one of estimation. Indeed, if a covariance matrix could be created, the bond optimization process could parallel the analysis for stock.

Worst Case Approach

An alternative approach defines risk as the worst case interest rate scenario or the outcome given the most adverse change (increase) in interest rates. The objective becomes to maximize bond portfolio expected return with risk defined as the level of return under the worst case interest rate scenario, constrained to some minimum level. Risk is specified in terms of minimally acceptable return levels that in turn are a direct result of the worst case interest rate scenario expectations. Because the analytical procedure is linear, a linear programming optimization algorithm may be used.

OTHER ACTIVE STRATEGIES OR TACTICS

There are other active strategies beyond relative return value and sector strategies. Their potential impact on total portfolio return may not be as great, but they can still make a significant contribution.

Trades or Exchanges

Trades or exchanges that managers use to enhance portfolio returns can be classified as pure yield pickup trades, substitution trades, and intermarket or sector spread trades. Trades or exchanges are also referred to as *swaps*.

Pure Yield Pickup Trade or Exchange: Switching to a security having a higher yield is called a pure yield trade or exchange. The transaction may be made to achieve either a higher coupon yield or a higher yield to maturity. While such transactions seem the reasonable action, as long as there is no significant shift in risk level (or liquidity), accounting rules or regulatory mandates bar some investors from making yield pickup trades that create a loss, usually unless offset by a gain else-where in the portfolio, even though a portfolio benefit would result.

Substitution Trade or Exchange: A substitution trade involves replacing one security with another that has a higher yield to maturity but is otherwise identical in terms of maturity, coupon, and quality. This type of trade depends on a capital market imperfection. Because the imper-fection is temporary, the portfolio manager expects the yields to ma-turity on the two securities to reestablish a normal yield spread rela-tionship, but usually resulting in a price increase and hence capital appreciation for the holder of the higher-yielding issue. The workout period (time for the yield realignment to occur) can be critical; the sooner it occurs, the greater the return on an annualized basis. If the substituted security must be held to maturity, the realized annual return may be marginal.

Intermarket or Sector Spread Trade or Exchange: There are expected nor-mal yield relationships between two different sectors of the bond market. An intermarket trade may be made when there is a perceived misalignment in a relationship. The trade may involve switching to the higher-yielding security when the yield spread is too wide and is expected to narrow, and to the lower-yielding security when the spread is too narrow and is expected to widen. The risk, especially of the latter switch, is that the anticipated adjustment will not occur, resulting in a reduced portfolio yield.

Maturity Spacing Strategies

Alternative portfolio maturity structures may be used as an active management strategy. These include a balanced maturity schedule with equal spacing of maturities held; an all-short or all-long maturity strategy; or a *barbell* structure, where bond holdings are concentrated in short maturities and long maturities, with little or no holdings of intermediates.

The rationale for an equal-maturity portfolio is minimization of reinvestment risk, as reinvestment of bond proceeds is spread out over the full interest rate cycle. That is, there will be a relatively constant cash flow over time from maturity *laddering*, so funds can be reinvested at then-current rates. The effects of overall interest rate change will tend to be averaged, and the risk/return extremes will be ameliorated.

An all-short or all-long maturity portfolio strategy is frequently a temporary strategy adopted in anticipation of interest rate change, but it is a strategy of potentially large reinvestment rate risk. A manager who stays with an all-short portfolio usually has either a preference for high liquidity or an extreme aversion to principal risk.

A barbell approach aims to achieve the best return-risk reward by balancing the defensive qualities of short-term securities with the aggressive qualities of long-term securities and avoiding the intermediates.

There has been no assurance found in empirical tests of these various strategies that any one has been consistently superior over time.[4]

Consistency of Style

As a general objective, consistency of management style is important. Given the range of strategies available and the expertise required for implementation, it is important to identify a style that is compatible with the investment policy established or that is most effective for the portfolio management organization. Emphasizing a particular style should provide the best results. This is not to say that other strategies should be neglected. In some cases, managers should attempt to insulate a portfolio from the effects of interest rate change or quality effects; in other cases, a subfocus might be, say, substitution trading. Basically, consistency of management style, assuming a clear rationalization for that style, should provide the best results over time.

SUMMARY

In this chapter we have explained several active management strategies and illustrated their application. Fixed income portfolio management is subject to many influences, and the portfolio manager must select from a menu of active strategies. The final strategy should depend on the portfolio manager's own strengths, fortified with complementary

---

4   See, for example, H. Russell Fogler and William A. Groves, "How Much Can Active Bond Management Raise Returns?" *Journal of Portfolio Management* (Fall 1976), pp. 35–40; and H. Russell Fogler, William A. Groves, and James G. Richardson, "Managing Bonds: Are 'Dumbbells' Smart?" *Journal of Portfolio Management* (Winter 1976), pp. 54–60.

techniques and tools. The final result should be superior returns and consistency of returns through risk control. Uncertainty is always with us, but the strategies discussed in this chapter can help portfolio managers to make the best investment decisions—by increasing understanding and decreasing uncertainty.

Chapter 8

Indexing

Indexing a portfolio is one form of passive investing. Indexing means designing a portfolio so that its performance will match the performance of some target index or bogey. Performance is measured in terms of total rate of return achieved over some investment horizon. An indexing strategy generally does not rely on expectations of interest rate movements or changes in yield spread relationships.

Several factors explain the recent popularity of bond indexing.[1] First, the empirical evidence suggests that historically the performance of active bond investment advisors has been poor. Second is that lower management fees are charged for an indexed portfolio than for actively managed portfolios. Some pension funds have decided to avoid management fees and manage some or all of their funds in-house employing an indexing strategy. Lower nonmanagement fees, such as custodian and master fees, than for actively managed portfolios is a third explanation. Finally, sponsors have greater control over investment managers when an indexing strategy is selected. A sponsor who specifies a restriction on an actively managed portfolio's duration still gives a manager ample leeway to pursue strategies that may significantly underperform the index selected as a benchmark. Requiring that a portfolio be constructed to track an index gives little leeway to the manager, and, as a result should result in performance that does not significantly depart from the benchmark.

---

1   Sharmin Mossavar-Rahmani, *Bond Index Funds* (Chicago: Probus Publishing, 1991), p. vii.

Critics of indexing are quick to point out that while a portfolio can be managed to match the performance of some index, the performance of that index does not necessarily represent optimal performance. Moreover, matching an index does not mean that the manager will satisfy the client's return requirement objective. For a life insurance company or a pension fund aiming to have sufficient funds to satisfy a predetermined liability, indexing merely reduces the likelihood that the performance will not lag the index materially. Indexing does not ensure that there will be sufficient funds to satisfy a predetermined liability. Finally, matching an index means a manager is restricted to the sectors of the bond market that are in the index, even though there may be attractive opportunities in market sectors outside the index. While the broad-based bond market indexes typically include agency passthrough securities, for example, other mortgage-backed securities such as private label passthroughs, stripped mortgage-backed securities, and collateralized mortgage obligations are generally not included. Yet it is in these markets that attractive returns to enhance performance may be available.

At the theoretical level, the indexing approach is supported by the work of Markowitz on the construction of efficient portfolios[2] and by capital market theory as developed by Sharpe,[3] Lintner,[4] and Mossin.[5] Markowitz demonstrates how portfolios can be constructed so as to maximize return for a given level of risk. Such portfolios are referred to as *efficient portfolios.*

The Sharpe-Lintner-Mossin analysis demonstrates that a "market" portfolio offers the highest level of return per unit of risk in an *efficient* market. An efficient market is one where market participants cannot consistently earn abnormal risk-adjusted returns after considering transactions costs. Combining securities in a portfolio with characteristics similar to the market allows the efficiency of the market to be captured.

2 Harry M. Markowitz, "Portfolio Selection," *Journal of Finance* (March 1952), pp. 71–91, and *Portfolio Selection: Efficient Diversification of Investment* (New York: John Wiley & Sons, 1959).

3 William F. Sharpe, "Capital Asset Prices: A Theory of Market Equilibrium under Conditions of Risk," *Journal of Finance* (September 1964), pp. 425–442.

4 John Lintner, "Security Prices, Risk, and Maximal Gains from Diversification," *Journal of Finance* (December 1965), pp. 587–616.

5 Jan Mossin, "Equilibrium in a Capital Asset Market," *Econometrica* (October 1966), pp. 76–83.

The theoretical market portfolio consists of all risky assets. The weight of each risky asset in the market portfolio is equal to the ratio of its market value to the aggregate market value of all risky assets. That is, the market portfolio is a capitalization-weighted (value-weighted) portfolio of all risky assets.[6]

FACTORS TO CONSIDER IN SELECTING AN INDEX

A manager who wishes to pursue an indexing strategy must determine which bond index to replicate. There are a number of bond indexes from which to select, and several factors influence the decision. The first is the investor's risk tolerance. Selection of an index that includes corporate bonds will expose the investor to credit risk. If this risk is unacceptable, an investor should avoid an index that includes this sector.

The second factor influencing the selection of an index is the investor's objective. For example, while the total return of the various indexes tends to be highly positively correlated, the variability of total returns has been quite different. Therefore, an investor whose objective is to minimize the variability of total returns will be biased toward one that has had, and expects to continue to have, low variability (i.e., a shorter duration relative to other indexes). Moreover, variability of total return may not be symmetric in rising and falling markets. Investors who have expectations about the future direction of interest rates will favor the index that is expected to perform better given their expectations. Finally, because the cash flow of different indexes can be quite different, if the objective of an investor is to meet projected liabilities, the index that best matches that liability stream may be the better choice.

A final consideration in selecting an index is constraints on acceptable investments that may be imposed by regulators. An index may include sectors of the bond market in which a regulated entity is not allowed to invest. For example, a regulated financial institution that is not permitted to invest in the high-yield sector of the corporate market should not select an index that includes that sector. Even without restrictions on investing in a given sector of the bond market, there may

---

6 Granito argues that while the theoretical arguments support indexing a common stock portfolio, they are inappropriate for justifying indexing of a bond portfolio. See Michael R. Granito, "The Problem with Bond Index Funds," *Journal of Portfolio Management* (Summer 1987), pp. 41–48.

be restrictions imposed on the proportion of the portfolio that can be allocated to a specific sector. The investor is then limited to indexes whose allocations comply with the regulations imposed.

BOND INDEXES

The wide range of bond market indexes available can be classified as *broad-based market indexes* or *specialized market indexes*. The three broad-based market indexes most commonly used by institutional investors are the Lehman Brothers Aggregate Index, the Salomon Brothers Broad Investment-Grade Bond Index, and the Merrill Lynch Domestic Market Index. The bond market sectors covered by these three indexes are the Treasury, agency, investment-grade corporate, mortgage-backed, and Yankee markets.

The specialized market indexes focus on only one sector or subsector of the bond market. Indexes on sectors of the market are published by the three investment banking firms that produce the broad-based market indexes. For example, Salomon Brothers publishes both a corporate bond index (a sector index) and a high-grade corporate bond index that includes AAA- and AA-rated corporate bonds (a subindex of the corporate bond index). Other firms also provide specialized indexes. Some examples are the Morgan Stanley Actively Traded MBS Index, the Donaldson Lufkin & Jenrette High Yield Index, the First Boston High Yield Index, the Goldman Sachs Convertible 100, and the Ryan Labs Treasury Index.

In recent years, money managers and clients have moved in the direction of "customized benchmarks," or a benchmark that is designed to meet a client's requirements and long-term objectives.[7] In December 1986, Salomon Brothers Inc. introduced its Large Pension Fund Baseline Bond Index as a standardized benchmark tailor-made for large pension funds "seeking to establish long-term core portfolios that more closely match the longer durations of their nominal dollar liabilities."[8]

---

7 For a discussion of customized benchmarks and the reasons for the growing interest in them, see Sharmin Mossavar-Rahmani, "Customized Benchmarks in Structured Management," *Journal of Portfolio Management* (Summer 1987), pp. 65–68.

8 Martin L. Leibowitz, Thomas Klaffky, and Steven Mandel, "Introducing the Salomon Brothers Large Pension Fund Baseline Bond Index" (New York, NY: Salomon Brothers Inc., December 1986), p. 1.

DIVERSIFICATION AND PORTFOLIO SIZE

One of the key considerations in an indexing strategy is how many bond issues are necessary to obtain adequate diversification. A study by McEnally and Boardman examines how diversification of bonds varies with portfolio size.[9] From 515 corporate bonds with quality ratings ranging from Aaa to Baa, they construct 1,000 randomly selected portfolios for a given number of issues. They then compute the variance of monthly returns. The results of the McEnally-Boardman study are summarized in Exhibit 8.1.

The first row of the exhibit shows the average variance of returns for the 515 issues. The last row presents the variance of returns for a portfolio consisting of all bond issues. The other rows show the average variance for the 1,000 randomly constructed portfolios as the number of issues in the portfolio increases. Note that as the number of issues in the portfolio increases, the average variance of the portfolio return decreases—approaching the variance of returns of the portfolio consisting of all issues. Also shown in Exhibit 8.1 is the nondiversifiable return variation (that is, the variance of the return for the all-bond portfolio) as a proportion of the total return variation (that is, the average variation of return) for the random portfolios.

If we look at the entire sample of bonds as the universe of all fixed income securities and the quality ratings as a sector, the McEnally-Boardman results have several interesting implications for indexing strategies.

First, the analysis supports a theoretical relationship between portfolio size and the variance of return of a portfolio consisting of n issues:

$$Var(P_n) = Var(M) + (1/n) Var(R_1)$$

where n $\quad$ = number of securities in the portfolio
$Var(P_n)$ = the expected value of the variance of returns of portfolios constructed by investing $1/n$ of the portfolio in each of n randomly selected securities
$Var(M)$ = the average systematic or market-related variance of returns from the universe from which the n securities are drawn

---

9 Richard W. McEnally and Calvin M. Boardman, "Aspects of Corporate Bond Portfolio Diversification," *Journal of Financial Research* (Spring 1979), pp. 27–36.

$Var(R_1)$ = the average nonsystematic (diversifiable or residual) variance of the one-security portfolios from which the n securities are drawn

Thus, as an additional security is added to the portfolio, the variance of the portfolio can be expected to decrease by $1/n$ times the average nonsystematic risk of the one-security portfolios.

This can be seen in Exhibit 8.2, which repeats the results for all corporate bonds in Exhibit 8.1, and also shows the theoretical expected value of the variance for a portfolio of size n. There is no statistically significant difference between the theoretical expected value and the observed average value for the variance for any of the portfolios.

Second, it appears that the effect of portfolio size on diversification closely parallels the relationship found in common stocks.[10] This suggests that once a desired target is selected, it can be replicated with a manageable number of securities, probably fewer than 40 issues.

Finally, when portfolios are constructed from different segments of the market, the number of securities necessary to diversify away nonsystematic risk in that segment may differ. For the segments represented by the quality rating of the issue, for example, the results in Exhibit 8.2 indicate that it takes fewer issues to eliminate systematic risk for higher-quality bonds than for lower-quality bonds. For example, a four-bond portfolio consisting of Aaa issues has an average variance that is 6% greater than a completely diversified portfolio of Aaa issues. On the other hand, a four-bond portfolio consisting of Baa issues has an average variance that is 40% larger than a completely diversified portfolio of Baa issues.

TRACKING AN INDEX

Once a target index is selected, a manager must construct a portfolio to track that index. We will refer to the portfolio as the *indexed portfolio*. Any discrepancy between the performance of the indexed portfolio and the index (whether positive or negative) is referred to as *tracking error*.

---

10 See John L. Evans and Stephen H. Archer, "Diversification and the Reduction of Dispersion: An Empirical Analysis," *Journal of Finance* (December 1968), pp. 761–767.

Exhibit 8.1

Monthly Return Variance of Corporate Bond Portfolios, January 1973 to June 1976 ($\times 10^4$)

	All issues	Aaa	Aa	A	Baa
All bonds in universe, individually [Var(P$_1$)]	9.257	7.756	8.419	9.912	10.977
Random portfolios of bonds [Var(P$_n$)]*					
1 bond	9.367 (1.85)**	7.737 (1.21)	8.308 (1.47)	9.721 (2.10)	10.974 (2.52)
2 bonds	7.469 (1.48)	7.175 (1.20)	7.234 (1.28)	7.316 (1.58)	7.557 (1.73)
4 bonds	6.004 (1.19)	6.777 (1.06)	6.298 (1.11)	5.827 (1.26)	6.100 (1.40)
6 bonds	5.782 (1.15)	6.630 (1.03)	6.096 (1.08)	5.503 (1.19)	5.446 (1.25)
8 bonds	5.591 (1.11)	6.644 (1.04)	6.075 (1.07)	5.309 (1.15)	5.229 (1.20)
10 bonds	5.376 (1.07)	6.482 (1.01)	5.965 (1.05)	5.133 (1.11)	4.982 (1.14)
12 bonds	5.401 (1.07)	6.537 (1.02)	5.894 (1.04)	5.050 (1.09)	4.912 (1.13)
14 bonds	5.341 (1.06)	6.549 (1.02)	5.871 (1.04)	5.003 (1.08)	4.845 (1.11)
16 bonds	5.299 (1.05)	6.484 (1.02)	5.876 (1.04)	4.940 (1.07)	4.768 (1.09)
18 bonds	5.266 (1.05)	6.524 (1.02)	5.784 (1.02)	4.917 (1.06)	4.760 (1.09)
20 bonds	5.274 (1.05)	6.410 (1.00)	5.809 (1.03)	4.928 (1.06)	4.699 (1.07)
40 bonds	5.155 (1.02)	6.449 (1.00)	5.767 (1.02)	4.776 (1.03)	4.513 (1.03)
All bond portfolio [Var(M)]	5.039	6.416	5.661	4.633	4.362

Key: Var(P$_1$) = mean variance of individual issues
      Var(P$_n$) = mean variance of portfolios constructed by investing 1/n of the portfolio in each of n randomly selected securities
      Var(M) = mean systematic or market-related variance for the universe

* Based on 1,000 portfolios in each cell.
** Var(P$_n$)/Var(M) = ratio of mean variance of portfolio to mean market-related variance. (Computed by authors)
Source: Richard W. McEnally and Calvin M. Boardman, "Aspects of Corporate Bond Portfolio Diversification," *Journal of Financial Research* (Spring 1979), p. 31.

Exhibit 8.2

Monthly Return Variance of Randomly Generated Portfolios of Corporate Bonds of All Quality Classes, January 1973 to June 1976 ($\times 10^4$)

Number of bonds in portfolio	Mean Var(P_n)*	Theoretical Var(P_n)*
1	9.367	9.257
2	7.469	7.148
4	6.004	6.094
6	5.782	5.742
8	5.591	5.566
10	5.376	5.461
12	5.401	5.391
14	5.341	5.340
16	5.299	5.303
18	5.266	5.273
20	5.274	5.250
40	5.155	5.144

* $Var(P_n)$ = mean (expected value in case of theoretical) variance of portfolios constructed by investing $1/n$ of the portfolio in each of n randomly selected securities.

Source: Richard W. McEnally and Calvin M. Boardman, "Aspects of Corporate Bond Portfolio Diversification," *Journal of Financial Research* (Spring 1979), p. 34.

Tracking Error

Tracking error has three sources: (1) transactions costs in constructing the indexed portfolio; (2) differences in the composition of the indexed portfolio and the index itself; and (3) discrepancies between prices used by the organization constructing the index and transactions prices available to the manager.

One approach in constructing the indexed portfolio is for the manager to purchase all the issues in the index according to their weight in the target index. Substantial tracking error will then result from transactions costs (and other fees) associated with purchasing all the issues and reinvesting cash flow (maturing principal and coupon interest). A broad-based market index could include over 5,000 issues, so large transactions costs may make this approach impractical. Moreover, some issues in the index may not be available at the prices used in constructing the index. Even small indexes, such as the Lehman Treasury Index, contain hundreds of securities, and some indexes may actually be based on universes of several thousand bonds.

Instead of purchasing all issues in the index, the manager may purchase just a sample of issues. While this approach reduces tracking error resulting from high transactions costs, it increases tracking error resulting from the mismatch of the indexed portfolio and the index.

Generally speaking, the fewer the number of issues used to replicate the target index, the smaller the tracking error due to transactions costs, but the greater the tracking error risk due to the mismatch of the characteristics of the indexed portfolio and the index. In contrast, the more issues purchased to replicate the index, the greater the tracking error due to transactions costs, and the smaller the tracking error risk due to the mismatch of the index portfolio and the index. Obviously, then, there is a trade-off between tracking error and the number of issues used to construct the indexed portfolio.

Typical Conditions

The question then arises as to the construction and maintenance of an actual portfolio that would replicate the given index as closely as possible in actual operating conditions. Specifically, typical conditions for a feasible strategy are that:

1. The portfolio should not contain more than a given number of securities (for example, 50).

2. The portfolio should not be rebalanced more often than monthly.

3. Any interest income should be kept as cash until the next rebalancing date or reinvested at a specified rate.

4. There should be a minimum amount for any purchase or sale (for example, $100,000 of face value).

5. All purchases or sales should be in round lots of a given size (for example, $10,000 of face value).

6.   Transactions costs should be included in the portfolio returns.

In addition to these requirements, there are two desiderata to make the investment strategy practical. First, the strategy should be flexible enough to allow the portfolio manager to be involved in the selection of the securities for the portfolio. Second, the strategy should include a quantitative algorithm that determines exactly the holdings in each security selected for the portfolio, as well as the transactions necessary to maintain the portfolio.

Index Tracking Methodology

The goal of any indexing methodology is to track the returns of the target index as closely as possible, subject to the requirements discussed above. The extent of the tracking accuracy can be assessed by historical simulations. The methodology we suggest consists of three steps.

The first step is to define the classes into which the index universe is to be divided. The number of classes should be made equal to the number of securities to be held in the portfolio. The classes should be as homogeneous as possible. This could be accomplished by dividing the universe into issuing sector/quality, maturity range, and coupon range. Suppose that the objective is to track the Lehman Government Index with a portfolio of at most 40 bonds. The classes can be defined by distinguishing Treasuries and agencies, breaking the maturity range into 10 intervals (for example, 1–2, 2–3, 3–4, 4–6, 6–8, 8–10, 10–12, 12–15, 15–20, and 20–30 years to maturity), and separating the securities with coupons of 10% or less from those with coupons over 10%. The total number of classes will then be 40 ($2 \times 10 \times 2$). Each class is reasonably homogeneous, because it includes only one type of security in a narrow maturity range and with similar coupon levels.

The second step is the selection of securities. On the initial date, as well as on each rebalancing date (typically monthly), one security is chosen from each class for inclusion in the investment portfolio. The methodology places no requirements on the selection of the security from the class. This gives the portfolio manager complete freedom to exercise personal judgment. The portfolio manager may review the list of bonds in the class and select the one that has the most appeal in terms of availability or liquidity, and so on. To keep turnover down, the portfolio manager will probably choose a security that is already held in the portfolio (if any), unless there are reasons to prefer a new security within the class. It is even possible to base the selection on a valuation model that ranks the securities in the class from the most underpriced to the most overpriced.

The third and final step is determination of the amount to be held in each security selection. This step does not involve any judgmental input and is accomplished completely by quadratic programming. This mathematical programming technique constructs the portfolio to be as representative of the target index as possible. The quadratic programming technique ensures that:

1. The duration of the portfolio is equal to that of the index.

2. Other characteristics are matched.

3. The amount held in each of the selected securities is as close to proportional to the total weight of that class in the index as is possible, given the two constraints above.[11]

After the quadratic programming solution is obtained, the solution can be modified to satisfy round lot and minimum trade requirements. The residual amount of cash at the rebalancing date can also be minimized.

Alternative Optimization Approaches

There are two possible optimization approaches for tracking an index. The first is a traditional tracking methodology developed by Gifford Fong Associates in the 1980s (BONDTRAC).[12] The second is to apply volatility analysis and control using a strategic optimization system (STRATOS) developed by Gifford Fong Associates and based on the stochastic volatility term structure described in Chapter 4.

The period October 1990 to March 1991 is chosen for our simulations, to include a six-month time period in which the implied volatilities changed significantly. We use the spot rate of the one-month T-bill for the risk-free short rate. The target index is the Shearson Lehman Treasury Index. The stochastic volatility term structure theory asserts

---

11 The first two conditions are the constraints in the quadratic program. The objective function is to minimize the sum of the square of the difference between the relative weights in the portfolio and the weights in the class.

12 The methodology is described in H. Gifford Fong and Frank J. Fabozzi, *Fixed Income Portfolio Management* (Homewood, IL: Dow Jones-Irwin, 1985), pp. 106–110.

that even noncallable bond pricing is affected by volatility, so we restrict ourselves to the noncallable securities to highlight the issue. To compare the effectiveness of BONDTRAC and STRATOS, both systems optimize a portfolio containing the same assets indexed against the same target index.

To replicate the index using the traditional approach (BONDTRAC), we separate the bonds in the index into 10 cells defined by coupon and maturity break points. The index is first partitioned into two groups by coupon (i.e., 0–10% and 10–30%). Then, both coupon groups are partitioned into five maturity groups (i.e., 1–2 years, 2–5 years, 5–10 years, 10–20 years, and 20–30 years). In total, there are ten cells. Partitioning the index into 10 cells allows us to maintain a fair representation of the characteristics of the target index since the target index was composed of high- and low-coupon bonds and short- to long-maturity bonds.

One Treasury issue is randomly selected from each cell to be included in the portfolio created by the traditional index tracking methodology and the volatility management index tracking methodology. Both approaches calculate the optimal composition of the ten issues. In the optimization procedure, BONDTRAC tries to match the duration, convexity, and cell representation of the portfolio with those of the index. STRATOS tries to match the duration, convexity, and volatility exposure without any explicit attempt to match the cell representation of the index.

Once we have the optimal portfolio compositions, the actual returns from each index tracking approach are calculated. The tracking error is defined as the deviation of the portfolio return from the index return. The actual tracking errors are reported in Exhibit 8.3.

Both approaches do a good job of tracking the target index. The average tracking error was 2.8 basis points for the portfolio constructed using BONDTRAC and 1.9 basis points for the portfolio constructed using STRATOS. Keep in mind that these are based on 10 randomly selected issues. STRATOS generates smaller tracking error in terms of absolute value in four out of six months. Statistical analysis of the results suggests that STRATOS tracked the index better, on average, than BONDTRAC during the period covered in the study. In particular, STRATOS tended to work better when the volatility of the short rate changed significantly, as it did from November 1990 to January 1991.

Exhibit 8.3

Tracking Error Using BONDTRAC and STRATOS

Period	Volatility (%)	Monthly returns (%):			Tracking error (%):	
		BONDTRAC	STRATOS	Index	BONDTRAC	STRATOS
Oct. 90	3.791	1.652	1.667	1.609	.043	.058
Nov. 90	3.710	2.267	2.150	2.107	.160	.043
Dec. 90	3.263	1.580	1.582	1.576	.004	.006
Jan. 91	4.037	1.071	1.042	1.042	.029	.000
Feb. 91	3.429	.519	.532	.548	.029	.016
Mar. 91	3.158	.439	.503	.477	.038	.026
Average	3.565				.028	.019
Std. Dev.	.338				.065	.025

LOGISTICAL PROBLEMS IN IMPLEMENTING AN INDEXING STRATEGY[13]

A manager pursuing an indexing strategy faces several logistical problems in constructing an indexed portfolio. First of all, the prices for each issue used by the organization that publishes the index may not be execution prices available to the indexer. In fact, they may be materially different from the prices offered by some dealers.

In addition, the prices used by organizations reporting the value of indexes are based on bid prices. Dealer ask prices, however, are the ones that the manager would have to transact at to construct or rebalance the indexed portfolio. Thus there will be a bias between the performance of the index and the indexed portfolio that is equal to the bid–ask spread.

Furthermore, there are logistical problems unique to certain sectors in the bond market. Consider first the corporate bond market. There are typically about 3,500 issues in the corporate bond sector of a broad-based index. Because of the illiquidity of this sector of the bond market, prices used may be unreliable, and many of the issues may not even be available. And in the mortgage-backed securities market, there are over 300,000 agency passthrough issues. The organizations that publish indexes lump all these issues into a few hundred generic issues. The indexer then has the difficult task of finding passthrough securities with the same risk/return profiles of these generic issues.

Finally, recall that the total return depends on the reinvestment rate available on coupon interest. According to one source, if the organization publishing the index regularly overestimates the reinvestment rate, the indexed portfolio could underperform the index by 10 to 15 basis points a year.[14]

ENHANCED INDEXING

So far we have discussed straight or "plain vanilla" indexing, whose objective is to replicate the total return performance of some predeter-

---

13 For a more detailed discussion, see Sharmin Mossavar-Rahmani, "Understanding and Evaluating Index Fund Management," in Frank J. Fabozzi and T. Dessa Garlicki (eds), *Advances in Bond Analysis and Portfolio Strategies* (Chicago, IL: Probus Publishing, 1987), pp. 433–440.

14 Fran Hawthorne, "The Battle of the Bond Indexes," *Institutional Investor* (April 1986), p. 122.

mined index. The objective of enhanced indexing (also called "indexing plus") is to exceed the total return performance of the index consistently, by an amount sufficient to justify a higher management fee and more risk of underperforming the index. The total return on the index becomes the minimum total return objective rather than the target total return. Thus enhanced indexing brings active strategies back into the portfolio management process, although they are assumed to employ only low-risk strategies.

Because the selection of a security from a class is an independent step in the indexing methodology, it is possible to combine the bond index tracking procedure with an approach that identifies securities that may be mispriced with respect to a valuation model, then choose the most underpriced securities for purchase and the most overpriced securities for sale. The result, if the valuation model is correct in pricing securities, would be an increase in the portfolio return.[15]

Another strategy for enhancing total return is to use securities not included in the index. For example, the broad-based indexes do not include derivative mortgage-backed securities (collateralized mortgage obligations and stripped mortgage-backed securities). Managers pursuing an enhanced index strategy who believe that derivative mortgage-backed securities will outperform the agency passthrough securities in the index can substitute the former securities for the latter. Or a manager may be able to create synthetic agency passthrough securities by using stripped mortgage-backed securities (interest-only and principal-only securities) that would exhibit better performance in certain interest rate environments.

SUMMARY

Indexing is a passive strategy, although the manager of the fund cannot be totally passive, as should be clear from our discussion. The first decision to be made is selection of the target index. Once a target index is selected, the manager must decide whether to replicate the target index exactly (full capitalization-weighted approach), or to select only a sample of issues from the target index using some optimization approach.

---

15 H. Gifford Fong and Frank J. Fabozzi, "How to Enhance Bond Returns with Naive Strategies," *Journal of Portfolio Management* (Summer 1989), pp. 57–60.

With either approach, there will be transactions costs associated with (1) purchase of the issues held to construct the indexed portfolio; (2) reinvestment of cash proceeds from coupon interest payments and principal repayment (at maturity or early redemption); and (3) rebalancing of the portfolio if the composition of the issues in the target index changes. Although the full-capitalization approach will track the index better, practical considerations generally preclude this approach. If a sample of issues are selected, initial portfolio construction cost is reduced. Transactions costs will be incurred to rebalance the indexed portfolio over time in order to track the target index.

Transactions costs and management fees will mean that returns on the target index and the indexed portfolio will diverge. The role of the portfolio manager in an indexing strategy is to minimize the tracking error.

Chapter 9

Immunization, Cash Flow Matching, and Combination Strategies

In this chapter we will explain three management strategies: immunization, cash flow matching, and combination strategies. Immunization is a hybrid strategy having elements of both active and passive strategies. It is used to minimize the risk of reinvestment over a specified investment horizon. Immunization can be employed to structure a portfolio designed to fund a single terminal period liability ("bullet" immunization). Where there are a number of liabilities to fund, advances in immunization theory provide a strategy to construct a *dedicated portfolio*. This is a portfolio designed to fund a schedule of liabilities from portfolio return and asset value, with the portfolio's value diminishing to zero after payment of the last liability. *Cash flow matching* is an alterative strategy for designing a dedicated portfolio. In the last section of this chapter we discuss combination strategies.

Immunization is appropriate for accumulation-maximizing investors who require a high degree of assurance of compounded return over a specified investment horizon. By accepting a more modest return than the highest that can be expected, they are more likely to realize the desired return. This is another example of the classic trade-off between risk and return. Potential users of immunization include life insurance companies, pension funds, and some banks for their own investment portfolios. Life insurance companies can use immunization to invest the proceeds from their guaranteed investment contracts (GICs) and fixed annuities. Both of these investment vehicles require a specific payment at a defined future date. GICs provide for a lump-sum payment at a specified time in the future and at a rate of return guaranteed by the insurance company. Annuities provide for a series of payments over a predetermined time period (sometimes until the holder's death). In both contracts, the specific terms are important, especially those governing premature redemption and reinvestment terms.

The difference between the promised return on the contract or annuity and the realized return is revenue available for expenses and profit. It is the ability to fund specified liabilities on a timely basis that makes immunization attractive. Banks and other savings institutions use immunization to structure the assets of the investment portfolio to match the liabilities of the balance sheet.

Pension funds seeking to fund the retired lives liability, or seeking an alternative to a GIC vehicle for the funding of such liabilities, also use immunization strategies. The latter application can include customization of an asset alternative for a pension fund sponsor.

CLASSICAL SINGLE-PERIOD IMMUNIZATION

Classical immunization can be defined as creation of a fixed income portfolio that produces an assured return for a specific time horizon, irrespective of interest rate changes.[1] In its most concise form, the important characteristics of immunization are:

1. Specified time horizon.

2. Assured rate of return during the holding period to a fixed horizon date.

---

1   The classical theory of immunization is set forth in F. M. Reddington, "Review of the Principles of Life Insurance Valuations," *Journal of the Institute of Actuaries*, 1952; and Lawrence Fisher and Roman Weil, "Coping with Risk of Interest Rate Fluctuations: Returns to Bondholders from Naive and Optimal Strategies," *Journal of Business* (October 1971), pp. 408–431.

3. Insulation from the effects of potential adverse interest rate changes on the portfolio value at the horizon date.

The fundamental mechanism supporting immunization is a portfolio structure that balances the change in the value of the portfolio at the end of the investment horizon with the return from the reinvestment of portfolio cash flows (coupon payments and maturing securities). That is, immunization requires offsetting interest rate risk and reinvestment risk. To accomplish this balancing requires the controlling of duration. Setting the duration of the portfolio equal to the desired portfolio time horizon assures the offsetting of positive and negative incremental return sources. This is a necessary condition for effectively immunized portfolios.

Illustration

Consider the situation that a life insurance company faces when it sells a GIC. For a lump sum payment, the life insurance company guarantees that specified dollars will be paid to the policyholder at a specified future date. Or, equivalently, the life insurance company guarantees a specified rate of return on the purchaser's investment. Suppose a life insurance company sells a five-year GIC that guarantees an interest rate of 7.5% per year on a bond-equivalent yield basis (3.75% every six months for the next ten six-month periods). Also suppose that the payment the policyholder makes is $9,642,899. The value that the life insurance company has guaranteed the policyholder five years from now is thus $13,934,413. That is, the target accumulated value for the manager of the portfolio of supporting assets is $13,934,413 after five years, which is the same as a target yield of 7.5% on a bond-equivalent basis.

Suppose the manager buys $9,642,899 par value of a bond selling at par with a 7.5% yield to maturity that matures in five years. The portfolio manager will not be assured of realizing a total return at least equal to the target yield of 7.5%, because to realize 7.5% the coupon interest payments must be reinvested at a minimum rate of 3.75% every six months. That is, the accumulated value will depend on the reinvestment rate.

To demonstrate this, suppose that immediately after investing the $9,642,899 in the 7.5% coupon, five-year maturity bond, yields in the

Exhibit 9.1

Accumulated Value and Total Return after 5 Years: 5-Year, 7.5% Bond Selling to Yield 7.5%

Investment horizon (years)	5
Coupon rate	7.50%
Maturity (years)	5
Yield to maturity	7.50%
Price	100.00000
Par value purchased	$9,642,899
Purchase price	$9,642,899
Target accumulated value	$13,934,413

After 5 years

New yield	Coupon	Interest on interest	Price of bond	Accumulated value	Total return
11.00%	$3,616,087	$1,039,753	$9,642,899	$14,298,739	8.04%
10.50	3,616,087	985,615	9,642,899	14,244,601	7.98
10.00	3,616,087	932,188	9,642,899	14,191,175	7.88
9.50	3,616,087	879,465	9,642,899	14,138,451	7.80
9.00	3,616,087	827,436	9,642,899	14,086,423	7.73
8.50	3,616,087	776,093	9,642,899	14,035,079	7.65
8.00	3,616,087	725,426	9,642,899	13,984,412	7.57
7.50	3,616,087	675,427	9,642,899	13,934,413	7.50
7.00	3,616,087	626,087	9,642,899	13,885,073	7.43
6.50	3,616,087	577,398	9,642,899	13,836,384	7.35
6.00	3,616,087	529,352	9,642,899	13,788,338	7.28
5.50	3,616,087	481,939	9,642,899	13,740,925	7.21
5.00	3,616,087	435,153	9,642,899	13,694,139	7.14
4.50	3,616,087	388,985	9,642,899	13,647,971	7.07
4.00	3,616,087	343,427	9,642,899	13,602,414	7.00

market change, and then stay at the new level for the remainder of the five years. Exhibit 9.1 illustrates what happens at the end of five years.

The first column shows the new yield level. The second column shows the total coupon interest payments. The third column gives the interest-on-interest over the entire five years if the coupon interest payments are reinvested at the new yield level shown in the first column. The price of the bond at the end of five years shown in the fourth column is the par value. The fifth column is the accumulated value from all three sources: coupon interest, interest-on-interest, and bond price. The percentage of total return is shown in the last column.[2]

If yields do not change, and the coupon payments can be reinvested at 7.5% (3.75% every six months), the portfolio manager will achieve the target accumulated value. If market yields rise, an accumulated value (total return) higher than the target accumulated value (target yield) will be achieved. This is because the coupon interest payments can be reinvested at a higher rate than the initial yield to maturity. Contrast this with what happens when the yield declines. The accumulated value (total return) is then less than the target accumulated value (target yield). Therefore investing in a coupon bond with a yield to maturity equal to the target yield and a maturity equal to the investment horizon does not assure that the target accumulated value will be achieved.

Suppose that instead of investing in a bond maturing in five years the portfolio manager invests in a 12-year bond with a coupon rate of 7.5% that is selling at par to yield 7.5%. Exhibit 9.2 presents the accumulated value and total return if the market yield changes immediately after the bond is purchased, and remains at the new yield level. The fourth column of the exhibit is the market price of a 7.5% coupon, seven-year bond (since five years have passed), assuming the market yields shown in the first column. If the market yield increases, the portfolio will fail to achieve the target accumulated value; the opposite will be true if the market yield decreases—the accumulated value (total return) will exceed the target accumulated value (target yield).

The reason for this result can be seen in Exhibit 9.3, which summarizes the change in interest-on-interest and the change in price resulting from a change in the market yield. For example, if the market yield rises instantaneously by 200 basis points, from 7.5% to 9.5%, interest-on-interest will be $154,040 greater; the market price of the bond, however, will decrease by $715,310. The net effect is that the accumulated value will be $561,270 less than the target accumulated value. The reverse will be true if the market yield decreases. The change in the price of the

---

2 The value in this column is found as follows:

$$2\left[\left(\frac{\text{Accumulated value}}{\$9,642,899}\right)^{1/10} - 1\right]$$

Exhibit 9.2

Accumulated Value and Total Return after 5 Years: 12-Year, 7.5% Bond Selling to Yield 7.5%

Investment horizon (years)	5
Coupon rate	7.50%
Maturity (years)	12
Yield to maturity	7.50%
Price	100.00000
Par value purchased	$9,642,899
Purchase price	$9,642,899
Target accumulated value	$13,934,413

After 5 years

New yield	Coupon	Interest on interest	Price of bond	Accumulated value	Total return
11.00%	$3,616,087	$1,039,753	$ 8,024,639	$12,680,479	5.55%
10.50	3,616,087	985,615	8,233,739	12,835,440	5.80
10.00	3,616,087	932,188	8,449,754	12,998,030	6.06
9.50	3,616,087	879,465	8,672,941	13,168,494	6.33
9.00	3,616,087	827,436	8,903,566	13,347,090	6.61
8.50	3,616,087	776,093	9,141,907	13,534,087	6.90
8.00	3,616,087	725,426	9,388,251	13,729,764	7.19
7.50	3,616,087	675,427	9,642,899	13,934,413	7.50
7.00	3,616,087	626,087	9,906,163	14,148,337	7.82
6.50	3,616,087	577,398	10,178,367	, 14,371,852	8.14
6.00	3,616,087	529,352	10,459,851	14,605,289	8.48
5.50	3,616,087	481,939	10,750,965	14,848,992	8.82
5.00	3,616,087	435,153	11,052,078	15,103,318	9.18
4.50	3,616,087	388,985	11,363,569	15,368,642	9.54
4.00	3,616,087	343,427	11,685,837	15,645,352	9.92

bond will more than offset the decline in the interest-on-interest, resulting in an accumulated value that exceeds the target accumulated value.

Now we can see what is happening to the accumulated value. There is a trade-off between interest rate (or price) risk and reinvestment risk. For this 12-year bond, the target accumulated value will be realized only if the market yield does not increase.

Because neither a coupon bond with the same maturity nor a bond with a longer maturity ensures realization of the target accumulated value, maybe a bond with a maturity shorter than five years will. Consider a 7.5% bond with six months remaining to maturity selling at par. Exhibit 9.4 shows the accumulated value and total return over

Exhibit 9.3

Change in Interest-on-Interest and Price Due to Interest Rate Change after 5 Years: 12-Year, 7-5% Bond Selling to Yield 7.5%

New yield	Change in interest-on-interest	Change in price	Total change in accumulated value
11.00%	$314,327	($1,363,612)	($1,049,285)
10.50	260,189	(1,154,513)	(894,324)
10.00	206,763	(938,497)	(731,735)
9.50	154,040	(715,310)	(561,270)
9.00	102.011	(484,685)	(382,674)
8.50	50,667	(246,344)	(195,677)
8.00	0	0	0
7.50	(49,999)	254,648	204,649
7.00	(99,339)	517,912	418,573
6.50	(148,028)	790,116	642,088
6.00	(196,074)	1,071,600	875,525
5.50	(243,486)	1,362,714	1,119,228
5.00	(290,272)	1,663,826	1,373,554
4.50	(336,440)	1,975,318	1,638,877
4.00	(381,998)	2,297,586	1,915,588

• the five-year investment horizon. The second column shows the accumulated value after six months. The third column shows the value that is accumulated after five years by reinvesting the value accumulated after six months at the yield shown in the first column.[3]

By investing in this six-month bond, the manager incurs no interest rate risk, although reinvestment risk remains. The target accumulated value will be achieved only if the market yield remains at 7.5% or rises. Once again, the manager is not assured of achieving the target accumulated value.

---

3 This value is found as follows:

$10,004,508 $(1 + \text{New yield}/2)^9$

Exhibit 9.4

Accumulated Value and Total Return: 6-Month, 7.5% Bond Selling to Yield 7.5%

Investment horizon (years)	5
Coupon rate	7.50%
Maturity (years)	0.50
Yield to maturity	7.50%
Price	100.00000
Par value purchased	$9,642,899
Purchase price	$9,642,899
Target accumulated value	$13,934,413

After 5 years

New yield	After six months	Accumulated value	Total return
11.00%	$10,004,508	$16,198,241	10.65%
10.50	10,004,508	15,856,037	10.20
10.00	10,004,508	15,520,275	9.75
9.50	10,004,508	15,190,848	9.30
9.00	10,004,508	14,867,650	8.85
8.50	10,004,508	14,550,580	8.40
8.00	10,004,508	14,239,534	7.95
7.50	10,004,508	13,934,413	7.50
7.00	10,004,508	13,635,117	7.05
6.50	10,004,508	13,341,549	6.60
6.00	10,004,508	13,053,613	6.15
5.50	10,004,508	12,771,214	5.70
5.00	10,004,508	12,494,259	5.25
4.50	10,004,508	12,222,656	4.80
4.00	10,004,508	11,956,313	4.35

If we assume there is a one-time instantaneous change in the market yield, is there a coupon bond a manager can purchase to assure the target accumulated value whether the market yield rises or falls? The answer is to look for a coupon bond so that, however the market yield changes, the change in the interest-on-interest will be offset by the change in the price.

Consider a six-year, 6.75% coupon bond selling at $96.42899 to yield 7.5%. Suppose $10,000,000 of par value of this bond is purchased for $9,642,899. Exhibit 9.5 provides the same information as in Exhibits 9.1 and 9.2 for the previous bonds. Looking at the last two columns, we see

Exhibit 9.5

Accumulated Value and Total Return after 5 Years: 6-Year, 6.75% Bond Selling to Yield 7.5%

Investment horizon (years)	5
Coupon rate	6.75%
Maturity (years)	6
Yield to maturity	7.50%
Price	96.42899
Par value purchased	$10,000,000
Purchase price	$9,642,899
Target accumulated value	$13,934,413

After 5 years

New yield	Coupon	Interest on interest	Price of bond	Accumulated value	Total return
11.00%	$3,375,000	$970,432	$ 9,607,657	$13,953,089	7.53%
10.50	3,375,000	919,903	9,652,592	13,947,495	7.52
10.00	3,375,000	870,039	9,697,846	13,942,885	7.51
9.50	3,375,000	820,831	9,743,423	13,939,253	7.51
9.00	3,375,000	772,271	9,789,325	13,936,596	7.50
8.50	3,375,000	724,350	9,835,556	13,934,906	7.50
8.00	3,375,000	677,061	9,882,119	13,934,180	7.50
7.50	3,375,000	630,395	9,929,017	13,934,413	7.50
7.00	3,375,000	584,345	9,976,254	13,935,599	7.50
6.50	3,375,000	538,902	10,023,832	13,937,734	7.50
6.00	3,375,000	494,059	10,071,755	13,940,814	7.51
5.50	3,375,000	449,808	10,120,027	13,944,835	7.52
5.00	3,375,000	406,141	10,168,650	13,949,791	7.52
4.50	3,375,000	363,051	10,217,628	13,955,679	7.53
4.00	3,375,000	320,531	10,266,965	13,962,495	7.54

that the accumulated value and the total return are never less than the target accumulated value and target yield. Thus the target accumulated value is assured, whatever happens to the market yield.

Exhibit 9.6 shows why. When the market yield rises, the increase in interest-on-interest more than offsets the decline in price. When the market yield declines, the increase in price exceeds the decline in interest-on-interest. What characteristic of this bond assures that the target accumulated value will be realized regardless of how the market

184

Chapter 9

Exhibit 9.6

Change in Interest-on-Interest and Price Due to Interest Rate Change after 5 Years: 6-Year, 6.75% Bond Selling to Yield 7.5%

New yield	Change in interest-on-interest	Change in price	Total change in accumulated value
11.00%	$293,371	($274,462)	$18,909
10.50	242,842	(229,527)	13,314
10.00	192,978	(184,273)	8,704
9.50	143,770	(138,697)	5,073
9.00	95,210	(92,794)	2,415
8.50	47,289	(46,563)	726
8.00	0	0	0
7.50	(46,666)	46,898	233
7.00	(92,716)	94,135	1,419
6.50	(138,159)	141,713	3,554
6.00	(183,002)	189,636	6,634
5.50	(227,253)	237,907	10,654
5.00	(270,920)	286,531	15,611
4.50	(314,010)	335,509	21,499
4.00	(356,530)	384,846	28,315

yield changes? Let's look at Macaulay durations. The Macaulay duration for each of the four bonds we have considered is:

Bond	Macaulay duration
5-year, 7.5% coupon, selling at par	4.26 years
12-year, 7.5% coupon, selling at par	8.12 years
6-month, 7.5% coupon, selling at par	0.50 years
6-year, 6.75% coupon, selling for 96.42899	5.00 years

Notice that the last bond, which assures that the target accumulated value will be achieved, whatever happens to the market yield, has a

Macaulay duration equal to the length of the investment horizon. This is the key. *To immunize a portfolio's target accumulated value (target yield) against a change in the market yield, a manager must invest in a bond (or a bond portfolio) whose (1) Macaulay duration is equal to the investment horizon, and (2) initial present value of cash flow equals the present value of the future liability.*

Rebalancing an Immunized Portfolio

Our illustration of the principles underlying immunization assumes a one-time instantaneous change in the market yield. In actuality, the market yield will fluctuate over the investment horizon. As a result, the duration of the portfolio will change as the market yield changes. The duration will also change simply because of the passage of time. In any interest rate environment different from a flat term structure, the duration of a portfolio will change at a different rate from time. Hence, starting with a portfolio of supporting assets with a duration of 5 for a five-year GIC, at the end of one year the portfolio duration will be greater (less) than four years if the term structure is upward sloping (downward sloping).

Even in the face of changing market yields, a portfolio can be immunized if it is rebalanced periodically so that its duration is readjusted to the remaining time of the investment horizon. For example, if the investment horizon is initially five years, the initial portfolio should have a Macaulay duration of five years. After six months, the investment horizon will be 4.5 years, but the duration of the portfolio will probably be different from 4.5 years. Now the portfolio must be rebalanced so that its Macaulay duration is equal to 4.5. Six months later, the portfolio must be rebalanced again so that its Macaulay duration will equal four years, and so on. In other words, as the portfolio matures, the portfolio duration must be kept equal to the remaining time to the horizon.

How often should a portfolio be rebalanced to adjust its Macaulay duration? This is a problem. On the one hand, more frequent rebalancing increases transactions costs, thereby reducing the likelihood of achieving the target return. On the other hand, less frequent rebalancing causes the duration to wander from the target duration, which also reduces the likelihood of achieving the target return. Thus the manager faces a trade-off: Some transactions costs must be accepted to prevent the duration from straying too far from its target; but some mismatch in the duration must be lived with, or transactions costs will become prohibitively high.

Determining the Target Return

Given the term structure of interest rates or the yield curve prevailing at the beginning of the horizon period, the assured rate of return of immunization can be determined. Theoretically, it is defined as the total return of the portfolio, assuming no change in the term structure. This will always differ from the portfolio's present yield to maturity unless the term structure is described by a flat line, because by virtue of the passage of time there is a return effect as the portfolio moves along the yield curve (matures). That is, for an upward-sloping yield curve, the yield to maturity of a portfolio would be quite different from its immunization target rate of return, while for a flat yield curve the yield to maturity would roughly approximate the assured return.

In general, for an upward-sloping yield curve, the immunization target rate of return will be less than the yield to maturity because of the lower reinvestment return; conversely, a negative or downward-sloping yield curve will result in an immunization target rate of return greater than the yield to maturity because of the higher reinvestment return.

Alternative measures of the immunization target rate of return include the yield implied by a zero coupon bond of comparable quality and duration as the bond portfolio, or results of a simulation that rebalances the initial portfolio, given scenarios of interest rate change. Granito has suggested the duration-weighted yield to maturity as a proxy that can be calculated directly from the initial portfolio holdings.[4]

Time Horizon

The range of time horizons depends on matching the investor's desired time horizon with the weighted average duration of the portfolio. In principle, duration-matching is straightforward: portfolio duration is equal to a weighted average of the individual security durations where the weights are the relative amounts or percentages invested in each.

The most typical immunized time horizon is five years. This is a common planning period for GICs and allows flexibility in security

---

4 Michael R. Granito, *Bond Portfolio Immunization* (Lexington, MA: D.C. Heath and Co., 1984).

selection because there is a fairly large population of securities to create the necessary portfolio duration. Securities in the portfolio should be limited to high-quality, very liquid instruments, because portfolio rebalancing is required to keep the portfolio duration synchronized with the horizon date.

EXTENSIONS OF CLASSICAL IMMUNIZATION THEORY

The sufficient condition for classical immunization is that the duration of the portfolio is equal to the length of the investment horizon. Classical theory is based on several assumptions:

1. Any changes in the yield curve are parallel changes, i.e., interest rates move either up or down by the same amount for all maturities.

2. The portfolio is valued at a fixed horizon date, and there are no cash inflows or outflows during the horizon.

3. The target value of the investment is defined as the portfolio value at the horizon date if the interest rate structure does not change (i.e., there is no change in forward rates).

Perhaps the most critical assumption of classical immunization techniques is the first one—the type of interest rate change anticipated. A property of a classically immunized portfolio is that the target value of the investment is the lower limit of the value of the portfolio at the horizon date if there are parallel interest rate changes.[5] This would appear to be an unrealistic assumption, because such interest rate behavior is rarely, if ever, experienced. According to the theory, if there is a change in interest rates that does not correspond to this shape-preserving shift, matching the duration to the investment horizon no longer assures immunization.[6]

Exhibit 9.7 illustrates the nature of the portfolio value, given an immunized portfolio and parallel shifts in rates. The curve ab represents the behavior of the portfolio value for various changes in rates,

---

5 Fisher and Weil.

6 For a more complete discussion of these issues, see John C. Cox, Jonathan E. Ingersoll, Jr., and Stephen A. Ross, "Duration and the Measurement of Basis Risk," *Journal of Business* (January 1979), pp. 51–61.

Exhibit 9.7

Changes in Portfolio Value Caused by Parallel Interest Rate Changes for
an Immunized Portfolio

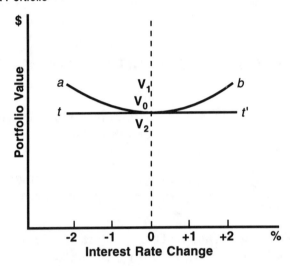

ranging from a decline to an increase as shown on the horizontal axis.
Point V_0 on line tt' is the level of the portfolio value assuming no change
in rates. As we note above, an immunized portfolio subjected to parallel
shifts in the yield curve will provide at least as great a portfolio value
at the horizon date as the assured target value, which therefore becomes the minimum value. Thus, if the assumptions of classical theory
hold, immunization provides a minimum-risk strategy.

Exhibit 9.8 illustrates the relationship when interest rates do not
shift in a parallel fashion. Here we can see the possibility that a portfolio
value can be less than the target. Depending on the shape of the
nonparallel shift, either the (a) or (b) relationship will occur. The
important point here is that merely matching the duration of the
portfolio to the investment horizon as the condition for immunization
may not prevent significant deviations from the target rate of return.

Empirical studies of the effectiveness of immunization strategies
based on Macaulay duration clearly demonstrate that immunization
does not work perfectly in the real world. In the first study of immunization, Fisher and Weil found that a duration-based immunization
strategy would have come closer to the target yield or exceeded it more

Exhibit 9.8

Two Patterns of Changes in Portfolio Value Caused by Nonparallel Interest Rate Shifts for an Immunized Portfolio

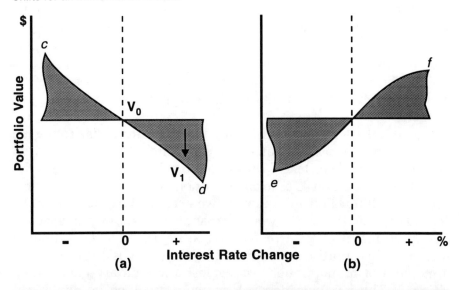

often than a strategy based on matching the maturity of the portfolio to the investment horizon (for the period 1925 through 1968), even after considering transactions costs.[7] When Ingersoll evaluated this Fisher-Weil study, using actual prices rather than the indexes they use, he did not find support for the claim that a duration-matching strategy out-performs a maturity strategy.[8] Studies by Bierwag, Kaufman, Schweitzer, and Toevs;[9] Hackett;[10] Lau;[11] and Leibowitz and Weinber-

---

7 Fisher and Weil.

8 Jonathan E. Ingersoll, "Is Immunization Feasible? Evidence from the CRSP Data," in George K. Kaufman, G.O. Bierwag, and Alden Toevs (eds.), *Innovations in Bond Portfolio Management: Durations and Analysis and Immunization* (Greenwich, CT: JAI Press, 1983).

9 G.O. Bierwag, George C. Kaufman, Robert Schweitzer, and Alden Toevs, "The Art of Risk Management in Bond Portfolios," *Journal of Portfolio Management* (Spring 1981), pp. 27–36.

10 T. Hackett, "A Simulation Analysis of Immunization Strategies Applied to Bond Portfolios," unpublished doctoral dissertation, University of Oregon, 1981.

11 Patrick W. Lau, "An Empirical Examination of Alternative Interest Rate Immunization Strategies," unpublished doctoral dissertation, University of Wisconsin at Madison, 1983.

ger,[12] however, all support the theory that a duration-matched portfolio will outperform a maturity-matched portfolio.

Yet, contrary to what immunization theory would lead us to expect, a common finding has been that use of a duration-matched strategy produces a total return frequently below the target yield. As for the magnitude of the divergence, Leibowitz and Weinberger found that for five-year investment horizons from January 1958 to January 1975, the total return did not fall below the target yield by more than 25 basis points. The divergence of total return from target yield arises out of the assumption that the yield curve is flat and changes only in a parallel fashion.

A natural extension of classical immunization theory is a technique for modifying the assumption of parallel shifts in interest rates. Two approaches have been taken. The first approach has been to modify the definition of duration so as to allow for nonparallel yield curve shifts, such as multifunctional duration as we explained in Chapter 3. The second approach is a strategy that can handle any arbitrary interest rate change so that it is not necessary to specify an alternative duration measure. This approach, developed by Fong and Vasicek, establishes a measure of immunization risk against any arbitrary interest rate change.[13] The immunization risk measure can then be minimized subject to the constraint that the duration of the portfolio be equal to the investment horizon, resulting in a portfolio with minimum exposure to any interest rate movements. This approach is discussed later in the chapter.

A second extension of classical immunization theory applies to overcoming the limitations of a fixed horizon (the second assumption on which immunization depends). Marshall and Yawitz demonstrate that, under the assumption of parallel rate changes, a lower bound exists on the value of an investment portfolio at any particular time, although this lower bound may be below the value realized if interest rates do not change.[14]

---

12 Martin L. Leibowitz and Alfred Weinberger, "Contingent Immunization—Part II: Problem Areas," *Financial Analysts Journal* (January–February 1983), pp. 35–50.

13 H. Gifford Fong and Oldrich A. Vasicek, "A Risk Minimizing Strategy for Portfolio Immunization,"*Journal of Finance* (December 1984), pp. 1541–1546.

14 William J. Marshall and Jess B. Yawitz, "Lower Bounds on Portfolio Performance: An Extension of the Immunization Strategy," *Journal of Financial and Quantitative Analysis* (March 1982), pp. 101–114.

Fong and Vasicek and Bierwag, Kaufman, and Toevs extend immunization to the case of multiple liabilities.[15] Multiple liability immunization involves an investment strategy that guarantees meeting a specified schedule of future liabilities, regardless of any type of shift in interest rate changes. The Fong and Vasicek study provides a generalization of the immunization risk measure for the multiple liability case. Moreover, it extends the theory to the general case of arbitrary cash flows (contributions as well as liabilities). Multiple liability immunization and the general case of arbitrary cash flows are discussed later in the chapter.

In some situations, the objective of immunization as strict risk minimization may be too restrictive. The third extension of classical immunization theory is to analyze the risk and return trade-off for immunized portfolios. Fong and Vasicek demonstrate how this trade-off can be analyzed. Their approach, called "return maximization," is explained later in this chapter.[16]

The fourth extension of classical immunization theory is to integrate immunization strategies with elements of active bond portfolio management strategies. The traditional objective of immunization has been risk protection, with little consideration of possible returns. Leibowitz and Weinberger have proposed a technique called *contingent immunization*, which provides a degree of flexibility in pursuing active strategies while ensuring a certain minimum return in the case of a parallel rate shift.[17] In this approach, immunization serves as a fall-back strategy if the actively managed portfolio does not grow at a certain rate. An alternative approach is possible. Both this approach and contingent immunization are discussed later in this chapter.

---

15 Fong and Vasicek, "A Risk Minimizing Strategy for Portfolio Immunization"; G. O. Bierwag, George G. Kaufman, and Alden Toevs, "Immunization for Multiple Planning Periods," Center for Capital Market Research, University of Oregon, October 1979.

16 H. Gifford Fong and Oldrich A. Vasicek, "Return Maximization for Immunized Portfolios," unpublished paper, June 1981.

17 Martin L. Leibowitz and Alfred Weinberger, "The Uses of Contingent Immunization," *Journal of Portfolio Management* (Fall 1981), pp. 51–55.

RISK MINIMIZATION FOR IMMUNIZED PORTFOLIOS

The Fong and Vasicek extension of classical immunization theory produces an immunized portfolio with a minimum exposure to any arbitrary interest rate change subject to the duration constraint. One way of minimizing immunization risk is shown in Exhibit 9.9.

The spikes in the two panels of Exhibit 9.9 represent actual portfolio cash flows. The taller spikes depict the actual cash flows generated by securities on maturity, while the smaller spikes represent coupon payments. Both portfolio A and portfolio B are composed of two bonds with a duration equal to the investment horizon. Portfolio A is, in effect, a "barbell" portfolio—a portfolio made up of short and long maturities and interim coupon payments. For portfolio B, the two bonds mature

Exhibit 9.9

Illustration of Immunization Risk Measure

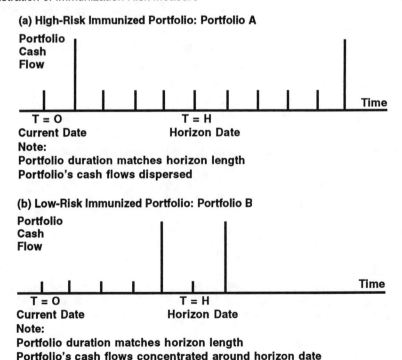

(a) High-Risk Immunized Portfolio: Portfolio A

Portfolio Cash Flow

Time

T = 0
Current Date

T = H
Horizon Date

Note:
Portfolio duration matches horizon length
Portfolio's cash flows dispersed

(b) Low-Risk Immunized Portfolio: Portfolio B

Portfolio Cash Flow

Time

T = 0
Current Date

T = H
Horizon Date

Note:
Portfolio duration matches horizon length
Portfolio's cash flows concentrated around horizon date

very close to the investment horizon, and the coupon payments are nominal over the investment horizon. A portfolio with these characteristics is called a "bullet" portfolio.

It is not hard to see why the barbell portfolio should be riskier than the bullet portfolio. Assume that both portfolios have durations equal to the horizon length, so that both portfolios are immune to parallel rate changes. This immunity is attained through balancing the effect of changes in reinvestment rates on coupon payments received against the effect of changes in capital value of the investment outstanding at the end of the investment horizon. When interest rates change in an arbitrary nonparallel way, however, the effect on the two portfolios is very different. Suppose, for instance, short rates decline while long rates go up. Both portfolios would realize a decline of the portfolio value at the end of the investment horizon below the target investment value, because they experience a capital loss in addition to lower reinvestment rates.

The decline would be substantially higher for the barbell portfolio, however, for two reasons. First, the barbell portfolio experiences the lower reinvestment rates longer than the bullet portfolio does, so the opportunity loss is much greater. Second, there is more of the barbell portfolio still outstanding at the end of the investment horizon, which means that the same rate increase causes much more of a capital loss. In other words, the bullet portfolio has less exposure to changes in the interest rate structure than the barbell portfolio.

It should be clear that immunization risk is defined by the risk of reinvestment. The portfolio that has the least reinvestment risk will have the least immunization risk. When there is a high dispersion of cash flows around the horizon date, as in the barbell portfolio, the portfolio is exposed to higher reinvestment risk. When the cash flows are concentrated around the horizon date, as in the bullet portfolio, the portfolio is subject to minimum reinvestment risk.

An example of a zero immunization risk portfolio is a portfolio consisting of a pure discount instrument maturing at the investment horizon. Here there is no reinvestment risk. Moving from pure discount instruments to coupon payment instruments, the portfolio manager is confronted with selecting coupon-paying securities that provide the best protection against immunization risk. If the manager can construct a portfolio that replicates a pure discount instrument that matures at the investment horizon, that portfolio will be the lowest immunization risk portfolio.

To formalize the measure of immunization risk, recall that the target accumulated value of an immunized portfolio is a lower bound on the terminal value of the portfolio at the investment horizon if yields on all maturities change by the same amount. If yields of different maturities change by different amounts, the target accumulated value is not necessarily the lower bound on the investment value.

Fong and Vasicek demonstrate that if forward rates change by any arbitrary function, the relative change in the portfolio value depends on the product of two terms.[18] The first term depends solely on the structure of the investment portfolio, while the second term is a function of interest rate movement only. The second term characterizes the nature of the interest rate shock. It is an uncertain quantity and therefore outside the control of the manager. The first term, however, is under the control of the manager, as it depends solely on the composition of the portfolio. This first term, which is a multiplier of the unknown rate change as given by the second term, is thus a measure of risk for immunized portfolios defined as follows:[19]

$$(1) \quad \frac{[PVCF_1(1 - H)^2 + PVCF_2(2 - H)^2 + \cdots + PVCF_n(n - H)^2]}{\text{Initial investment value}}$$

where $PVCF_t$ = the present value of the cash flow in period t discounted at the prevailing yield-to-maturity

  H = length of the investment horizon

  n = the time to receipt of the last portfolio cash flow

---

18 Fong and Vasicek, "A Risk Minimizing Strategy for Portfolio Immunization." This result is derived by expansion of the terminal value function into the first three terms of a Taylor series.

19 The only assumption about the interest rate changes necessary to justify this measure of risk is that the interest rate change is a sufficiently smooth function of maturity so that the Taylor series expansion is valid. Beyond that, no assumptions are necessary about the nature or dimensionality of the stochastic process that governs the behavior of the term structure of interest rates.

It is interesting to compare this measure of immunization risk with the definition of Macaulay duration. The denominator of both is the value of the portfolio. The numerator of both includes the present value of cash flows. In the case of duration, the present value of the cash flow is weighted by the time it will be received. For the immunization risk measure, however, the present value of the cash flow is weighted by the square of the difference between the time it will be received and the investment horizon. Consequently, while duration is a weighted average of time to payments on the portfolio, immunization risk is a similarly weighted variance of times to payment around the horizon date.

Given the measure of immunization risk that is to be minimized, and the constraint that the duration of the portfolio equal the investment horizon, the optimal immunized portfolio can be found using linear programming. Linear programming is appropriate because the risk measure is linear in the portfolio payments.

The immunization risk measure can be used to construct approximate confidence intervals for the target return over the horizon period and the target end-of-period portfolio value. A confidence interval represents an uncertainty band around the target return within which the realized return can be expected with a given probability. The general expression for a confidence interval is:

Target return ± k (standard deviation of target return)

where k is the number of standard deviations around the expected target return. The confidence level determines k. The higher the probability, the smaller the k, and the smaller the band around the expected target return.

Fong and Vasicek demonstrate that the standard deviation of the expected target return can be approximated by the product of three terms:[20] (1) the immunization risk measure; (2) the standard deviation of the variance of the one-period change in the slope of the yield curve;[21] and (3) an expression that is a function of the horizon length only.[22]

MULTIPLE LIABILITY IMMUNIZATION

Immunization with respect to a single investment horizon is appropriate where the objective of the investment is to preserve the value of the investment at the horizon date. This may be the case when a single given liability is payable at the horizon date, or a target investment value is to be attained at that date. More often, however, there are a number of liabilities to be paid from the investment funds, and no

---

20 Fong and Vasicek, "Return Maximization for Immunized Portfolios." The derivation is based on the assumption that the immunization risk measure of an optimally immunized portfolio periodically rebalanced decreases in time in approximate proportion to the third power of the remaining horizon length.

21 This term can be estimated empirically from historical yield changes.

22 The expression for the third term for the standard deviation of the expected target return of a single-period liability immunized portfolio is $(7H)^{-1/2}$, where H is the length of the horizon.

single horizon that corresponds to the schedule of liabilities. A portfolio is said to be immunized with respect to a given liability stream if there are enough funds to pay all the liabilities when due even if interest rates change by a parallel shift.

Bierwag, Kaufman, and Toevs demonstrate that matching the duration of the portfolio to the duration of the liabilities is not a sufficient condition for immunization in the presence of multiple liabilities.[23] Instead the portfolio payment stream must be decomposed in such a way that each liability is separately immunized by one of the component streams. The key notion here is that it is the payment stream on the portfolio, not the portfolio itself, that can be decomposed in this manner. There may be no actual securities that would give the component payment streams.

Fong and Vasicek demonstrate the conditions that must be satisfied to assure multiple liability immunization in the case of parallel rate shifts.[24] The necessary and sufficient conditions are:

1. The (composite) duration of the portfolio must equal the (composite) duration of the liabilities.[25]

2. The distribution of durations of individual portfolio assets must have a wider range than the distribution of the liabilities.[26]

An implication of the first condition is that to immunize a liability stream that extends 30 years it is not necessary to have a portfolio with a duration of 30 years. The condition requires that the manager construct a portfolio so that the portfolio duration matches the weighted average of the liability durations. This is important, because in any reasonable interest rate environment it is unlikely that a portfolio of investment-grade coupon bonds could be constructed with a duration

---

23 Bierwag, Kaufman, and Toevs, "Immunization for Multiple Planning Periods."

24 Fong and Vasicek, "A Risk Minimizing Strategy for Portfolio Immunization."

25 The duration of the liabilities is found as follows:

$$\frac{(1)\ PVL_1 + (2)\ PVL_2 + \cdots + (m)PVL_m}{\text{Total present value of liabilities}}$$

where PVL_t = present value of the liability at time t
        m = time of the last liability payment

26 More specifically, the mean absolute deviation of the portfolio payments must be greater than or equal to the mean absolute deviation of the liabilities at each payment date.

in excess of 15 years. Yet for corporate pension funds retired lives, the liability stream is typically a diminishing amount. That is, liabilities in the earlier years are the greatest, and liabilities farther out toward the 30-year end are generally lower. Taking a weighted average duration of the liabilities usually brings the portfolio duration to something manageable, say, eight or nine years.

The second condition requires portfolio payments to be more dispersed in time than the liabilities. That is, there must be an asset with a duration equal to or less than the duration of the shortest-duration liability in order to have funds to pay the liability when it is due. And there must be an asset with a duration equal to or greater than the longest-duration liability in order to avoid the reinvestment rate risk that might jeopardize payment of the longest duration. This bracketing of shortest- and longest-duration liabilities with even shorter- and longer-duration assets balances changes in portfolio value with changes in reinvestment return.

To understand why the portfolio payments have to be more spread out in time than the liabilities to assure immunization, consider the single investment horizon case. Here immunization is achieved by balancing changes in reinvestment return on coupon payments with changes in investment value at the investment horizon. The same bracketing of each liability by the portfolio payments is necessary in the multiple liability case, which implies that the payments have to be more dispersed in time than the liabilities. This means that managers selecting securities to be included in the portfolio not only must keep track of the matching of duration between assets and liabilities but also must maintain a specified distribution for assets in the portfolio.

The two conditions for multiple liability immunization assure immunization against parallel rate shifts only. Reitano has explored the limitations of the parallel shift assumption.[27] He has also developed models that generalize the immunization of multiple liabilities to arbitrary yield curve shifts. His research indicates that classical multiple-period immunization can mask the risks associated with nonparallel yield curve shifts and that a model that protects against one type of yield curve shift may expose a portfolio to other types of shifts.

---

27 Robert R. Reitano, "A Multivariate Approach to Immunization Theory," *Actuarial Research Clearing House*, Vol. 2, 1990; and "Multivariate Immunization Theory," *Transactions of the Society of Actuaries*, Vol. XLIII, 1991. For a detailed illustration of the relationship between the underlying yield curve shift and immunization, see Reitano, "Non-Parallel Yield Curve Shifts and Immunization," *Journal of Portfolio Management* (Spring 1992), pp. 36–43.

Fong and Vasicek also address the question of the exposure of an immunized portfolio to an arbitrary interest rate change and generalize the immunization risk measure to the multiple liability case.[28] Just as in the single investment horizon case, they find that the relative change in the portfolio value if forward rates change by any arbitrary function depends on the product of two terms—a term solely dependent on the structure of the portfolio and a term solely dependent on the interest rate movement. The immunization risk measure in the multiple liability case is:

$$
(2) \quad \frac{[\mathrm{PVCF}_1\,(1-D)^2 + \mathrm{PVCF}_2\,(2-D)^2 + \cdots + \mathrm{PVCF}_n\,(n-D)^2]}{\text{Initial investment value}}
$$

$$
- \frac{[\mathrm{PVL}_1\,(1-D)^2 + \mathrm{PVL}_2\,(2-D)^2 + \cdots + \mathrm{PVL}_m\,(m-D)^2]}{\text{Initial investment value}}
$$

where D = duration of the portfolio (which by the first condition is equal to the weighted average duration of the liabilities)

PVL_t = present value of the liability at time t

m   = time of the last liability payment

PVCF and n are as defined earlier.[29]

An optimal immunization strategy is to minimize the immunization risk measure subject to the constraints imposed by the two conditions (and any other applicable portfolio constraints). Constructing minimum-risk immunized portfolios can be accomplished by the use of linear programming.

Approximate confidence intervals can also be constructed in the multiple liability case. The standard deviation of the expected target return is the product of the three terms indicated in the section on risk minimization.[30]

---

28 Fong and Vasicek, "A Risk Minimizing Strategy for Portfolio Immunization."

29 Note that this risk measure attains its extreme value of zero if and only if the portfolio payments coincide exactly in amount and timing with the liabilities.

30 Fong and Vasicek, "Return Maximization for Immunized Portfolios." The expression for the third term in the multiple liability case is a function of the dates and relative sizes of the liabilities, as well as the horizon length.

IMMUNIZATION FOR GENERAL CASH FLOWS

In both the single investment horizon and multiple liability cases, we have assumed that the investment funds are initially available in full. What if instead a given schedule of liabilities to be covered by an immunized investment must be met by investment funds that are not available at the time the portfolio is to be constructed?

Suppose a manager has a given obligation to be paid at the end of a two-year horizon. Only one-half of the necessary funds, however, are now available; the rest are expected at the end of the first year, to be invested at the end of the first year at whatever rates are then in effect. Is there is an investment strategy that would guarantee the end-of-horizon value of the investment regardless of the development of interest rates?

Under certain conditions this is indeed possible. The expected cash contributions can be considered the payments on hypothetical securities that are part of the initial holdings. The actual initial investment can then be invested in such a way that the real and hypothetical holdings taken together represent an immunized portfolio.

We can illustrate this using the two-year investment horizon. The initial investment should be constructed with a three-year duration. Half of the funds are then in an actual portfolio with a duration of three years, and the other half in a hypothetical portfolio with a duration of one year. The total stream of cash inflow payments for the portfolio has a duration of two years, matching the horizon length. This is a sufficient condition for immunization with respect to a single horizon.

At the end of the first year, any decline in the interest rates at which the cash contribution is invested will be offset by a corresponding increase in the value of the initial holdings. The portfolio is at that time rebalanced by selling the actual holdings and investing the proceeds together with the new cash in a portfolio with a duration of one year to match the horizon date. Note that the rate of return guaranteed on the future contributions is not the current spot rate but rather the forward rate for the date of contribution.

This strategy can be extended to apply to multiple contributions and liabilities. This produces a general immunization technique that is applicable to the case of arbitrary cash flows over a period. Fong and Vasicek have derived the conditions for the general cash flow case.[31]

---

31 Fong and Vasicek, "A Risk Minimizing Strategy for Multiple Liability Immunization."

The construction of an optimal immunized portfolio can then be achieved by minimizing the immunization risk measure, which is equal to:

$$
\begin{aligned}
(3) \quad & \frac{[PVCF_1 (1-D)^2 + PVCF_2 (2-D)^2 + \cdots + PVCF_n (n-D)^2]}{\text{Present value of liabilities}} \\
+ & \frac{[PVCC_1 (1-D)^2 + PVCC_2 (2-D)^2 + \cdots + PVCC_k (k-D)^2]}{\text{Present value of liabilities}} \\
- & \frac{[PVL_1 (1-D)^2 + PVL_2 (2-D)^2 + \cdots + PVL_m (m-D)^2]}{\text{Present value of liabilities}}
\end{aligned}
$$

where $PVCF_t$ = present value of the cash flow payments from the securities held in the portfolio at time t

D = duration of the *liability stream*

n = time of the last cash flow payment from the securities held in the portfolio

$PVCC_t$ = present value of the cash contribution at time t

k = time of the last cash contribution

PVL_t = present value of the liability at time t

m = time of the last liability payment

Once again linear programming methods can be used to obtain the optimal portfolio.

RETURN MAXIMIZATION FOR IMMUNIZED PORTFOLIOS

The objective of risk minimization for an immunized portfolio may be too restrictive in certain situations. If a substantial increase in the expected return can be accomplished with little effect on immunization risk, the higher-yielding portfolio may be preferred in spite of its higher risk. Suppose that an optimally immunized portfolio has a target return of 8% over the horizon with a 95% confidence interval at ± 20 basis points. This means that the minimum-risk portfolio would have a 1 in 40 chance of a realized return less than 7.8%. Suppose that another portfolio less well-immunized can produce a target return of 8.3% with a 95% confidence interval of ±30 basis points. In all but one case out of 40, this portfolio would realize a return above 8% compared to 7.8% on the minimum-risk portfolio. For many investors, this may be the preferred trade-off.

Fong and Vasicek's approach to the risk/return trade-off for immunized portfolios maintains the duration of the portfolio at all times equal to the horizon length.[32] Thus the portfolio stays fully immunized in the classical sense. Instead of minimizing the immunization risk against nonparallel rate changes, however, a trade-off between risk and return is considered. The immunization risk measure can be relaxed if the compensation in terms of expected return warrants it. Specifically, the strategy maximizes a lower bound on the portfolio return. The lower bound is defined as a confidence interval on the realized return for a given probability level.

Linear programming can be used to solve for the optimal portfolio when return maximization is the objective. In fact, parametric linear programming can be employed to determine an efficient frontier for immunized portfolios analogous to those in the mean/variance framework that will be discussed in Chapter 11.

CASH FLOW MATCHING

Cash flow matching is an alternative to multiple liability immunization for creating a dedicated portfolio. It is an appealing strategy because the portfolio manager need only select securities to match liabilities. A bond is selected with a maturity that matches the last liability, and an amount of principal equal to the amount of the last liability is invested in this bond. The remaining elements of the liability stream are then reduced by the coupon payments on this bond, and another bond is chosen for the next-to-last liability, adjusted for any coupon payments received on the first bond selected. Going backward in time, this sequence is continued until all liabilities have been matched by payments on the securities selected for the portfolio. Linear programming techniques can be employed to construct a least-cost cash flow matching portfolio from an acceptable universe of bonds.

Exhibit 9.10 provides a simple illustration of this process for a five-year liability stream. Exhibit 9.11 displays a portfolio chosen to match the sequence of liability payments shown in the second-to-last column of Exhibit 9.12. These bonds range in maturity from cash

---

32 Fong and Vasicek, "Return Maximization for Immunized Portfolios." In the multiple liability case, the two conditions are maintained.

Exhibit 9.10

Illustration of Cash Flow Matching Process

Assume: 5-year liability stream.   Cash flow from bonds is annual.

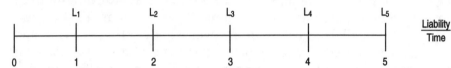

Step 1—Cash flow from Bond A selected to satisfy L_5
Coupons = A_c; Principal = A_p and $A_c + A_p = L_5$;   Unfunded liabilities remaining:

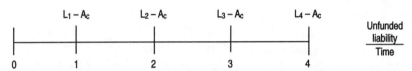

Step 2—Cash flow from Bond B selected to satisfy L_4
Unfunded liability = $L_4 - A_c$;   Coupons = B_c; Principal= B_p and $B_c + B_p = L_4 - A_c$
Unfunded liabilities remaining:

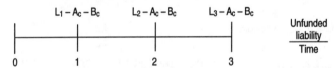

Step 3—Cash flow from Bond C selected to satisfy L_3
Unfunded liability = $L_3 - A_c - B_c$
Coupons = C_c; Principal = C_p and $C_c + C_p = L_3 - A_c - B_c$
Unfunded liabilities remaining:

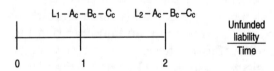

Step 4—Cash flow from Bond D selected to satisfy L_2
Unfunded liability = $L_2 - A_c - B_c - C_c$
Coupons = D_c; Principal = D_p and $D_c + D_p = L_2 - A_c - B_c - C_c$
Unfunded liabilities remaining:

$$L_1 - A_c - B_c - C_c - D_c$$

```
|——————————————|                          Unfunded
                                          liability
|——————————————|                          Time
0              1
```

Step 5—Select Bond E with a cash flow of $L_1 - A_c - B_c - C_c - D_c$

Exhibit 9.11

Characterization of a Sample Universe for Cash Flow Matching (Evaluation Date 6-30-88)

Forward Rates Date: 6-30-88
Long Rate: 8.964%
Short Rate: 6.395%
Interest Rate Model:
  Speed of Reversion: .880
  Volatility Parameter: .200 (Yr)$^{-\frac{1}{2}}$
Analysis Includes Accrued Interest

Bond No.	Par value ($)	% of Total	CUSIP	Issuer name	Quality	Coupon (%)	Effective maturity date	Price ($)	Adj. Y-T-M (%)	Adj. duration (yrs)
17	$2800.	10.2%	912794QD	Bill	AAA	.000%	12/22/88	$ 96.709	7.117%	.463
19	153.	.6	666666ZZ	Cash	UNRTD	.00	12/31/86	100.000	6.862	.487
1	1600.	6.3	313586NB	Federal Natl Mtg Assn	AAA	11.300	12/11/89	104.344	8.052	1.317
2	1700.	6.4	313368PF	Federal Home Ln Bks	AAA	8.700	12/26/90	100.656	8.402	2.197
3	1700.	7.0	313388MU	Federal Home Ln Bks	AAA	11.400	12/26/91	106.594	8.501	2.873
6	1800.	6.5	795498AD	Salomon Inc	A1	10.700	8/ 1/92	103.152	9.741	3.135
4	100.	.4	318388KR	Federal Home Ln Bks	AAA	11.100	11/25/92	106.375	8.781	3.451
13	2500	10.2	002624AD	Abbott Labs	AA1	11.000	2/ 1/93	103.771	9.951	3.415
18	1200.	5.2	912627RM	United States Treas Nts	AAA	11.625	11/15/94	114.500	8.617	4.544
16	1800.	6.6	958118AA	Western Elec Inc	AA1	8.375	10/ 1/95	95.933	8.709	3.794
10	500.	1.8	462506AU	Iowa Pwr & Lt Co	AA3	8.250	7/ 1/96	91.584	9.639	5.011
14	1400.	5.0	239753AN	Dayton Hudson Corp	AA3	8.375	10/ 1/96	92.036	9.641	5.204
12	1800.	5.5	744567AX	Public Svc Elec & Gas Co	A1	6.250	6/ 1/97	80.214	9.576	6.282
7	400.	1.4	441812CC	Household Fin Corp	A1	8.250	3/ 1/98	68.725	10.003	5.833
5	1500.	4.8	341061AX	Florida Pwr & Lt Co	AA3	7.000	12/ 1/98	83.969	9.411	6.766
8	1700.	5.6	441812AU	Household Fin Corp	A1	7.750	10/ 1/99	85.581	9.843	6.682
15	1800.	5.1	812387AL	Sears Roebuck & Co	AA2	6.000	5/ 1/00	74.750	9.617	7.596
11	1700	5.7	665772AV	North Sts Pwr Co Minn	AA1	8.250	6/ 1/01	88.602	9.765	7.218
9	1700.	5.8	066365AE	Bankers Trust Ny Corp	A1	8.625	11/ 1/02	88.929	10.029	7.297

Exhibit 9.11 continues

Exhibit 9.11 (Continued)

PORTFOLIO TOTALS

Average Adjusted Duration (yrs)	4.221
Average Adjusted Yield (%)	9.057
Dur Wtd. Avg Yield (%)	9.449
Average Coupon (%)	7.976
Average Effective Maturity	1-30-95
Avg Time To Maturity (yrs)	6.585
Average Quality	AA2
Total Par Value ($000)	27652.870
Total Market Value($000)	26581.790
Total Principal Value ($000)	26164.470
Total Accrued Interest ($)	417.328
Number of Issues	19

Exhibit 9.12

Cash Flow Analysis of a Sample Universe for Cash Flow Matching: Reinvestment Rate—6% (Evaluation Date 6/30/88)

Date	Previous cash balance ($000)	+	Interest on balance ($000)	+	Principal payments ($000)	+	Coupon payments ($000)	+	Reinvestment of payments ($000)	−	Liability due ($000)		New cash balance ($000)
12-31-88	$ .0		$ .0		$2960.2		$1102.8		$ 14.8		$4038.0		$ 39.804
12-31-89	39.8		2.4		1600.0		2205.7		63.9		3900.0		11.851
12-31-90	11.9		.7		1700.0		2024.9		56.8		3762.0		32.272
12-31-91	32.3		2.0		1700.0		1877.0		54.5		3624.0		41.690
12-31-92	41.7		2.5		1700.0		1683.2		90.4		3474.0		43.813
12-31-93	43.8		2.7		2500.0		1363.4		178.5		3330.0		758.402
12-31-94	756.4		46.2		1200.0		1225.9		40.9		3174.0		97.317
12-31-95	97.3		5.9		1800.0		1066.4		55.3		3012.0		32.952
12-31-96	33.0		2.0		1900.0		935.6		59.8		2850.0		80.422
12-31-97	80.4		4.9		1800.0		720.9		81.5		2682.0		5.670
12-31-98	5.7		.3		1900.0		648.1		43.6		2514.0		83.765
12-31-99	83.8		5.1		1700.0		526.6		38.4		2346.0		7.894
12-31-00	7.9		.5		1800.0		340.9		80.9		2178.0		52.198
12-31-01	52.2		3.2		1700.0		216.8		65.7		2004.0		33.854
12-31-02	33.9		2.1		1700.0		146.6		20.5		1900.0		2.996

(shortest) to just before the date of the longest liability. (Exhibit 9.11 also includes a number of descriptive statistics for the individual securities held and the portfolio as a whole.)

Exhibit 9.12 provides a cash flow analysis of sources and application of funds. The last column in the exhibit shows the excess funds remaining at each period, which are reinvested at the assumed 6% reinvestment rate supplied by the portfolio manager. The more excess cash, the greater the risk of the strategy.

Cash Flow Matching versus Multiple Liability Immunization

If all the liability flows are perfectly matched by the asset flows of the portfolio, the resulting portfolio would have no reinvestment risk and, therefore, no immunization or cash flow match risk. Given typical liability schedules and bonds available for cash flow matching, however, perfect matching is unlikely. Under such conditions, a minimum immunization risk approach would, at worst, be equal to cash flow matching and would probably be better, because an immunization strategy would require less money to fund liabilities. This is the result of two factors.

First, cash flow matching requires a relatively conservative rate of return assumption for short-term cash, which may be occasionally substantial, throughout the life of the plan; an immunized portfolio is essentially fully invested at the remaining horizon duration. Second, funds from a cash flow-matched portfolio must be available when (and usually before) each liability is due, because of the difficulty in perfect matching. An immunized portfolio needs to meet the target value only on the date of each liability, because funding is achieved by a rebalancing of the portfolio. Because the reinvestment assumption for excess cash for cash flow matching extends many years into the future, a conservative assumption is appropriate.

Thus, even with the sophisticated linear programming techniques used, in most cases cash flow matching will be technically inferior to immunization. Using the cost of the initial portfolio as an evaluation measure, Gifford Fong Associates has found that cash flow-matched portfolios, using a universe of corporate bonds rated at least double-A, cost from 3% to 7% more in dollar terms than multiple liability immunized portfolios. Cash flow matching is easier to understand than multiple liability immunization, though, which occasionally supports its selection in dedicated portfolio strategies.

Extensions of Basic Cash Flow Matching

In basic cash flow matching, only asset cash flows occurring prior to a liability date can be used to satisfy the liability. The basic technique can be extended to allow cash flows occurring both before and after the liability date to be used to meet a liability.[33] This technique, called *symmetric cash matching*, allows for the short-term borrowing of funds to satisfy a liability prior to the liability due date. The opportunity to borrow short-term so that symmetric cash matching can be employed results in a reduction in the cost of funding a liability.

A popular variation of multiple liability immunization and cash flow matching to fund liabilities is one that combines the two strategies. This strategy, referred to as *combination matching* or *horizon matching*, creates a portfolio that is duration-matched with the added constraint that it be cash-matched in the first few years, usually five years. The advantage of combination matching over multiple liability immunization is that liquidity needs are provided for in the initial cash flow-matched period. Also, most of the positive slope or inversion of a yield curve tends to take place in the first few years. Cash flow matching the initial portion of the liability stream reduces the risk associated with nonparallel shifts of the yield curve. The disadvantage of combination matching over multiple liability immunization is that it costs more.

APPLICATION CONSIDERATIONS

Universe Considerations

Selection of the universe for construction of a single period immunized portfolio or a dedicated portfolio is extremely important. The lower the quality of the securities considered, the higher the potential risk and return. Dedication assumes there will be no defaults, and immunization theory further assumes securities are responsive only to overall changes in interest rates. The lower the quality, the greater the possibility that these assumptions will not be met. Further, securities with embedded options such as call features or mortgage-backed prepayments complicate and may even prevent the accurate measure of cash

---

33 T. Dessa Fabozzi, Tom Tong, and Yu Zhu, "Extensions of Dedicated Bond Portfolio Techniques," Chapter 44 in Frank J. Fabozzi (ed.), *The Handbook of Fixed Income Securities: Third Edition* (Homewood, IL: BusinessOne-Irwin, 1991).

flow, and hence duration, frustrating the basic requirements of immunization and cash flow matching. Finally, liquidity is a consideration for immunized portfolios, because they must be rebalanced periodically.

Optimization

Optimization procedures can be used for the construction of immunized and cash flow-matched portfolios. For an immunized portfolio, this typically takes the form of minimizing maturity variance subject to the constraints of duration and necessary duration dispersion (in multiple liability immunization). For cash flow matching, it takes the form of minimizing the initial portfolio cost subject to the constraint of having sufficient cash at the time a liability arises. Further considerations such as average quality, minimum and maximum concentration constraints, and, perhaps, issuer constraints may be included. Throughout the process, it is critical to establish realistic guidelines and objectives. Accurate pricing is important because optimization is very sensitive to the pricing of the universe under consideration. Because there are many inputs and variations available, the optimization process should be approached iteratively, with a final solution the result of a number of trials.

Monitoring

Monitoring of an immunized or cash flow-matched portfolio requires periodic performance measurement. For a bullet portfolio (single horizon date), performance monitoring may take the form of regular observations of the return to date linked with the current target return and annualized. This return should fluctuate only slightly about the original target return.

The performance of a multiple liability immunized plan can be monitored most easily by comparing the current market value of the assets to the present value of the remaining liabilities. (The current internal rate of return on the immunized portfolio can be used to discount the remaining liabilities.) These two quantities should track one another closely. It may also be useful to monitor the estimated standard deviation of the terminal value of the fund to make sure that it falls more or less uniformly to zero as the horizon date approaches.

Transactions Costs

Transactions costs are important in meeting the target rate for an immunized portfolio. They must be considered not only in the initial immunization (when the immunized portfolio is first created) but also in the periodic rebalancing necessary to avoid duration mismatch. If the portfolio undertakes too many trades, it will enjoy only marginal benefits from risk minimization. Fortunately, transactions costs can be included into the optimization framework in order to strike a balance between transactions costs and risk minimization.

COMBINATION STRATEGIES

While we have explained a number of basic portfolio strategies, the range of portfolio strategies really represents a continuum. At various phases during an interest rate cycle, a particular strategy may be most appropriate, but more often than not a mix of alternatives is best for part or all of the cycle. The determination of what is optimal may be made either by the investor or pension plan sponsor or, alternatively, by the portfolio manager.

When decision makers have strong convictions, a one-strategy approach may be optimal; in the more likely case of uncertainty, strategy combinations may produce the best risk/return trade-off. A trade-off, for example, might be to tie a portion of the portfolio risk and return to some baseline portfolio whose performance over the long term should provide satisfactory results, and actively manage the remaining portion.

Retaining an active component preserves the opportunity for superior performance. Determination of the proportion to be allocated to each strategy could be made following the procedure for asset allocation discussed in Chapter 11. This, in effect, would be an allocation among strategies within the fixed income asset category.

Managers are frequently selected on the basis of expertise in specific strategies. Specialization might be in any of the continuum of strategies available. It is particularly attractive in the multimanager situation typical of large pension plan sponsors.

Two of the most popular combination strategies are active/passive and active/immunization combinations. An active/passive combination allocates a core component of the portfolio to a passive strategy and the balance to an active component. The passive strategy would replicate an index or some sector of the market. In the active portion, the manager is free to pursue a return maximization strategy (at some given level of risk). A large pension fund might have a large allocation to a core strategy, consisting of an indexed portfolio, with additional active strategies chosen on the margin to enhance overall portfolio returns.

An active/immunization combination also consists of two components. The immunized portfolio provides an assured return over the planning horizon, and the balance of the portfolio is managed using an active high return/high risk strategy. The immunization component is intended to provide a guaranteed absolute return source. A surplus protection strategy, managing the surplus of a pension fund actively and immunizing the liabilities, is an example of a possible application.

Two specific forms of active/immunization combinations have been suggested: *contingent immunization* and *combination by formula*.

Contingent Immunization

Contingent immunization requires specification of both the available immunization target rate and a lower "safety net-level" return to meet minimal expectations.[34] The manager can continue to pursue an active strategy until an adverse investment experience drives the then-available potential return—combined active return (from actual past experience) and immunized return (from expected future experience)—down to the safety net level; at that time the manager would be obligated to immunize the portfolio completely and lock in the safety net-level return. As long as this safety net is not violated the manager can continue to manage the portfolio actively. Once the immunization is activated, the manager cannot return to the active mode unless, of course, the contingent immunization plan is abandoned.

The key considerations in implementing a contingent immunization strategy are: (1) establishing accurate immunized initial and ongoing available target returns, (2) identifying a suitable and immunizable safety net, and (3) implementing an effective monitoring procedure to ensure that the safety net is not violated.

---

34 Martin L. Leibowitz and Alfred Weinberger, "Contingent Immunization—Part I: Risk Control Procedures," *Financial Analysts Journal* (November-December 1982), pp. 17–31.

To illustrate the basic principles of the contingent immunization strategy, suppose that a sponsor is willing to accept a 6% return over a five-year planning horizon at a time when a possible immunized rate of return is 7.5%. The 6% rate of return is called the safety net (or minimum target or floor) return. The difference between the possible immunized rate of 7.5% and the safety net rate is called the *cushion spread* or *excess achievable return*. It is this cushion spread of 150 basis points that offers the manager latitude in pursuing an active strategy. The greater the cushion spread, the more scope the manager has to pursue an active management policy.

Assuming an initial portfolio of $100 million, the required terminal asset value when the safety net return is 6% is $134.39 million.[35] At the current available return of 7.5%, the assets required at inception in order to generate the required terminal value of $134.39 million are $93 million.[36] The safety cushion of 150 basis points translates, therefore, into an initial dollar safety margin of $7 million.

Now suppose the portfolio manager places the initial $100 million in a portfolio of 30-year par bonds with a coupon of 7.5%. Let us see what happens if there is a change in the yield level immediately following the purchase of these bonds.

---

35 Assuming semiannual compounding, the general formula for the required terminal value is:

Required terminal value $= I(1 + s/2)^{2H}$

where   I   = Initial portfolio value
          s   = safety net or floor rate
         H = number of years in the planning horizon

In our example, the initial portfolio value is $100 million, s is 6%, and H is five years. Therefore, the required terminal value is:

$100 million $(1.03)^{10} = 134.39 million

36 Assuming semiannual compounding, the required assets at any given time t necessary to achieve the required terminal value is:

$$\text{Required assets at time } t = \frac{\text{Required terminal value}}{(1 + i_t)^{2(H-t)}}$$

where i_t = the immunized semiannual yield available at time t and the other variables are as defined previously.

Because in the example, the required terminal value is $134.39 million and the market yield that can be realized if the immunization mode is activated is 7.5%, the required assets are:

$$\frac{\$134.39 \text{ million}}{(1.0375)^{10}} = \$120 \text{ million}$$

First suppose the yield level decreases to 5.6% from 7.5%. The value of the portfolio of 30-year bonds would increase to $127.46 million. The asset value required to achieve the required terminal value if this portfolio is immunized at a 5.6% rate is $102 million.[37] The asset value above and beyond the required asset value or dollar safety margin is now $25.46 million. This amount is $18.46 million more than the initial dollar safety margin, and therefore allows the manager more freedom to pursue active management.

Suppose instead of a decline in yield levels there is an increase in yield levels to 8.6%. At that yield level the portfolio of 30-year bonds would decline in value to $88.23 million. The required asset value to achieve the terminal value of $134.39 million is $88.23 million. A rise in the yield by 110 basis points to 8.6% will reduce the dollar safety margin to zero. At this yield level, the immunization mode would be triggered with an immunization target rate of 8.6% to ensure that the required terminal value will be realized. If this did not happen, further adverse movements of interest rates would threaten the required terminal value or portfolio floor of $134.39 million. The yield level at which the immunization mode is activated is called the "trigger point."

For monitoring purposes, it is useful to recast the dollar safety margin in terms of the potential return. This return, also called the *return achievable with immunization strategy*, measures the yield that would be realized if the current value of the portfolio is immunized at the prevailing market yield at a particular time.

Trigger yields can be computed for portfolios of different duration so that the manager will know how much leeway there is for a given risk position with respect to an adverse movement in the market yield; that is, how much of an adverse movement in the market yield can be tolerated before the immunization mode must be activated. The key to a contingent immunization plan is controlling and monitoring the performance of the portfolio over time so that the manager has information about its sensitivity.

An accurate immunization target is critical. It determines not only the basis for the initial immunization plan (e.g., the safety net is usually a certain basis point difference from the target over a specified time

---

37 Using the formula in the previous footnote, the required terminal value is $134.39 million and the market yield for immunizing (following the yield change) is 5.6%; therefore:

$$\frac{\$134.39 \text{ million}}{(1.028)^{10}} = \$102 \text{ million}$$

period), but also the immunization levels that are available over the management horizon. A safety net too close to the initial target return makes triggering of the immunization process highly likely, while too low a safety net defeats the purpose of the process—the very low satisfactory minimum return would probably never trigger immunization. Finally, the benefits of the strategy may be lost without an adequate monitoring procedure.

Even with good control and monitoring procedures, attainment of the minimum target return may be impossible because of factors beyond the control of the manager. There are two reasons for this.[38] The first is that a rapid adverse movement in market yields may be so large that the manager will not have time to shift from the active to immunization mode quickly enough to achieve the minimum target. Successive market yield jumps of several hundred basis points would immobilize a contingent immunization strategy. The second reason why the minimum target return may not be attained is that simply triggering the immunization mode does not guarantee achievement of the immunized rate, even if the portfolio is reconfigured at the required rate.

Combination by Formula

Another strategy combining active and immunization approaches has been described by Gifford Fong Associates.[39] In contrast to contingent immunization, this procedure allocates a portion of the initial portfolio to active management, and immunizes the balance according to a relationship that assumes that the immunization target return is greater than either the minimum or the expected worst-case active returns:

Active component
$$= \frac{\text{Immunization target rate} - \text{Minimum return}}{\text{Immunization target rate} - \text{Worst case active return}}$$

As an example, assuming that the available immunization target is 10% per year, the minimum return acceptable to the fund sponsor is 10%, and the worst-case return for the actively managed portion of the portfolio is anticipated to be 4%, the percentage in the active portion of the portfolio would be:

---

38 Leibowitz and Weinberger, "Contingent Immunization—Part II: Problem Areas."
39 Gifford Fong Associates, "The Costs of Cash Flow Matching," 1981.

$$\text{Active component} = \frac{.10 - .07}{.10 - .04} = 50\%$$

For any given immunization target return, the smaller the minimum acceptable return and the larger the expected active return, the greater the proportion of the portfolio under active management. Note that the percentages assumed will change over time in some relationship; it is the manager's responsibility to monitor these factors constantly, adjusting and rebalancing the portfolio as appropriate.

As long as the worst-case scenario is not violated—that is, as long as the actual return experienced does not drop below the expected active return—the desired minimum return will be achieved.

Chapter 10

Strategies with Interest Rate Derivatives

With the advent of interest rate futures, options, and swaps it is now possible for managers to alter the interest-rate sensitivity of a bond portfolio or an asset/liability position economically and quickly. These *derivative contracts*, so-called because they derive their value from an underlying asset, offer managers risk and return patterns that were once either unavailable or too costly to achieve. This chapter provides an overview of the risk/return characteristics of these contracts and describes how they can be used by fixed income portfolio managers.

INTEREST RATE FUTURES

A futures contract is a firm legal agreement between a buyer (seller) and an established exchange or its clearinghouse in which the buyer (seller) agrees to take (make) delivery of something at a specified price at the end of a designated period of time. We shall refer to the "something" that can be bought or sold as the *underlying*. The price at which parties agree to transact in the future is called the *futures price*. The designated date at which the parties must transact is called the *settlement* or *delivery date*.

Most financial futures contracts have settlement dates in the months of March, June, September, or December. This means that at a predetermined time in the contract settlement month the contract stops trading, and a price is determined by the exchange for settlement of the contract. The contract with the closest settlement date is called the *nearby futures contract*. The next futures contract is the one that settles just after the nearby contract. The contract farthest away in time from settlement is called the *most distant futures contract*.

When an investor takes a position in the market by buying a futures contract, the investor is said to be in a *long position* or to be *long futures*. If, instead, the investor's opening position is the sale of a futures contract, the investor is said to be in a *short position* or *short futures*.

A party to a futures contract has two choices on liquidation of the position. First, the position can be liquidated prior to the settlement date. For this purpose, the party must take an offsetting position in the same contract. For the buyer of a futures contract, this means selling the same number of identical futures contracts; for the seller of a futures contract, this means buying the same number of identical futures contracts.

The alternative is to wait until the settlement date. At that time the party purchasing a futures contract accepts delivery of the underlying at the agreed-upon price; the party that sells a futures contract liquidates the position by delivering the underlying at the agreed-upon price. For some futures contracts, settlement is made in cash only. Such contracts are referred to as *cash settlement contracts*.

Associated with every futures exchange is a clearinghouse, which performs several functions. One of these functions is guaranteeing that the contractual obligations of the two parties to the transaction will be met. Thus, when an investor takes a position in the futures market, the clearinghouse takes the opposite position and agrees to satisfy the terms set forth in the contract. Besides its guarantee function, the clearinghouse makes it simple for parties to a futures contract to unwind their positions prior to the settlement date by taking an offsetting position.

When a position is first taken in a futures contract, the investor must deposit a minimum dollar amount per contract as specified by the exchange. This amount is called *initial margin*. As the price of the futures contract fluctuates, the value of the investor's margin account changes. At the end of each trading day, the exchange determines the settlement price for the futures contract. This price is used to mark to market the investor's position, so that any gain or loss from the position is reflected in the investor's margin account.

Maintenance margin is the minimum level (specified by the exchange) by which an investor's margin account may fall as a result of an unfavorable price movement before the investor is required to deposit additional margin. The additional margin required is called *variation margin*, and it is an amount necessary to bring the margin account back to its initial margin level.

Futures versus Forward Contracts

A *forward contract*, just like a futures contract, is an agreement for the future delivery of something at a specified price at the end of a designated period of time. Futures contracts are standardized agreements as to the delivery date (or month) and quality of the deliverable, and are traded on organized exchanges. A forward contract differs in that it is usually nonstandardized (that is, the terms of each contract are negotiated individually between buyer and seller), there is no clearinghouse, and secondary markets are often nonexistent or extremely thin. Unlike a futures contract, which is an exchange-traded product, a forward contract is an over-the-counter instrument.

Although both futures and forward contracts set forth terms of delivery, futures contracts are not intended to be settled by delivery. In fact, fewer than 2% of outstanding contracts are settled by delivery. Forward contracts, in contrast, are intended for delivery.

Futures contracts are marked to market at the end of each trading day, while forward contracts usually are not. Consequently, futures contracts are subject to interim cash flows as additional margin may be required in the case of adverse price movements, or as cash is withdrawn in the case of favorable price movements. There are no interim cash flow effects with forward contracts because no variation margin is typically required.

Finally, the parties in a forward contract are exposed to credit risk because either party may default on the obligation. Credit risk is minimal in the case of futures contracts because the clearinghouse associated with the exchange guarantees the other side of the transaction.

Other than these differences, most of what we say about futures contracts applies equally to forward contracts.

Risk and Return Characteristics

The buyer of a futures contract will realize a profit if the futures price increases; the seller of a futures contract will realize a profit if the futures price decreases. When a position is taken in a futures contract, the party need not put up the entire amount of the investment. Instead, only initial margin must be put up. Consequently, the futures contract allows a manager to create leverage.

At first, the leverage available in the futures market may suggest that the market benefits only those who want to speculate on price movements. This is not true. Futures markets can be used to reduce price risk. Without the leverage possible in futures transactions, the cost of reducing price risk using futures would be too high for many market participants.

Treasury Bond Futures

Interest rate futures contracts in the United States are traded on short-term instruments, the Treasury bill futures contract and the Eurodollar CD futures contract, and longer-term instruments, the Treasury notes and bonds futures contracts. Because the Treasury bond futures contract plays an important role in the strategies we discuss below, it is worth reviewing the nuances of this contract, which make it particularly interesting. The government bond futures of other countries such as Japan and Germany are modeled on the U.S. Treasury bond futures contract.

The underlying instrument for a Treasury bond futures contract is $100,000 par value of a hypothetical 20-year, 8% coupon bond. While price and yield of the Treasury bond futures contract are quoted in terms of this hypothetical Treasury bond, the seller of the futures contract has the choice of several actual Treasury bonds that are acceptable to deliver. The Chicago Board of Trade (CBT) allows the seller to deliver any Treasury bond that has at least 15 years to maturity from the date of delivery if not callable; in the case of callable bonds, the issue must not be callable for at least 15 years from the first day of the delivery month. To settle the contract an acceptable bond must be delivered.

The minimum price fluctuation for the Treasury bond futures contract is a 32nd of 1%. The dollar value of a 32nd for a $100,000 par value (the par value for the underlying Treasury bond) is $31.25. Thus, the minimum price fluctuation is $31.25 for this contract.

The delivery process for the Treasury bond futures contract makes the contract interesting. In the settlement month, the seller of a futures contract (the short) is required to deliver to the buyer (the long) $100,000 par value of an 8%, 20-year Treasury bond. No such bond exists, however, so the seller must choose from other acceptable deliverable bonds that the exchange has specified.

To make delivery equitable to both parties, and to tie cash to futures prices, the CBT has introduced *conversion factors* for determining the invoice price of each acceptable deliverable Treasury issue against the Treasury bond futures contract. The conversion factor is determined by the CBT before a contract with a specific settlement date begins trading. The conversion factor is based on the price that a deliverable bond would sell for at the beginning of the delivery month if it were to yield 8%. The conversion factor is constant throughout the trading period of the futures contract. The short must notify the long of the actual bond that will be delivered one day before the delivery date.

The invoice price paid by the buyer of the Treasury bonds delivered by the seller is determined using the formula:

Invoice price =

$$\begin{array}{ccccc} \text{Contract} \\ \text{size} \end{array} \times \begin{array}{c} \text{Futures contract} \\ \text{settlement price} \end{array} \times \begin{array}{c} \text{Conversion} \\ \text{factor} \end{array} + \begin{array}{c} \text{Accrued} \\ \text{interest} \end{array}$$

Suppose the Treasury bond futures contract settles at 96 (0.96 in decimal form) and that the short elects to deliver a Treasury bond issue with a conversion factor of 1.15. As the contract size is $100,000, the invoice price is:

$$\$100,000 \times .96 \times 1.15 + \begin{array}{c}\text{Accrued} \\ \text{interest}\end{array} = \$110,400 + \begin{array}{c}\text{Accrued} \\ \text{interest}\end{array}$$

In selecting the issue to be delivered, the short will select from all the deliverable issues and bond issues auctioned during the contract life the one that is cheapest to deliver. This issue is referred to as the *cheapest-to-deliver* (CTD). The CTD plays a key role in the pricing of this futures contract.

In addition to the option of which acceptable Treasury issue to deliver—sometimes referred to as the *quality* or *swap option*—the short position has two more options granted under CBT delivery guidelines. The short position is permitted to decide when in the delivery month actual delivery will take place. This is called the *timing option*. The other option is the right of the short position to give notice of intent to deliver up to 8:00 p.m. Chicago time after the closing of the exchange (3:15 p.m. Chicago time) on the date when the futures settlement price has been fixed. This option is referred to as the *wild card option*. The quality option, the timing option, and the wild card option (in sum referred to as the *delivery options*) mean that the long position can never be sure which Treasury bond will be delivered or when it will be delivered.

Modeled after the Treasury bond futures contract, the underlying for the Treasury note futures contract is $100,000 par value of a hypothetical 10-year, 8% Treasury note. There are several acceptable Treasury issues that may be delivered by the short. An issue is acceptable if the maturity is not less than 6.5 years and not greater than 10 years from the first day of the delivery month. The delivery options granted to the short position and the minimum price fluctuation are the same as for the Treasury bond futures contract.

Pricing of Futures Contracts

One of the primary concerns that most portfolio managers have when taking a position in futures contracts is whether the futures price at which they transact will be a "fair" price. Buyers are concerned that the price may be too high, and that they will be picked off by more experienced futures traders waiting to profit from the mistakes of the uninitiated. Sellers worry that the price is artificially low, and that savvy traders may have manipulated the markets so that they can buy at bargain basement prices. Furthermore, prospective participants frequently find no rational explanation for the sometimes violent ups and downs that occur in the futures markets. Theories about efficient markets give little comfort to anyone who knows of or has experienced the sudden losses that can occur in the highly leveraged futures markets.

Fortunately, the futures markets are not as irrational as they may at first seem; if they were, they would not have become so successful. The interest rate futures markets are not perfectly efficient markets, but they probably come about as close as any market. Furthermore, there are both very clear reasons why futures prices are what they are and useful methods by which market participants can and will quickly eliminate any discrepancy between futures prices and their fair levels.

There are several different ways to price futures contracts. Fortunately, all lead to the same fair price for a given contract. Each approach relies on the "Law of One Price." This law states that a given financial asset must have the same price regardless of the means by which it is created. The Law of One Price implies that a synthetically created cash security must have the same price as an actual cash security. Similarly, cash instruments can be combined to create cash flows that are identical to futures contracts. By the Law of One Price, the futures contract must have the same price as the synthetic futures created from cash instruments.

Theoretical Futures Price Based on Arbitrage Model

The theoretical futures price can be determined on the basis of the following information: (1) the price of the bond in the cash market, (2) the coupon rate on the bond, and (3) the interest rate for borrowing and lending until the settlement date. The borrowing and lending rate is referred to as the *financing rate*.
   Letting

r = financing rate
c = current yield, or coupon rate divided by the cash market price
P = cash market price
F = futures price
t = time, in years, to the futures delivery date

consider a strategy initiated on a coupon date:

Sell the futures contract at F.
Purchase the bond for P.
Borrow P until the settlement date at r.

The outcome at the settlement date is

From settlement of the futures contract:

Flat price of bond	=	F
Accrued interest	=	ctP
Total proceeds	=	$F + ctP$

From the loan:

Repayment of principal of loan	=	P
Interest on loan	=	rtP
Total outlay	=	P + rtP

The profit will equal:

$$\text{Profit} = \text{Total proceeds} - \text{Total outlay}$$
$$\text{Profit} = F + ctP - (P + rtP)$$

In equilibrium the theoretical futures price occurs where the profit from this trade is zero. Thus to have equilibrium, the following must hold:

$$0 = F + ctP - (P + rtP)$$

Solving for the theoretical futures price, we have

(1) $$F = P + Pt(r - c)$$

Alternatively, consider another strategy:

Buy the futures contract at F.
Sell (short) the bond for P.
Invest (lend) P at r until the settlement date.

The outcome at the settlement date would be

From settlement of the futures contract:

Flat price of bond	=	F
Accrued interest	=	ctP
Total outlay	=	F + ctP

From the loan:

Proceeds received from maturing investment	=	P
Interest earned	=	rtP
Total proceeds	=	P + rtP

The profit will equal:

$$\text{Profit} = \text{Total proceeds} - \text{Total outlay}$$
$$\text{Profit} = P + rtP - (F + ctP)$$

Setting the profit equal to zero so that there will be no arbitrage profit and solving for the futures price, we obtain the same equation for the futures price as equation (1).

Let's apply equation (1). Suppose that

$$r = .08; c = .12; P = 100; \text{ and } t = .25$$

Then the theoretical futures price is

$$F = 100 + 100\,(.25)\,(.08 - .12) = 100 - 1 = 99$$

The theoretical futures price may be at a premium to the cash market price (higher than the cash market price) or at a discount from the cash market price (lower than the cash market price), depending on $(r - c)$. The term $r - c$ is called the *net financing cost* because it adjusts the financing rate for the coupon interest earned. The net financing cost is more commonly called the *cost of carry*, or simply *carry*. *Positive carry* means that the current yield earned is greater than the financing cost; *negative carry* means that the financing cost exceeds the current yield.

In the case of interest rate futures, carry (the relationship between the short-term financing rate and the current yield on the bond) depends on the shape of the yield curve. When the yield curve is upward-sloping, the short-term financing rate will generally be less than the current yield on the bond, resulting in positive carry. The futures price will then be at a discount to the cash price for the bond. The opposite holds when the yield curve is inverted.

A Closer Look at the Theoretical Futures Price

To derive the theoretical futures price using the arbitrage argument, several assumptions are made that have certain implications.

Interim Cash Flows: No interim cash flows due to variation margin or coupon interest payments are assumed in the model, although we know that interim cash flows can occur for both of these reasons.

Because we assume no variation margin, the price derived is technically the theoretical price for a forward contract (which is not marked
to market at the end of each trading day).

Incorporating interim coupon payments into the pricing model is
not difficult. The value of the coupon payments at the settlement date
will depend on the interest rate at which they can be reinvested. The
shorter the maturity of the futures contract, and the lower the coupon
rate, the less important the reinvestment income is in determining the
futures price.

The Short-Term Interest Rate (Financing Rate): In deriving the theoretical
futures price, it is assumed that the borrowing and lending rates are
equal. Typically, however, the borrowing rate is higher than the lending rate.

Letting r_B and r_L denote the borrowing rate and the lending rate,
then consider the following strategy:

Sell the futures contract at F.
Purchase the bond for P.
Borrow P until the settlement date at r_B.

The futures price that would produce no arbitrage profit is

(2) $$F = P + Pt\,(r_B - c)$$

Now consider another strategy:

Buy the futures contract at F.
Sell (short) the bond for P.
Invest (lend) P at r_L until the settlement date.

The futures price that would produce no profit is

(3) $$F = P + Pt\,(r_L - c)$$

Equations (2) and (3) together provide boundaries for the futures
price equilibrium. Equation (2) provides the upper boundary and
equation (3) the lower boundary. For example, assume that the borrowing rate is 8% per year, while the lending rate is 6% per year. Then using
equation (2) and the previous example, the upper boundary is

$$F \text{ (upper boundary)} = 100 + 100 \, (.25) \, (.08 - .12) = 99$$

The lower boundary using equation (3) is

$$F \text{ (lower boundary)} = 100 + 100 \, (.25) \, (.06 - .12) = 98.50$$

In calculating these boundaries, we assume no transactions costs are involved in taking the position. In actuality, the transactions costs of entering into and closing the cash position as well as the round-trip transactions costs for the futures contract must be considered and do affect the boundaries for the futures contract.

Deliverable Bond Is Known: In the pricing model based on arbitrage arguments, it is assumed that only one instrument is deliverable. But the futures contracts on Treasury bonds and Treasury notes are designed to allow the short the choice of delivering one of a number of deliverable issues (the quality or swap option). Because there may be more than one deliverable, market participants track the price of each deliverable bond and determine which bond is the cheapest to deliver. The futures price will then trade in relation to the cheapest-to-deliver bond.

There is the risk that while an issue may be the cheapest to deliver at the time a position in the futures contract is taken, it may not be the cheapest to deliver after that time. A change in the cheapest-to-deliver can dramatically alter the futures price.

What are the implications of the quality (swap) option for the futures price? Because the swap option is an option granted by the long to the short, the long will want to pay less for the futures contract. Therefore, the theoretical futures price after adjusting for the quality option granted to the short should be less than the theoretical futures price given above. The derivation of the theoretical futures price and the value of the delivery options are described in Appendix C. Also described in Appendix C are the risk parameters of the futures contract such as duration and convexity. These risk parameters form the basis of various strategies with interest rate futures.

Delivery Date Is Known: In the pricing model based on arbitrage arguments, a known delivery date is assumed. For Treasury bond and note futures contracts, the short has timing and wild card options, so the long does not know when the securities will be delivered. The effect of the timing and wild card options on the theoretical futures price is the same as with the quality option. These delivery options should result in a theoretical futures price that is lower than the one suggested above.

Strategies with Interest Rate Futures

There are various strategies for which interest rate futures contracts can be used.

Hedging: Hedging with futures calls for taking a futures position as a temporary substitute for transactions to be made in the cash market at a later date. If cash and futures prices move together, any loss realized by the hedger from one position (whether cash or futures) will be offset by a profit on the other position.

In practice, hedging is not that simple. The outcome of a hedge will depend on the relationship between the cash price and the futures price both when a hedge is placed and when it is lifted. The difference between the cash price and the futures price is called the *basis*. From the theoretical pricing model, we know that the basis should equal carry. Departures from carry result because of the delivery options granted to the short. The risk that the basis will change in an unpredictable way is called *basis risk*.

In most hedging applications, the bond to be hedged is not identical to the bond underlying the futures contract. This kind of hedging is referred to as *cross hedging*. There may be substantial basis risk in cross hedging. An unhedged position is exposed to price risk, the risk that the cash market price will move adversely. A hedged position substitutes basis risk for price risk.

A *short* (or *sell*) *hedge* is used to protect against a decline in the cash price of a bond. To execute a short hedge, futures contracts are sold. By establishing a short hedge, the hedger has fixed the future cash price and transferred the price risk of ownership to the buyer of the futures contract. To understand why a short hedge might be executed, suppose that a pension fund manager knows that bonds must be liquidated in 40 days to make a $5 million payment to the beneficiaries of the pension fund. If interest rates rise during the 40-day period, more bonds will have to be liquidated to realize $5 million. To guard against this possibility, the manager can sell bonds in the futures market to lock in a selling price.

A *long* (or *buy*) *hedge* is undertaken to protect against an increase in the cash price of a bond. In a long hedge, the hedger buys a futures contract to lock in a purchase price. A pension fund manager might use a long hedge when substantial cash contributions are expected, and the manager is concerned that interest rates will fall. Also, a money manager who knows that bonds are maturing in the near future and expects that interest rates will fall can employ a long hedge to lock in a rate for the proceeds to be reinvested.

Conceptually, cross hedging is somewhat more complicated than hedging deliverable securities, because it involves two relationships. First, there is the relationship between the cheapest-to-deliver security and the futures contract. Second, there is the relationship between the security to be hedged and the cheapest-to-deliver security.

The key to minimizing risk in a cross hedge is to choose the right *hedge ratio*. The hedge ratio depends on volatility weighting, or weighting by relative changes in value. The purpose of a hedge is to use gains or losses from a futures position to offset any difference between the target sale price and the actual sale price of the asset. Accordingly, the hedge ratio is chosen with the intention of matching the volatility (that is, the dollar change) of the futures contract to the volatility of the asset. Consequently, the hedge ratio is given by:

$$\text{Hedge ratio} = \frac{\text{Volatility of bond be hedged}}{\text{Volatility of hedging instrument}}$$

As the formula shows, if the bond to be hedged is more volatile than the hedging instrument, more of the hedging instrument will be needed.

While it might be fairly clear why volatility is the key variable in determining the hedge ratio, "volatility" has many definitions. For hedging purposes, we are concerned with volatility in absolute dollar terms. To calculate the dollar volatility of a bond, one must know the precise time at which volatility is to be calculated (because volatility generally declines as a bond ages) as well as the price or yield at which to calculate volatility (because higher yields generally reduce dollar volatility for a given yield change).

The relevant point in the life of the bond for calculating volatility is the point at which the hedge will be lifted. Volatility at any other point is essentially irrelevant, because the goal is to lock in a price or rate only on that particular day. Similarly, the relevant yield at which to calculate volatility initially is the target yield. Consequently, the "volatility of the bond to be hedged" referred to in the formula is the dollar duration of the bond on the hedge lift date, calculated at its current implied forward rate. The dollar duration is the product of the price of the bond and its duration.

The relative price volatilities of the bonds to be hedged and the cheapest-to-deliver bond are easily obtained from the assumed sale date and target prices. In the formula for the hedge ratio we need the volatility not of the cheapest-to-deliver bond, but of the hedging instrument, that is, of the futures contract. Fortunately, knowing the volatility of the bond to be hedged relative to the cheapest-to-deliver bond and the volatility of the cheapest-to-deliver bond relative to the futures contract, the relative volatilities that define the hedge ratio can be easily obtained as follows:

$$\text{Hedge ratio} = \frac{\text{Volatility of bond to be hedged}}{\text{Volatility of futures contract}}$$

$$= \frac{\text{Volatility of bond to be hedged}}{\text{Volatility of CTD bond}} \times \frac{\text{Volatility of CTD bond}}{\text{Volatility of futures contract}}$$

Or, more concisely, assuming a fixed yield spread between the bond to be hedged and the cheapest-to-deliver bond:

$$\text{Hedge ratio} = \frac{D_H \, P_H}{D_{CTD} \, P_{CTD}} \times \text{Conversion factor for the CTD bond}$$

where D_H = the duration of the bond to be hedged
P_H = the price of the bond to be hedged
D_{CTD} = the duration of the cheapest-to-deliver bond
P_{CTD} = the price of the cheapest-to-deliver bond

The product of the duration and the price is the dollar duration.

Another refinement in the hedging strategy is usually necessary for hedging nondeliverable securities. This refinement concerns the assumption about the relative yield spread between the cheapest-to-deliver bond and the bond to be hedged. In the discussion so far, we have assumed that the yield spread is constant over time. Yield spreads, however, are not constant over time. They vary with the maturity of the instruments in question and the level of rates, as well as with many unpredictable and nonsystematic factors.

A hedger can use regression analysis to capture the relationship between yield levels and yield spreads. For hedging purposes, the variables are the yield on the bond to be hedged and the yield on the cheapest-to-deliver bond. The regression equation takes the form:

Yield on bond to be hedged = a + b (Yield on CTD bond) + error

The regression procedure provides an estimate of b, called the *yield beta*, which is the expected relative change in the two bonds. The "error" term accounts for the fact that the relationship between the yields is not perfect and contains a certain amount of "noise." The regression will, however, give an estimate of a and b so that over the sample period the error is on average zero. Our formula for the hedge ratio assumes a constant spread and implicitly assumes that the yield beta in the regression equals 1.0.

The formula for the hedge ratio can be revised to incorporate the impact of the yield beta by multiplying by the yield beta.

Controlling the Interest Rate Risk of a Portfolio: Hedging is a special case of controlling interest rate risk where the target duration for the portfolio is zero. Managers can use interest rate futures to alter the interest rate sensitivity of a portfolio. Those with strong expectations about the direction of the future course of interest rates will adjust the durations of their portfolios so as to capitalize on their expectations. Specifically, a manager who expects rates to increase will shorten duration; a manager who expects interest rates to decrease will lengthen duration. While managers can use cash market instruments to alter the durations of their portfolios, futures contracts provide a quicker and less expensive means for doing so (on either a temporary or permanent basis).

Besides adjusting a portfolio for anticipated interest rate movements, managers can use futures in strategies such as immunization (described in Chapter 9) to construct a portfolio with a longer duration than would be available with cash market securities. Suppose that in a given interest rate environment a pension fund manager must structure a portfolio to have a duration of 10 years to accomplish a particular investment objective. Bonds with such a long duration may not be available, but buying the appropriate number and kind of interest rate futures contracts can allow a pension fund manager to increase the portfolio's duration to the target level of 10.

A formula to approximate the number of futures contracts necessary to adjust the portfolio duration to a new level is:

$$\text{Approximate number of contracts} = \frac{(D_T - D_I) P_I}{D_{CTD} P_{CTD}} \times \text{Conversion factor for the CTD bond}$$

where D_T = target modified duration for the portfolio
       D_I = initial modified duration for the portfolio
       P_I = initial market value of the portfolio

Notice that if the manager wishes to increase the duration, then D_T will be greater than D_I, and the equation will have a positive sign. This means that futures contracts will be purchased. The opposite is true if the objective is to shorten the portfolio duration. Also note that if the target duration is zero, the approximation formula is equivalent to the hedge ratio given earlier.

Allocating Funds between Stocks and Bonds: The costs associated with changing the asset allocation of a fund between common stock and bonds using the cash market are: (1) transactions costs with respect to commissions and bid-ask spreads, (2) market impact costs, and (3) disruption of the activities of managers employed by the client.

An alternative course of action is to use interest rate futures and stock index futures. Positions in an appropriate number of interest rate futures and stock index futures can achieve the desired exposure to stocks and bonds. Futures positions can be maintained or liquidated slowly as funds invested in the cash markets are actually shifted. The advantages of using the futures market rather than the cash market are: (1) transactions costs are lower, (2) market impact costs are avoided or reduced as the sponsor has more time to buy and sell securities in the cash market, and (3) activities of the managers employed by the pension sponsor are not disrupted.

To determine the approximate number of interest rate futures contracts needed to change the market value of the portfolio allocated to bonds, assuming that the duration of the portfolio is to remain constant, we can use the formula:

$$\begin{matrix} \text{Approximate number} \\ \text{of contracts} \end{matrix} = \frac{(P_T - P_I)\,D_I}{D_{CTD}\,P_{CTD}} \times \begin{matrix} \text{Conversion factor} \\ \text{for the CTD bond} \end{matrix}$$

where P_T is the target market value allocated to bonds and the other terms are as identified earlier.

Notice that if the market value of the portfolio allocated to bonds is to be increased, the numerator of the equation will be positive. This means that futures contracts will be purchased. If funds are to be reallocated to stocks and withdrawn from bonds, the numerator of the equation will be negative, which means that interest rate futures contracts will be sold.

Creating Synthetic Securities for Yield Enhancement: A cash market security can be created synthetically by using a position in the futures contract together with the deliverable instrument. The yield on the synthetic security should be the same as the yield on the cash market security. Any difference between the two yields can be exploited so as to enhance the yield on the portfolio.

To see how, consider an investor who owns a 20-year Treasury bond and sells Treasury futures that call for the delivery of that particular bond three months from now. While the maturity of the Treasury bond is 20 years, the investor has effectively shortened the maturity of the bond to three months.

Consequently, the long position in the 20-year bond and the short futures position are equivalent to a long position in a three-month riskless security. The position is riskless because the investor is locking in the price to be received three months from now—the futures price. By being long the bond and short the futures, the investor has synthetically created a three-month Treasury bill. The return the investor should expect to earn from this synthetic position should be the yield on a three-month Treasury bill. If the yield on the synthetic three-month Treasury bill is greater than the yield on the cash market Treasury bill, the investor can realize an enhanced yield by creating the synthetic short-term security. The fundamental relationship for creating synthetic securities is:

(4)   RSP = CBP − FBP

where RSP = riskless short-term security position
      CBP = cash bond position
      FBP = bond futures position

A negative sign before a position means a short position. In terms of our previous example, CBP is the long cash bond position; the negative sign before FBP refers to the short futures position; and RSP is the riskless synthetic three-month security or Treasury bill.

Equation (4) states that an investor who is long the cash market security and short the futures contract should expect to earn the rate of return on a risk-free security with the same maturity as the futures delivery date. In fact, one way to determine the CTD is to find the issue that gives the greatest short-term money market rate by buying the cash market security and selling the futures contract. This rate is called the *implied repo rate*.

Solving equation (4) for the long bond position, we have

(5) $CBP = RSP + FBP$

Equation (5) states that a cash bond position equals a short-term riskless security position plus a long bond futures position. Thus, a cash market bond can be created synthetically by buying a futures contract and investing in a Treasury bill.

Solving equation (5) for the bond futures position, we have

(6) $FBP = CBP - RSP$

Equation (6) tells us that a long position in the futures contract can be created synthetically by taking a long position in the cash market bond and shorting the short-term riskless security. But shorting the short-term riskless security is equivalent to borrowing money. If we reverse the signs on both sides of equation (6), we can see how a short futures position can be created synthetically.

In an efficient market the opportunities for yield enhancement should not exist very long.

INTEREST RATE SWAPS

In an interest rate swap, two parties (called *counterparties*) agree to exchange periodic interest payments. The dollar amount of the interest payments exchanged is based on some predetermined dollar principal, which is called the *notional principal amount*. The dollar amount each counterparty pays to the other is the agreed-upon periodic interest rate times the notional principal amount. The only dollars that are exchanged between the parties are the interest payments, not the notional principal amount.

In the most common type of swap, one party agrees to pay the other party fixed interest payments at designated dates for the life of the contract. This party is referred to as the *fixed-rate payer*. The other party, who agrees to make interest rate payments that float with some reference interest rate, is referred to as the *floating-rate payer*.

For example, suppose that for the next five years party X agrees to pay party Y 10% per year, while party Y agrees to pay party X six-month LIBOR. Party X is a fixed-rate payer/floating-rate receiver, while party Y is a floating-rate payer/fixed-rate receiver. Assume that the notional principal amount is $50 million, and that payments are exchanged every six months for the next five years. This means that every six months, party X (the fixed-rate payer/floating-rate receiver) will pay party Y $2.5 million (10% times $50 million divided by 2). The amount that party Y (the floating-rate payer/fixed-rate receiver) will pay party X will be six-month LIBOR times $50 million divided by 2. If six-month LIBOR is 7%, party Y will pay party X $1.75 million (7% times $50 million divided by 2). Note that we divide by two because one-half year's interest is being paid.

The benchmark interest rates used for the floating rate in an interest rate swap are those on various money market instruments: Treasury bills, the London Interbank Offered Rate (LIBOR), commercial paper, bankers acceptances, certificates of deposit, the federal funds rate, and the prime rate.

Risk/Return Characteristics of a Swap

The value of an interest rate swap will fluctuate with market interest rates. To see how, let's consider our hypothetical swap. Suppose that interest rates change immediately after parties X and Y enter into the swap. First, consider what would happen if the market demanded that in any five-year swap the fixed-rate payer must pay 11% in order to receive six-month LIBOR. If party X (the fixed-rate payer) wants to sell its position to party A, then party A will benefit by having to pay only 10% (the original swap rate agreed upon) rather than 11% (the current

swap rate) to receive six-month LIBOR. Party X will want compensation for this benefit. Consequently, the value of party X's position has
increased. Thus, if interest rates increase, the fixed-rate payer will
realize a profit, and the floating-rate payer will realize a loss.

Next, consider what would happen if interest rates decline to, say,
6%. Now a five-year swap would require the fixed-rate payer to pay
6% rather than 10% to receive six-month LIBOR. If party X wants to sell
its position to party B, the latter would demand compensation to take
over the position. In other words, if interest rates decline, the fixed-rate
payer will realize a loss, while the floating-rate payer will realize a
profit. The risk/return profile of the two positions when interest rates
change is summarized below:

	Interest rates decrease	*Interest rates increase*
Floating-rate payer	Gain	Loss
Fixed-rate payer	Loss	Gain

Interpreting a Swap Position

There are two ways a swap position can be interpreted: (1) as a package
of forward/futures contracts, and (2) as a package of cash flows from
buying and selling cash market instruments.

Package of Forward Contracts: Contrast the position of the counterparties
in the interest rate swap summarized above with the position of the
long and short futures (forward) contract. The long futures position
gains if interest rates decline and loses if interest rates rise—this is
similar to the risk/return profile for a floating-rate payer. The risk/re-
turn profile for a fixed-rate payer is similar to that of the short futures
position: a gain if interest rates increase and a loss if interest rates
decrease. By taking a closer look at the interest rate swap we can
understand why the risk/return relationships are similar.

Consider party X's position. Party X has agreed to pay 10% and
receive six-month LIBOR. More specifically, assuming a $50 million
notional principal amount, X has agreed to buy a commodity called
"six-month LIBOR" for $2.5 million. This is effectively a six-month
forward contract where X agrees to pay $2.5 million in exchange for
delivery of six-month LIBOR. If interest rates increase to 11%, the price
of that commodity (six-month LIBOR) is higher, resulting in a gain for

the fixed-rate payer, who is effectively long a six-month forward contract on six-month LIBOR. The floating-rate payer is effectively short a six-month forward contract on six-month LIBOR. There is therefore an implicit forward contract corresponding to each exchange date.

Now we can see why there is a similarity between the risk/return relationship for an interest rate swap and a forward contract. If interest rates increase to, say, 11%, the price of that commodity (six-month LIBOR) increases to $2.75 million (11% times $50 million divided by 2). The long forward position (the fixed-rate payer) gains, and the short forward position (the floating-rate payer) loses. If interest rates decline to, say, 9%, the price of our commodity decreases to $2.25 million (9% times $50 million divided by 2). The short forward position (the floating-rate payer) gains, and the long forward position (the fixed-rate payer) loses.

Consequently, interest rate swaps can be viewed as a package of more basic interest rate control tools, such as forwards. The pricing of an interest rate swap will then depend on the price of a package of forward contracts with the same settlement dates in which the underlying for the forward contract is the same reference rate.

While an interest rate swap may be nothing more than a package of forward contracts, it is not a superfluous contract for several reasons. First, maturities for forward or futures contracts do not extend out as far as those of an interest rate swap; an interest rate swap with a term of 15 years or longer can be obtained. Second, an interest rate swap is a more transactionally efficient instrument. By this we mean that in one transaction an entity can effectively establish a payoff equivalent to a package of forward contracts. The forward contracts would each have to be negotiated separately. Third, interest rate swaps now provide more liquidity than forward contracts, particularly long-dated (i.e., long-term) forward contracts.

Package of Cash Market Instruments: It can be shown that a fixed-rate payer has a cash market position that is equivalent to a long position in a floating-rate bond and borrowing the funds to purchase the floating-rate bond on a fixed-rate basis. But the borrowing can be viewed as issuing a fixed-rate bond, or, equivalently, being short a fixed-rate bond. Consequently, the position of a fixed-rate payer can be viewed as being long a floating-rate bond and short a fixed-rate bond.

It can be easily demonstrated that the position of a floating-rate payer is equivalent to purchasing a fixed-rate bond and financing that purchase at a floating rate, where the floating rate is the reference interest rate for the swap. That is, the position of a floating-rate payer is equivalent to a long position in a fixed-rate bond and a short position in a floating-rate bond.

Pricing a Swap

The price of any financial asset is equal to the present value of the expected cash flow. The proper methodology for discounting the cash flow is to use spot or zero-coupon rates. In the case of a swap, each cash flow should be discounted at the zero-coupon rate applicable to the time period when the cash flow will be realized (paid or received). Although there is no active market for zero-coupon swaps from which to determine the appropriate rates, a theoretical zero-coupon swap curve can be extrapolated from the existing coupon swap curve. These zero-coupon rates can then be used to price any swap, whether generic or one of the more complex swaps described later.

Dollar Duration of a Swap

As with any fixed-income contract, the value of a swap will change as interest rates change, and dollar duration is a measure of the interest-rate sensitivity of a fixed-income security. From the perspective of the party who pays floating and receives fixed, the interest rate swap position can be viewed as:

Long a fixed-rate bond + Short a floating-rate bond

This means that the dollar duration of an interest rate swap from the perspective of a floating-rate payer is just the difference between the dollar duration of the two bond positions that make up the swap. That is,

$$\text{Dollar duration of a swap} = \text{Dollar duration of a fixed--rate bond} - \text{Dollar duration of a floating--rate bond}$$

Most of the interest-rate sensitivity of a swap will result from the dollar duration of the fixed-rate bond because the dollar duration of the floating-rate bond will be small.

Applications of a Swap to Asset/Liability Management

An interest rate swap can be used to alter the cash flow characteristics of an institution's assets or liabilities so as to provide a better match between assets and liabilities. More specifically, it lets an institution alter the cash flow characteristics of its assets or liabilities: from fixed to floating or from floating to fixed. In general, swaps can be used to change the duration of a portfolio or an entity's surplus (the difference between the market value of the assets and the present value of the liabilities).

Rather than using an interest rate swap, the same objectives can be accomplished by taking an appropriate position in a package of forward contracts or appropriate positions in cash market positions. The advantage of an interest rate swap is that it is a more transactionally efficient vehicle for accomplishing an asset/liability objective. In fact, this is the primary reason for the growth of the interest rate swap market, a market that initially developed to exploit perceived credit arbitrages.

INTEREST RATE OPTIONS

Thus far in this book we have focused on options embedded in fixed income securities. We turn our attention here to the way standalone options can be used to control the interest rate risk of a portfolio.

Interest rate options can be written on cash instruments or futures. At one time, there were several exchange-traded option contracts whose underlying instrument was a debt instrument. These contracts are referred to as *options on physicals*. The most liquid exchange-traded option on a fixed income security at the time of this writing is an option on Treasury bonds traded on the Chicago Board Options Exchange. *Options on futures* have been far more popular than options on physicals. In recent years, market participants have made increasingly greater use of over-the-counter options on Treasury and mortgage-backed securities.

Certain institutional investors who want to purchase an option on a specific Treasury security or a Ginnie Mae passthrough can do so on an over-the-counter basis. There are government and mortgage-backed securities dealers who make a market in options on specific securities. Over-the-counter (or dealer) options typically are purchased by institutional investors who want to hedge the risk associated with a specific security. For example, a thrift may be interested in hedging its position in a specific mortgage passthrough security. Typically, the maturity of the option will coincide with the time period over which the buyer of the option wants to hedge, so the option's liquidity is not an issue.

Besides options on fixed income securities, there are OTC options on the shape of the yield curve or the yield spread between two securities (such as the spread between mortgage passthrough securities and Treasuries or between double-A corporates, and Treasuries). A discussion of these options is beyond the scope of this chapter.

Exchange-Traded Futures Options

An option on a futures contract, commonly referred to as a *futures option*, gives the buyer the right to buy from or sell to the writer a designated futures contract at the strike price at any time during the life of the option. If the futures option is a call option, the buyer has the right to purchase one designated futures contract at the strike price. That is, the buyer has the right to acquire a long futures position in the designated futures contract. If the buyer exercises the call option, the writer acquires a corresponding short position in the futures contract.

A put option on a futures contract grants the buyer the right to sell one designated futures contract to the writer at the strike price. That is, the option buyer has the right to acquire a short position in the designated futures contract. If the buyer exercises the put option, the writer acquires a corresponding long position in the designated futures contract.

There are futures options on all the interest rate futures contracts mentioned earlier.

As the parties to the futures option will realize a position in a futures contract when the option is exercised, the question is: What will the futures price be? That is, at what price will the long be required to pay for the instrument underlying the futures contract, and at what price will the short be required to sell the instrument underlying the futures contract?

Upon exercise, the futures price for the futures contract will be set equal to the strike price. The position of the two parties is then immediately marked to market in terms of the then-current futures price. Thus, the futures positions of the two parties will be at the prevailing futures price. At the same time, the option buyer will receive from the option seller the economic benefit from exercising. In the case of a call futures option, the option writer must pay the option buyer the difference between the current futures price and the strike price. In the case of a put futures option, the option writer must pay the option buyer the difference between the strike price and the current futures price.

For example, suppose an investor buys a call option on some futures contract in which the strike price is 85. Assume also that the futures price is 95 and that the buyer exercises the call option. Upon exercise, the call buyer is given a long position in the futures contract at 85, and the call writer is assigned the corresponding short position in the futures contract at 85. The futures positions of the buyer and the writer are immediately marked to market by the exchange. Because the prevailing futures price is 95 and the strike price is 85, the long futures position (the position of the call buyer) realizes a gain of 10, while the short futures position (the position of the call writer) realizes a loss of 10. The call writer pays the exchange 10, and the call buyer receives from the exchange 10.

The call buyer, who now has a long futures position at 95, can either liquidate the futures position at 95 or maintain a long futures position. If the former course of action is taken, the call buyer sells a futures contract at the prevailing futures price of 95. There is no gain or loss from liquidating the position. Overall, the call buyer realizes a gain of 10. The call buyer who elects to hold the long futures position will face the same risk and reward of holding such a position, but still realizes a gain of 10 from the exercise of the call option.

Suppose instead that the futures option is a put rather than a call, and the current futures price is 60 rather than 95. Then if the buyer of this put option exercises it, the buyer would have a short position in the futures contract at 85; the option writer would have a long position in the futures contract at 85. The exchange then marks the position to market at the then-current futures price of 60, resulting in a gain to the put buyer of 25 and a loss to the put writer of the same amount. The put buyer who now has a short futures position at 60 can either liquidate the short futures position by buying a futures contract at the prevailing futures price of 60 or maintain the short futures position. In either case the put buyer realizes a gain of 25 from exercising the put option.

There are no margin requirements for the buyer of a futures option once the option price has been paid in full. Because the option price is the maximum amount that the buyer can lose, regardless of how adverse the price movement of the underlying instrument, there is no need for margin.

Because the writer (seller) of an option has agreed to accept all of the risk (and none of the reward) of the position in the underlying instrument, the writer (seller) is required to deposit not only the margin required on the interest rate futures contract position if that is the underlying instrument, but also (with certain exceptions) the option price that is received for writing the option. In addition, as prices adversely affect the writer's position, the writer would be required to deposit variation margin as it is marked to market.

Options and Duration

The price of an interest rate option will depend on the price of the underlying instrument, which depends in turn on the interest rate on the underlying instrument. Thus, the price of an interest rate option depends on the interest rate on the underlying instrument. Consequently, the interest-rate sensitivity or duration of an interest rate option can be determined.

The modified duration of an option can be shown to be equal to:

Modified duration for an option =

$$\begin{array}{c}\text{Modified duration} \\ \text{of underlying} \\ \text{instrument}\end{array} \times \text{Delta} \times \frac{\begin{array}{c}\text{Price of underlying} \\ \text{instrument}\end{array}}{\text{Price of option}}$$

As expected, the modified duration of an option depends on the modified duration of the underlying instrument. It also depends on the price responsiveness of the option to a change in the underlying instrument, as measured by the option's delta. The leverage created by a position in an option comes from the last ratio in the formula. The higher the price of the underlying instrument relative to the price of the option, the greater the leverage (i.e., the more exposure to interest rates for a given dollar investment).

It is the interaction of all three factors that affects the modified duration of an option. For example, a deep out-of-the-money option offers higher leverage than a deep-in-the-money option, but the delta of the former is less than that of the latter.

Since the delta of a call option is positive, the modified duration of an interest rate call option will be positive. Thus, when interest rates decline, the value of an interest rate call option will rise. A put option, however, has a delta that is negative. Thus, modified duration is negative. Consequently, when interest rates rise, the value of a put option rises.

Hedging with Options

The most common application of options is to hedge a portfolio. There are two hedging strategies in which options are used to protect against a rise in interest rates: *protective put buying and covered call writing*. The protective put buying strategy establishes a minimum value for the portfolio but allows the manager to benefit from a decline in rates. The establishment of a floor for the portfolio is not without a cost. The performance of the portfolio will be reduced by the cost of the put option.

Unlike the protective put strategy, covered call writing is not entered into with the sole purpose of protecting a portfolio against rising rates. The covered call writer, believing that the market will not trade much higher or much lower than its present level, sells out-of-the-money calls against an existing bond portfolio. The sale of the calls brings in premium income that provides partial protection in case rates increase. The premium received does not, of course, provide the kind of protection that a long put position provides, but it does provide some additional income that can be used to offset declining prices. If, on the other hand, rates fall, portfolio appreciation is limited because the short call position constitutes a liability for the seller, and this liability increases as rates go down. Consequently, there is limited upside potential for the covered call writer. Of course, this is not so bad if prices are essentially going nowhere; the added income from the sale of options is obtained without sacrificing any gains.

Options can also be used to protect against a decline in interest rates. In such situations, managers seek to protect against a fall in reinvestment rates. The purchase of call options can be used in such situations. The sale of put options provides limited protection in much the same way as a covered call writing strategy does in protecting against a rise in interest rates.

SUMMARY

In this chapter, we describe interest rate futures, interest rate swaps, and interest rate options contracts. We look closely at the Treasury bond futures contract because it is commonly used in bond portfolio management. We explain that the reasons why actual futures prices depart from the theoretical futures price of a Treasury bond futures contract have to do with the delivery options granted to the seller.

Managers can use interest rate futures contracts to speculate on the movement of interest rates, to control the interest rate risk of a portfolio, and to enhance returns when futures are mispriced. Swaps can be used for asset/liability management.

Interest rate options include options on fixed income securities and options on interest rate futures contracts. The latter, called futures options, are the preferred vehicle for implementing investment strategies. Because of the difficulties of hedging particular bond issues or passthrough securities, many institutions find over-the-counter options more useful; these contracts can be customized to meet specific investment goals. Protective put buying and covered call writing strategies are used to hedge a portfolio against a rise in interest rates. There are similar strategies to protect against a decline in interest rates.

Chapter 11

Asset Allocation Models

One of the major steps in the investment management process that we described in Chapter 1 is the allocation of funds among major asset categories. The term "asset allocation" means different things to different people in different contexts. Asset allocation can be divided into three general categories: *policy asset allocation, dynamic asset allocation,* and *tactical asset allocation.*[1]

The policy asset mix decision can be characterized as long-term asset allocation, where the investor seeks to assess an appropriate long-term "normal" asset mix that represents an ideal blend of controlled risk and enhanced return. There are a host of different tools useful in assessing the policy asset allocation.

Some of the more intriguing strategies to emerge in recent years are the *dynamic strategies,* where the asset mix is shifted mechanically in response to changing market conditions.[2] In essence, dynamic strategies enable reshaping of the entire return distribution. By dynamically shifting the asset mix, investors can control both downside risk and surplus volatility, and can directly build a "shortfall constraint" into their strategy. Dynamic strategies are mechanistic in the sense that any action in the capital markets triggers a prescribed reaction in the portfolio of assets.

---

1 For a more detailed discussion, see Robert D. Arnott and Frank J. Fabozzi, "The Many Dimensions of the Asset Allocation Decision," Chapter 1 in Arnott and Fabozzi (eds.), *Active Asset Allocation* (Chicago: Probus Publishing, 1992).

2 The most well-publicized variant of these dynamic strategies is *portfolio insurance.*

Once the policy asset allocation has been established, the manager can turn to consideration of active departures from the normal asset mix established by policy. Suppose the long-run asset mix is established as 60% equities and 40% fixed income. Under certain circumstances a departure from this mix may be permitted. If a decision to deviate from this mix is based upon rigorous objective measures of value, it is often called tactical asset allocation (TAA). Tactical asset allocation is not a single, clearly defined strategy but takes many approaches.[3]

In this chapter we describe several asset allocation optimization models that can be used to implement an appropriate long-term allocation mix. The underlying theory is Markowitz portfolio theory, which is cast in terms of individual assets.[4] Asset allocation, of course, is cast in terms of asset classes. The basic Markowitz model has been embellished in several ways to provide investors with information about the risks associated with achieving a specified return and to allow for short-term/long-term asset allocations. At the end of the chapter, we discuss one strategy that falls into the category of dynamic asset allocation.

We begin with the two-asset class problem and introduce the notion of an efficient portfolio and an efficient frontier (or efficient set). The asset allocation model with more than two asset classes is then explained and extended to (1) provide supplementary measures of risk, which we refer to as the *risk-of-loss*, (2) multiple scenarios, and (3) short-term/long-term asset allocations.

The basic inputs for the asset allocation models are the expected returns, expected yields, risk estimates, and correlations (or covariances) for each asset class included in the analysis. The appropriate source for these inputs is the portfolio manager, who is most directly concerned with these factors on a day-to-day basis. Additional insights can be achieved by using historical estimates, either from a lengthy past period or from more recent experience. The objective is to use the proxy that best represents the future horizon of interest.

Typically, portfolio managers use their own return expectations in conjunction with historical risk measures based on the variance and

---

3 For a detailed description of these approaches, see Charles H. DuBois, "Tactical Asset Allocation: A Review of the Current Techniques," Chapter 12 in Arnott and Fabozzi, *Active Asset Allocation*.

4 Harry M. Markowitz, *Portfolio Selection* (New Haven, CT: Yale University Press, 1959) and Harry M. Markowitz, "Portfolio Selection," *Journal of Finance* (March 1952), pp. 77–91.

covariance from a historical series. Other inputs may include constraints such as target minimum or maximum concentration constraints of individual or group-of-asset types and corresponding yield constraints on part or all of the portfolio.

TWO-ASSET CLASS ALLOCATION MODEL

The simplest asset allocation model applies to allocation of funds between only two asset classes, stocks and bonds. Exhibit 11.1 summarizes the expectational inputs (expected return, variance, standard deviation, and correlation of returns). Exhibit 11.2 presents the formulas for calculating the portfolio expected return and variance of a two-asset class portfolio. When two assets are combined to form a portfolio, the expected return for the portfolio is simply the weighted average of the expected return for the two asset classes. The weight for each asset class is equal to the dollar value of the portfolio. The sum of the two weights, of course, must equal one.

Unlike the portfolio's expected return, the portfolio's variance (standard deviation) is not simply a weighted average of the variance (standard deviation) of the two asset classes. Instead, the portfolio variance depends on the correlation (covariance) between the two asset classes.

The portfolio expected return, variance, and standard deviation for different allocations, using the input in Exhibit 11.1 and the formulas in Exhibit 11.2, are shown in tabular form in Exhibit 11.3. Exhibit 11.4 graphs the portfolio expected return and standard deviation presented in Exhibit 11.3.

Exhibit 11.1
Expectational Inputs for Two Asset Classes

Asset class	Expected return	Variance	Standard deviation
Stocks	.13	.0342	.185
Bonds	.08	.0036	.060

Correlation between stocks and bonds = .20

Exhibit 11.2

Formulas for Expected Return and Variance for a Two-Asset Class Portfolio

Portfolio expected return

$$E(R_p) = W_1 E(R_1) + W_2 E(R_2)$$

where $E(R_p)$ = expected return for the portfolio
       $E(R_1)$ = expected return for asset class 1
       $E(R_2)$ = expected return for asset class 2
       W_1 = percentage of the portfolio invested in asset class 1
       W_2 = percentage of the portfolio invested in asset class 2
       $W_1 + W_2$ = 1

Portfolio variance

$$Var(R_p) = W_1^2 \, Var(R_1) + W_2^2 \, Var(R_2) + 2W_1 W_2 \, Covar(R_1, R_2)$$

where $Var(R_1)$ = variance of return for asset class 1
       $Var(R_2)$ = variance of return for asset class 2
       $Covar(R_1, R_2)$ = covariance between the returns for asset classes 1 and 2

In terms of correlation:

$$Var(R_p) = W_1^2 \, Var(R_1) + W_2^2 \, Var(R_2) + 2W_1 W_2 \, Std(R_1) Std(R_2) \, Corr(R_1, R_2)$$

where $Std(R_1)$ = standard deviation of asset class 1
       $Std(R_2)$ = standard deviation of asset class 2
       $Corr(R_1, R_2)$ = correlation between asset classes 1 and 2

Note in Exhibit 11.4 that:

1. Every point on line XYZ describes a portfolio consisting of a specific allocation of funds between stocks and bonds. Not all of the portfolios are shown in Exhibit 11.3. We filled in the gaps when we plotted the results.

2. XYZ represents all possible portfolios consisting of these two asset classes. XYZ is therefore called the *investment opportunity set,* or the *feasible set.*[5]

---

5   The portfolios on line XYZ include portfolios in which there is short selling of either asset class.

Exhibit 11.3

Portfolio Expected Return, Variance, and Standard Deviation for Different
Allocations of Funds between Stocks and Bonds*

Allocation		Expected return	Variance	Standard deviation
W_1	W_2	$E(R_p)$	$Var(R_p)$	$Std(R_p)$
.0	1.0	.080	.0036000	.0600000
.1	.9	.085	.0036570	.0604769
.2	.8	.090	.0043820	.0661978
.3	.7	.095	.0057740	.0759872
.4	.6	.100	.0078330	.0885054
.5	.5	.105	.0105596	.1027600
.6	.4	.110	.0139532	.1181240
.7	.3	.115	.0180141	.1342160
.8	.2	.120	.0227421	.1508050
.9	.1	.125	.0281375	.1677420
1.0	.0	.130	.0342000	.1849321

*   Asset class 1 = stocks.
    Asset class 2 = bonds.

See Exhibit 11.1 for the expectational inputs for these two asset classes.

3. It would never be beneficial for an investor to allocate funds
    between stocks and bonds to produce a portfolio on that portion
    of XYZ between Y and Z (excluding portfolio Z).[6] The reason is
    that for every portfolio on segment YZ there is a portfolio that
    dominates it on the XY segment of the opportunity set. That is,
    for a given portfolio standard deviation (risk level), an investor
    can realize a higher portfolio expected return. This can be seen
    in Exhibit 11.4 by comparison of portfolios A and A'. These
    portfolios have the same portfolio standard deviation, but the
    expected return for portfolio A is more than for that of portfolio

---

6 The portfolio represented by point Y offers the minimum variance that can be
   obtained by holding these two asset classes in any combination.

Exhibit 11.4

Investment Opportunity Set and Efficient Set for Two Asset Classes
(Stocks and Bonds)

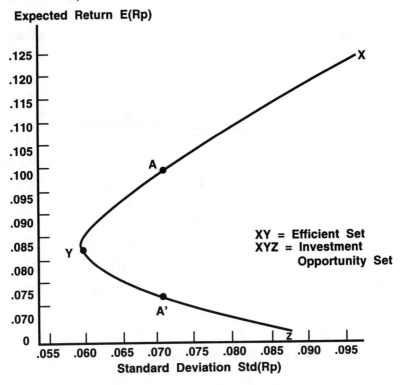

A'. Consequently, all portfolios on XY of the investment opportunity set dominate the portfolios on YZ of the investment
opportunity set. XY, therefore, is called the *efficient set*, or *efficient frontier*. We use these two terms interchangeably. A portfolio on the efficient set is said to be an *efficient portfolio*.

The efficient set indicates the expected trade-off between risk
(standard deviation) and return. Just which portfolio in the efficient set
the investor selects depends on the investor's preference.

To see the impact of the correlation on the efficient set, Exhibit 11.5
shows the expected return, variance, and standard deviation for portfolios consisting of stocks and bonds for various assumed correlations

of returns. The efficient set for each assumed correlation is plotted in Exhibit 11.6. Note that the lower the correlation of returns, the better off the investor is. That is, for a given set of expected returns and standard deviations for the two asset classes, the investor is exposed to less risk (standard deviation) for a given portfolio if the correlation of returns is lower. Notice also that, if the correlation is 1, the efficient set is a straight line, and the portfolio standard deviation is therefore a weighted average of the standard deviations of the two asset classes.

N-ASSET CLASS ALLOCATION MODEL

The principles we have discussed for the efficient set for the two-asset class allocation model are easily extended to the general case of N-asset classes. The formulas for the portfolio expected return and variance are shown in Exhibit 11.7. Exhibit 11.8 graphs all possible portfolios for the N-asset class case.

Exhibit 11.8 is similar to Exhibit 11.4, except that the investment opportunity set in the two-asset class case does not include points (portfolios) in the interior of XYZ. In the N-asset class case, interior points are also feasible portfolios. As in the two-asset class case, the portfolios represented by the segment XY dominate portfolios in the interior of the investment opportunity set.

Although the efficient set for the simple two-asset class case can be easily determined, computation of the efficient set when funds are to be allocated to more than two asset classes is more difficult. Fortunately, the efficient set of the N-asset class problem can be solved using quadratic programming. This algorithm can also accommodate other constraints that might be imposed, such as limitations on the concentration of funds in a given asset class.

Assume an investor wants to allocate available investment funds among three asset classes: stocks, bonds, and Treasury bills. Exhibit 11.9 presents the annual expected return, expected yield, standard deviation, and correlations for the three asset classes for two scenarios. The expected yield component of the expected return is the amount of the return attributable to dividends in the case of stocks, and interest payments in the case of bonds. The difference between the expected return and the expected yield is therefore the return attributable to capital appreciation.

Exhibit 11.5

Portfolio Expected Returns and Standard Deviation for Different Correlations between the Two Asset Classes (Stocks and Bonds)*

Weight for each asset class		Expected return	Portfolio standard deviation if the correlation is:				
W_1	W_2	$E(R_p)$	-.2	.0	.2	.5	1.0
.0	1.0	.080	.0600000	.0600000	.0600000	.0600000	.0600000
.1	.9	.085	.0534654	.0570789	.0604769	.0667560	.0724932
.2	.8	.090	.0544230	.0605970	.0661978	.0761736	.0849865
.3	.7	.095	.0625295	.0695845	.0759872	.0873967	.0974797
.4	.6	.100	.0755168	.0822679	.0885054	.0998180	.1099730
.5	.5	.105	.0913258	.0972111	.1027600	.1130430	.1224660
.6	.4	.110	.1087330	.1135250	.1181240	.1268210	.1349590
.7	.3	.115	.1270820	.1306980	.1342160	.1409900	.1474530
.8	.2	.120	.1460200	.1484320	.1508050	.1554430	.1599460
.9	.1	.125	.1653440	.1665470	.1677420	.1701070	.1724390
1.0	.0	.130	.1849320	.1849320	.1849320	.1849320	.1849320

* Asset class 1 = stocks.
  Asset class 2 = bonds.

Exhibit 11.6

Comparison of Efficient Set for Different Correlations between Two Asset Classes
(Stocks and Bonds)

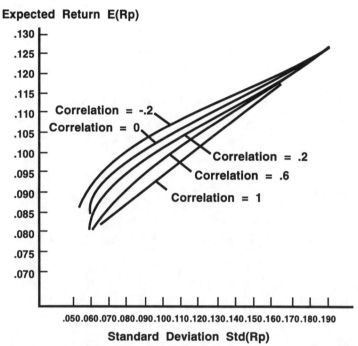

Using quadratic programming, the efficient set can be determined. The results for scenario 1, assuming a one-year horizon and no constraints, are shown in Exhibit 11.10; the results for scenario 2 are shown in Exhibit 11.11. For each identified level of portfolio expected return, the corresponding standard deviation, annual expected yield, and minimum risk concentrations (weights) of each class are shown.

Let's interpret results for scenario 1. The minimum risk (standard deviation) that the investor is exposed to in seeking a 9% return for the 12-month period is 6.552%. There is no other allocation producing a 9% return with a standard deviation less than 6.552%. The asset mix associated with this efficient or optimal portfolio is 24.8% in stocks, 64.2% in bonds, and 10.9% in Treasury bills. (The total does not equal one because of rounding.) The annual expected return of 9% amounts

---

Exhibit 11.7

Formulas for Expected Return and Variance for an N-Asset Class Portfolio

Portfolio expected return

$$E(R_p) = \sum_{i=1}^{N} E(R_i)W_i$$

where $E(R_i)$ = expected return for asset class i
        W_i = percent of the portfolio invested in asset class i

$$\sum_{i=1}^{N} W_i = 1$$

Portfolio variance

$$Var(R_p) = \sum_{i=1}^{N} W_i^2 \, Var(R_i) + \sum_{\substack{i=1 \\ \text{for } i \neq j}}^{N} \sum_{j=1}^{N} W_i W_j \, Covar(R_i, R_j)$$

In terms of correlation:

$$Var(R_p) = \sum_{i=1}^{N} W_i^2 \, Var(R_i) + \sum_{\substack{i=1 \\ \text{for } i \neq j}}^{N} \sum_{j=1}^{N} W_i W_j Std(R_j) \, Std(R_j) \, Corr(R_i, R_j)$$

---

to an expected yield of 7.04%. Therefore, 1.96% of the total annual expected return is attributable to capital appreciation.

EXTENSION OF THE ASSET ALLOCATION MODEL TO RISK-OF-LOSS

In the portfolio risk minimization process, the variance (standard deviation) of returns is the proxy measure for portfolio risk. A supplementary measure is the probability of not achieving a portfolio ex-

Exhibit 11.8

Feasible Set and Efficient Set in an N-Asset Class Portfolio Case

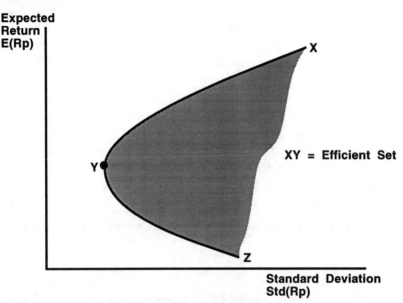

pected return. This type of analysis would be useful in determining the most appropriate mix from the set of optimal portfolio allocations.

We refer to this analysis as the *risk-of-loss.* A technical description of the analysis is presented in Appendix E. The columns under the heading "Probability of annual return of less than," in Exhibits 11.10 and 11.11 show the results of the risk-of-loss analysis for four annual levels. For the 9% expected return for scenario 1 in Exhibit 11.10, there is a 9.3% probability that the annual return will be negative, a 28.3% probability that the annual return will be less than 5%, a 38.8% probability that the annual return will be less than 7%, and a 55.6% probability that the annual return will be less than 10%.

EXTENSION OF THE ASSET ALLOCATION MODEL TO MULTIPLE SCENARIOS

In Exhibit 11.9, the expected return and expected yield are shown for two scenarios. Each scenario assumes asset performance in the long run over some investment horizon. If a probability can be assigned to each scenario, an efficient set can be constructed for the composite scenario. Appendix F explains how to compute the optimal asset allocation when there are multiple discrete or mutually exclusive scenarios, and each can be assigned a probability of occurrence.

Assuming a probability of 50% for each of the two scenarios in Exhibit 11.9, Exhibit 11.12 displays the optimal asset allocation for the composite scenario for a 12-month investment horizon. Exhibit 11.13 provides the minimum-risk portfolio for specified return levels for the composite scenario results for a 60-month horizon. Both exhibits also show the risk-of-loss analysis results.

Let's take a closer look at these results to see how useful they can be in the asset allocation decision. Exhibit 11.14 graphs the optimal mixes for the 12-month horizon for the composite scenario. The height of each of the three lines represents the amount to be allocated to an

---

Exhibit 11.9

Expectational Inputs for Three Asset Classes for Two Scenarios

Asset class	Expected return	Expected yield	Variance	Standard deviation
Scenario 1:				
Stocks	.13	.05	.034200	.185
Bonds	.08	.08	.003600	.060
Treasury bills	.06	.06	.000016	.004
Scenario 2:				
Stocks	.15	.05	.034200	.185
Bonds	.08	.08	.003600	.060
Treasury bills	.05	.05	.000016	.004

	Correlations for both scenarios		
	Stocks	Bonds	Treasury bills
Stocks	1.00	.20	–.15
Bonds	.20	1.00	–.12
Treasury bills	–.15	–.12	1.00

Exhibit 11.10

Optimal Asset Allocation for Scenario 1: Sample Portfolios in the Efficient Set (12-Month Horizon)

Annual expected return	Annual standard deviation	Annual expected yield	Probability of annual return of less than				Minimum risk asset mix		
			.0%	5.0%	7.0%	10.0%	Stocks	Bonds	T-bills
6.00%	.400%	6.00%	.9%	.9%	99.1%	100.0%	.0%	.0%	100.0%
6.04	.389	6.02	.0	.5	99.0	100.0	.3	1.0	98.7
6.50	1.097	6.18	.0	9.7	66.7	99.8	4.1	10.9	84.9
7.00	2.174	6.35	.1	19.2	50.0	90.0	8.3	21.7	70.0
7.50	3.271	6.52	1.3	23.5	44.3	76.0	12.5	32.4	55.1
8.00	4.368	6.70	3.8	25.8	41.5	66.4	16.6	43.1	40.3
8.50	5.462	6.84	6.6	27.3	39.9	60.0	20.7	53.7	25.6
9.00	6.552	7.04	9.3	28.3	38.8	55.6	24.8	64.2	10.9
9.50	7.649	7.09	11.6	29.0	38.1	52.4	30.4	69.6	.0
10.00	8.918	6.79	14.1	30.0	37.7	50.0	40.5	59.5	.0
10.50	10.356	6.48	16.5	31.0	37.7	48.2	50.5	49.5	.0
11.00	11.895	6.19	18.8	31.9	37.8	46.9	60.5	39.5	.0
11.50	13.497	5.89	20.8	32.7	37.9	46.0	70.4	29.6	.0
12.00	15.142	5.59	22.5	33.3	38.0	45.2	80.3	19.7	.0
12.50	16.813	5.29	24.0	33.9	38.2	44.6	90.2	9.8	.0
13.00	18.500	5.00	25.2	34.4	38.3	44.2	100.0	.0	.0

Exhibit 11.11

Optimal Asset Allocation for Scenario 2: Sample Portfolios in the Efficient Set (12-Month Horizon)

Annual expected return	Annual standard deviation	Annual expected yield	Probability of annual return of less than				Minimum risk asset mix		
			.0%	5.0%	7.0%	10.0%	Stocks	Bonds	T-bills
5.00%	.400%	5.00%	.0%	50.1%	100.0%	100.0%	.0%	.0%	100.0%
5.06	.389	5.03	.0	44.3	100.0	100.0	.3	1.0	98.7
5.50	.784	5.24	.0	27.2	96.5	100.0	2.8	7.9	89.3
6.00	1.501	5.47	.0	26.3	73.5	99.3	5.5	15.7	78.7
6.50	2.248	5.70	.2	26.3	58.3	92.6	8.3	23.5	68.2
7.00	3.003	5.94	1.2	26.4	50.0	82.3	11.0	31.2	57.7
7.50	3.757	6.17	2.6	26.4	45.0	73.1	13.8	38.9	47.3
8.00	4.509	6.40	4.3	26.5	41.8	65.9	16.5	46.6	36.9
8.50	5.258	6.63	5.9	26.5	39.5	60.4	19.2	54.2	26.6
9.00	6.005	6.85	7.4	26.5	37.8	56.1	21.9	61.8	16.3
9.50	6.750	7.08	8.8	26.6	36.5	52.7	24.6	69.4	6.0
10.00	7.505	7.13	10.0	26.6	35.5	50.0	29.1	70.9	.0
10.50	8.374	6.91	11.5	26.9	34.9	47.8	36.4	63.6	.0
11.00	9.345	6.69	13.0	27.4	34.6	46.1	43.6	56.4	.0
11.50	10.386	6.48	14.5	28.0	34.4	44.8	50.7	49.3	.0
12.00	11.478	6.26	15.9	28.5	34.4	43.7	57.8	42.2	.0

Exhibit continues

Exhibit 11.11 (Concluded)

Optimal Asset Allocation for Scenario 2: Sample Portfolios in the Efficient Set (12-Month Horizon)

Annual expected return	Annual standard deviation	Annual expected yield	Probability of annual return of less than				Minimum risk asset mix		
			.0%	5.0%	7.0%	10.0%	Stocks	Bonds	T-bills
12.50%	12.605%	6.05%	17.3%	29.0%	34.4%	42.9%	64.9%	35.1%	.0%
13.00	13.756	5.84	18.5	29.5	34.4	42.2	72.0	28.0	.0
13.50	14.927	5.63	19.6	29.9	34.5	41.6	79.1	29.9	.0
14.00	16.109	5.42	20.5	30.3	34.5	41.1	86.1	13.9	.0
14.50	17.302	5.21	21.4	30.6	34.6	40.7	93.0	7.0	.0
15.00	18.500	5.00	22.2	30.9	34.7	40.4	100.0	.0	.0

Exhibit 11.12

Optimal Asset Allocation for Composite Scenarios: Sample Portfolios in the Efficient Set (12-Month Horizon)

Annual expected return	Annual standard deviation	Annual expected yield	Probability of annual return of less than				Minimum risk asset mix		
			.0%	5.0%	7.0%	10.0%	Stocks	Bonds	T-bills
5.50%	.422%	5.50%	.0%	24.8%	99.5%	100.0%	.0%	.0%	100.0%
5.55	.412	5.53	.0	21.8	99.4	100.0	.3	1.1	98.6
6.00	.918	5.71	.0	16.7	82.4	100.0	3.3	9.2	87.5
6.50	1.777	5.92	.0	21.3	59.9	96.3	6.6	18.3	75.1
7.00	2.666	6.13	.6	23.8	49.7	84.8	10.0	27.3	62.8
7.50	3.560	6.34	2.1	25.2	44.5	73.9	13.3	36.2	50.5
8.00	4.452	6.55	4.1	26.2	41.5	65.8	16.6	45.2	38.3
8.50	5.342	6.75	6.3	26.8	39.5	59.9	19.8	54.0	26.1
9.00	6.228	6.96	8.3	27.3	38.1	55.6	23.1	62.9	14.0
9.50	7.113	7.16	10.0	27.6	37.1	52.4	26.3	71.7	2.0
10.00	8.063	6.98	11.8	28.1	36.4	49.8	33.9	66.1	.0
10.50	9.168	6.73	13.7	28.7	36.1	47.8	42.3	57.7	.0
11.00	10.377	6.48	15.6	29.5	36.0	46.4	50.7	49.3	.0
11.50	11.655	6.23	17.4	30.2	36.0	45.2	59.0	41.0	.0
12.00	12.981	5.98	19.0	30.6	36.1	44.3	67.3	32.7	.0
12.50	14.338	5.73	20.5	31.4	36.2	43.6	75.5	24.5	.0
13.00	15.715	5.49	21.7	31.9	36.3	43.1	83.7	16.3	.0
13.50	17.110	5.24	22.9	32.3	36.4	42.6	91.9	8.1	.0

Exhibit 11.13

Optimal Asset Allocation for Composite Scenarios: Sample Portfolios in the Efficient Set (60-Month Horizon)

Annual expected return	Annual standard deviation	Annual expected yield	Probability of annual return of less than				Minimum risk asset mix		
			.0%	5.0%	7.0%	10.0%	Stocks	Bonds	T-bills
5.50%	.422%	5.50%	.0%	23.7%	100.0%	100.0%	.0%	.0%	100.0%
5.55	.412	5.53	.0	17.3	100.0	100.0	.3	1.1	98.6
6.00	.918	5.71	.0	4.0	95.3	100.0	3.3	9.2	87.5
6.50	1.777	5.92	.0	4.5	70.2	100.0	6.6	18.3	75.1
7.00	2.666	6.13	.0	5.8	49.4	98.8	10.0	27.3	62.8
7.50	3.560	6.34	.0	6.8	38.0	92.3	13.3	36.2	50.5
8.00	4.452	6.55	.0	7.7	31.6	81.8	16.6	45.2	38.3
8.50	5.342	6.75	.0	8.3	27.6	71.3	19.8	54.0	26.1
9.00	6.228	6.96	.1	8.8	25.0	62.4	23.1	62.9	14.0
9.50	7.113	7.16	.2	9.2	23.1	55.3	26.3	71.7	2.0
10.00	8.063	6.98	.4	9.7	21.9	49.6	33.9	66.1	.0
10.50	9.168	6.73	.7	10.6	21.4	45.2	42.3	57.7	.0
11.00	10.377	6.48	1.2	11.5	21.3	41.9	50.7	49.3	.0
11.50	11.655	6.23	1.8	12.4	21.3	39.4	59.0	41.0	.0
12.00	12.981	5.98	2.6	13.2	21.4	37.5	67.3	32.7	.0
12.50	14.338	5.73	3.3	14.0	21.6	36.0	75.5	24.5	.0
13.00	15.715	5.49	4.1	14.7	21.7	34.8	83.7	16.3	.0
13.50	17.110	5.24	4.9	15.4	21.9	33.9	91.9	8.1	.0

asset for an expected return level shown on the horizontal axis. The optimal concentrations for an expected return of 8% are about 17% stocks, 45% bonds, and 38% Treasury bills, corresponding to the results shown in Exhibit 11.12 of 16.6% stocks, 45.2% bonds, and 38.3% Treasury bills. (Again the optimal mix may not equal one because of rounding.)

The yield component of the optimal mixes is shown for each scenario and the composite scenario in Exhibit 11.15. Remember that the yield is the amount of return attributable to dividends and interest payments for the range of optimal portfolios. For the 8% expected return level, Exhibit 11.15 indicates that the yield component is 6.55%, which leaves 1.45% as the return attributable to capital appreciation.

Exhibit 11.16 depicts the risk-of-loss or probability of not achieving the specified return benchmarks of 0%, 5%, 7%, and 10% over a one-year horizon for the composite case. From the expected return range

Exhibit 11.14

Risk-of-Loss Analysis: Minimum Risk Allocations

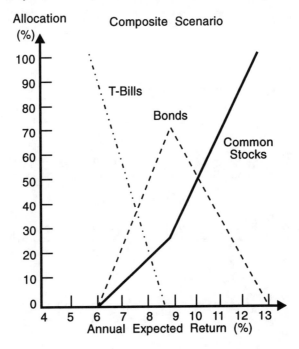

on the horizontal axis, the probability of not achieving a given bench-mark can be determined by measuring vertically on the return bench-mark curves. For example, if the 8% expected return optimal portfolio were assumed, there would be a 4% probability of not achieving a positive return over the next year (probabilities on the vertical axis). In the tabular results in Exhibit 11.12 we find the more precise value of 4.1%. Exhibit 11.17 is a graphic of the risk-of-loss for the composite scenario for the five-year horizon results tabulated in Exhibit 11.13.

A comparison of Exhibits 11.16 and 11.17 is particularly interesting. We can see the influence of the passage of time by comparing the 12-month horizon of Exhibit 11.16 and the 60-month horizon for Exhibit 11.17. The most striking difference is the significant downward shift of all risk-of-loss curves for the longer time horizon. This is consistent with the fact that return increases at a greater rate than risk over time.

Figure 11.15

Risk-of-Loss Analysis: Cash Yield of Minimum-Risk Portfolio

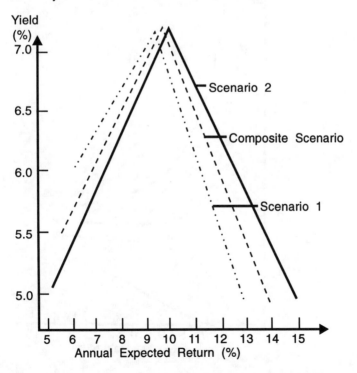

The longer the time horizon, the more the incentive to seek higher expected return/higher expected risk portfolios.

The effect of the high risk associated with high-return portfolios is most significant for short time horizons. If risk exposure over short horizons is important, it is apparent that lower-return portfolios are appropriate. In other words, if the investor is concerned with near-term portfolio fluctuation, a portfolio consisting entirely of common stock (highest expected return and risk class in our example) is clearly not fitting. As the relevant horizon increases, however, a higher proportion of stocks is possible—and even desirable—to achieve higher return.

Exhibit 11.16

Risk-of-Loss Analysis: Probability of Loss for Minimum-Risk Portfolio—
Composite Scenario One-Year Projection

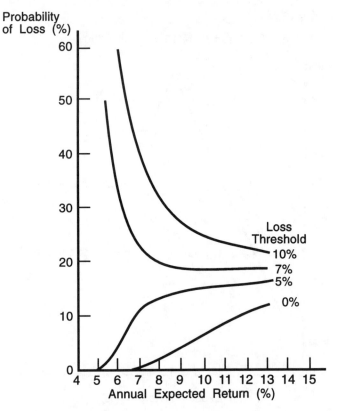

In reality, there is probably a trade-off between short-term risk tolerance and long-term return desirability. How much short-term risk is tolerable may therefore determine the proportion of higher-return assets and hence the expected return attainable. Formats such as Exhibits 11.16 and 11.17 and their supporting exhibits, Exhibits 11.12 and 11.13, can assist the investor in choosing the most desirable return/risk trade-off.

As an alternative to visual inspection of the return/risk trade-off, it is possible to calculate the best trade-off mathematically in terms of the most return per unit of risk. This procedure involves evaluation of a chosen risk-of-loss curve for the point along the curve where the second derivative of the curve is zero (i.e., where its slope is steepest).

Exhibit 11.17

Risk-of-Loss Analysis: Probability of Loss for Minimum-Risk Portfolio

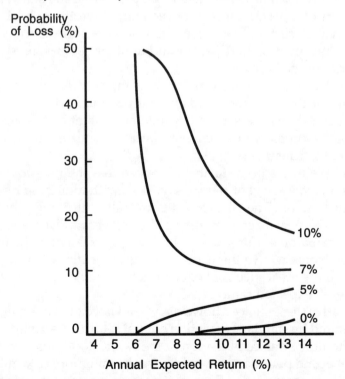

This provides the greatest decrease in risk-of-loss for an increment of expected return.

EXTENSION OF MODEL TO SHORT-TERM/LONG-TERM ASSET ALLOCATION

In the multiple scenario case, we have assumed that the investor has certain expectations about performance of the asset classes in terms of expected returns, expected yields, standard deviations, and correlations of return for each scenario. These values are used to assess asset class performance under various scenarios over some long-run investment horizon.

It is often the case, however, that the investor expects a very different set of values to be applicable in the short run, say, the next 12 months. For example, long-term expected annual return on stocks may be estimated at 12%, but over the next year the expected return on stocks is only 5%. The investment objectives are all still stated in terms of the portfolio performance over the entire investment horizon. The return characteristics of each asset class, however, are described by one set of values over a short period and another set of values over the remainder of the horizon.

In such a case, the investment strategy may involve investing in one portfolio for the short term and another portfolio over the remaining horizon. It is then necessary to take into consideration the subsequent asset allocation as well as current, because both relate to the total horizon investment objectives.

To explain this point further, suppose that the investor wants to achieve a certain level of return, say, 10%, with minimum risk over a five-year horizon. The 10% expected overall return might be accomplished by being very conservative in the first year and more aggressive over the remaining four years, or by being aggressive in the first year and more conservative thereafter. For the asset allocations in the two periods, there are a spectrum of choices that would produce the same 10% overall expected return.

Not all of these choices, however, would have the same overall risk, as measured by standard deviation of total returns. As a matter of fact, there should be one combination of the asset allocations over the first and the second periods that would have the minimum risk and overall expected return of 10%. Such a strategy represents a point on the overall efficient set. By varying the required total expected return, one can generate the whole efficient set for the investment horizon.

A procedure to identify the overall efficient frontier and characterize the investment strategies that produce it has been developed by Gifford Fong Associates. Notice that in this context we refer to optimal "strategies," rather than optimal asset allocations, because a strategy is made up of two asset allocations over the two separate periods of the horizon.

Extension of basic asset allocation has considerable flexibility. It allows an investor to specify different values, both for the short period and the remainder of the horizon, for any of the basic data required in the asset allocation model. The investor can also specify different portfolio constraints in the two periods. In fact, it is even possible to consider different asset classes in periods that make up the horizon.

The techniques to generate the efficient strategies characterized in terms of risk and return, as well as the probabilities of meeting threshold returns (risk-of-loss analysis), for a horizon and two subperiods are fairly complex. Because the model simultaneously optimizes over two periods, quadratic programming alone is no longer sufficient. Although detailed description of the computational procedure is beyond the scope of this chapter, briefly, the approach is as follows.

For a given level of the total expected return, the overall standard deviation is expressed as a function of the first-period expected return. This is possible because a value of the first-period expected return determines the second-period expected return necessary to generate the given overall return expectation required. Two separate quadratic algorithms give the two one-period minimum standard deviations corresponding to the one-period returns. These standard deviations are then combined by an appropriate formula to provide the overall standard deviation. Once the total standard deviation is expressed as a function of the first-period return expectation, this function is minimized to obtain a point on the overall efficient set.[7]

The process is repeated for different values of the total expected return in the feasible range to generate the whole efficient set, producing the optimal asset allocation strategies in the process. No assumptions beyond serial independence of returns are necessary for calculation of the mean/variance efficient strategies. Lognormality of the

---

7   The method used for the minimization of this function is the three-point Newton
    iteration method.

return distributions is assumed for calculation of the probabilities of exceeding threshold returns.

To illustrate this extension of the asset allocation model, certain assumptions are made:

1. There are six asset classes over which funds are to be allocated. They are: (1) government/agencies, (2) intermediate-term industrials, (3) long-term corporates, (4) S&P 500 stocks, (5) AMEX stocks, and (6) Treasury bills.

2. The investment horizon is 60 months.

3. The investor has expectations for a 12-month horizon that differs from the 60-month horizon.

4. Basic expectational values for the 60-month (long-term) and 12-month (short-term) horizons are as shown in Exhibits 11.18 and 11.19.

5. Minimum and maximum concentration constraints imposed for each subperiod are as shown in Exhibits 11.18 and 11.19.

6. The minimum yield for both subperiods is set at 6%.

Exhibit 11.20 displays the optimal strategies for the 12-month horizon. Exhibit 11.21 shows the optimal strategies for the residual term horizon of 48 months. Exhibit 11.22 presents the optimal composite statistics for the 60-month horizon based on the optimal strategies shown in Exhibits 11.20 and 11.21.

ASSET ALLOCATION MODELS WITH LIABILITIES CONSIDERED

Other asset allocation optimization models have been developed at Salomon Brothers Inc. for application to asset/liability problems of various financial institutions.[8] One of the problems that these models overcome is the incorporation of liabilities. That is, an optimization model must consider return distributions of not only asset classes but also liabilities.

---

8 Martin L. Leibowitz, Stanley Kogelman, and Lawrence N. Bader, "Asset Performance and Surplus Control—A Dual-Shortfall Approach," Chapter 9 in Arnott and Fabozzi, *Active Asset Allocation*.

Exhibit 11.18

Long-Term/Short-Term Asset Allocation: Long-Term Specifications (60-Month Period)

Name	Annual expected return	Annual expected yield	Annual standard deviation	Correlation with					
				G/A	ITI	LTC	S&P500	AMEX	T-bills
G/A	8.00%	8.00%	4.00%	1.000					
ITI	9.00	9.00	6.00	.974	1.000				
LTC	10.00	10.00	12.00	.965	.965	1.000			
S&P500	15.00	5.00	16.00	.353	.401	.387	1.000		
AMEX	20.00	5.00	25.00	.281	.356	.327	.845	1.000	
T-bills	6.00	6.00	1.00	.611	.560	.508	–.032	–.097	1.000

Constraints:

	G/A	ITI	LTC	S&P500	AMEX	T-bills
Minimum concentration (percent)	20.00	.0	.0	.0	.0	.0
Maximum concentration (percent)	100.00	100.00	100.00	80.00	80.00	60.00
Minimum yield (percent)	6.00					

Key

G/A	=	government/agencies
ITI	=	intermediate-term industrials
LTC	=	long-term corporates
S&P500	=	Standard & Poor's 500
AMEX	=	American Stock Exchange Index
T-bills	=	U.S. Treasury bills

Exhibit 11.19

Long-Term/Short-Term Asset Allocation: Short-Term Specifications (12-Month Period)

Name	Annual expected return	Annual expected yield	Annual standard deviation	Correlation with					
				G/A	ITI	LTC	S&P500	AMEX	T-bills
G/A	15.00%	8.00%	4.00%	1.000					
ITI	13.00	9.00	4.00	.965	1.000				
LTC	25.00	10.00	6.00	.972	.970	1.000			
S&P500	10.50	5.00	10.00	−.200	−.200	−.300	1.000		
AMEX	5.00	5.00	12.00	−.100	−.200	−.200	.848	1.000	
T-bills	7.00	7.00	.0	.0	.0	.0	.0	.0	1.000

Constraints:

Minimum concentration (percent)				20.00	.0	.0	.0	.0	.0
Maximum concentration (percent)				100.00	100.00	100.00	80.00	80.00	100.00
Minimum yield (percent)				6.00					

Key G/A   = government/agencies
     ITI   = intermediate-term industrials
     LTC   = long-term corporates
     S&P500 = Standard & Poor's 500
     AMEX   = American Stock Exchange Index
     T-bills   = U.S. Treasury bills

Exhibit 11.20

Long-Term/Short-Term Asset Allocation: Optimal Initial Strategy (12-Month Period)

Strategy	Annual expected return	Annual standard deviation	Annual expected yield	Probability of annual return less than					Minimum risk asset mix					
				.0%	8.0%	10.0%	12.0%	20.0%	G/A	ITI	LTC	S&P500	AMEX	T-bills
1	8.66%	.784%	7.17%	.0%	20.0%	95.7%	100.0%	100.0%	20.0%	.0%	.0%	1.6%	.0%	78.4%
2	10.10	1.214	7.34	.0	4.0	46.9	94.1	100.0	20.0	.0	7.5	4.2	.0	68.2
3	12.49	1.938	7.66	.0	.9	9.9	40.4	100.0	20.0	.0	20.2	7.3	.0	52.5
4	14.92	2.680	7.98	.0	.4	3.1	13.7	96.9	20.0	.0	33.1	10.4	.0	36.5
5	17.41	3.440	8.32	.0	.2	1.3	5.5	77.6	20.0	.0	46.3	13.6	.0	20.1
6	19.96	4.216	8.66	.0	.1	.7	2.6	51.1	20.0	.0	59.8	16.9	.0	3.3
7	21.69	4.861	9.15	.0	.1	.6	2.0	37.0	20.0	.0	71.0	8.0	.0	.0
8	23.00	5.581	9.60	.0	.2	.7	2.1	30.1	20.0	.0	80.0	.0	.0	.0
9	23.00	5.581	9.60	.0	.2	.7	2.1	30.1	20.0	.0	80.0	.0	.0	.0
10	23.00	5.581	9.60	.0	.2	.7	2.1	30.1	20.0	.0	80.0	.0	.0	.0
11	23.00	5.581	9.60	.0	.2	.7	2.1	30.1	20.0	.0	80.0	.0	.0	.0
12	23.00	5.581	9.60	.0	.2	.7	2.1	30.1	20.0	.0	80.0	.0	.0	.0
13	23.00	5.581	9.60	.0	.2	.7	2.1	30.1	20.0	.0	80.0	.0	.0	.0
14	23.00	5.581	9.60	.0	.2	.7	2.1	30.1	20.0	.0	80.0	.0	.0	.0
15	23.00	5.581	9.60	.0	.2	.7	2.1	30.1	20.0	.0	80.0	.0	.0	.0
16	23.00	5.581	9.60	.0	.2	.7	2.1	30.1	20.0	.0	80.0	.0	.0	.0
17	23.00	5.581	9.60	.0	.2	.7	2.1	30.1	20.0	.0	80.0	.0	.0	.0
18	23.00	5.581	9.60	.0	.2	.7	2.1	30.1	20.0	.0	80.0	.0	.0	.0
19	23.00	5.581	9.60	.0	.2	.7	2.1	30.1	20.0	.0	80.0	.0	.0	.0
20	23.00	5.581	9.60	.0	.2	.7	2.1	30.1	20.0	.0	80.0	.0	.0	.0
21	23.00	5.581	9.60	.0	.2	.7	2.1	30.1	20.0	.0	80.0	.0	.0	.0
22	23.00	5.581	9.60	.0	.2	.7	2.1	30.1	20.0	.0	80.0	.0	.0	.0
23	23.00	5.581	9.60	.0	.2	.7	2.1	30.1	20.0	.0	80.0	.0	.0	.0
24	23.00	5.581	9.60	.0	.2	.7	2.1	30.1	20.0	.0	80.0	.0	.0	.0

Exhibit 11.21

Long-Term/Short-Term Asset Allocation: Optimal Residual Strategy (48-Month Period)

Strategy	Annual expected return	Annual standard deviation	Annual expected yield	Probability of annual return less than					Minimum risk asset mix					
				.0%	8.0%	10.0%	12.0%	20.0%	G/A	ITI	LTC	S&P500	AMEX	T-bills
1	6.80%	2.023%	6.80%	.0%	88.5%	99.8%	100.0%	100.0%	40.0%	.0%	.0%	.0%	.0%	60.0%
2	6.86	2.031	6.78	.0	87.2	99.8	100.0	100.0	39.2	.0	.0	.6	.1	60.0
3	6.91	2.042	6.76	.0	86.1	99.8	100.0	100.0	38.8	.0	.0	.6	.4	60.0
4	6.95	2.056	6.75	.0	85.0	99.8	100.0	100.0	38.3	.0	.0	1.0	.7	60.0
5	6.99	2.072	6.74	.0	83.8	99.8	100.0	100.0	37.9	.0	.0	1.2	.9	60.0
6	7.03	2.091	6.73	.0	82.7	99.8	100.0	100.0	37.5	.0	.0	1.4	1.1	60.0
7	7.26	2.246	6.66	.0	75.2	99.3	100.0	100.0	35.2	.0	.0	2.4	2.4	60.0
8	7.58	2.589	6.56	.0	63.6	97.0	100.0	100.0	31.9	.0	.0	3.8	4.3	60.0
9	8.19	3.415	6.72	.0	46.9	86.1	98.7	100.0	41.7	.0	.0	5.3	6.2	46.7
10	8.80	4.266	6.99	.0	36.8	72.6	93.6	100.0	56.8	.0	.0	6.5	7.7	29.0
11	9.41	5.125	7.27	.0	30.6	60.9	85.3	100.0	71.9	.0	.0	7.7	9.1	11.3
12	10.02	5.997	7.38	.0	26.6	51.9	76.1	99.9	79.2	.0	.0	9.5	11.3	.0
13	10.63	6.951	7.24	.1	24.1	45.3	67.5	99.6	69.6	3.7	.0	12.1	14.5	.0
14	11.24	7.946	7.36	.2	22.4	40.4	60.3	98.6	41.2	28.2	.0	14.4	16.3	.0
15	11.85	8.956	7.39	.3	21.3	36.8	54.5	96.7	20.0	44.7	.0	16.5	18.8	.0
16	12.47	10.018	7.14	.5	20.5	34.1	49.8	93.9	20.0	38.5	.0	18.0	23.5	.0
17	13.08	11.134	6.89	.8	20.1	32.1	46.1	90.4	20.0	32.2	.0	19.6	28.3	.0
18	13.70	12.290	6.63	1.1	19.9	30.7	43.2	86.6	20.0	25.9	.0	21.1	33.0	.0
19	14.31	13.474	6.38	1.5	19.8	29.5	40.9	82.7	20.0	19.6	.0	22.7	37.7	.0
20	14.93	14.682	6.13	2.0	19.8	28.7	39.0	79.0	20.0	13.2	.0	24.3	42.5	.0
21	15.55	15.917	6.00	2.4	19.8	28.1	37.5	75.5	20.0	10.0	.0	19.1	50.9	.0
22	16.16	17.217	6.00	3.0	20.0	27.7	36.4	72.2	20.0	.0	8.0	12.7	59.3	.0
23	16.78	18.573	6.00	3.6	20.3	27.5	35.5	69.2	20.0	.0	8.0	.4	71.6	.0
24	16.80	18.613	6.00	3.6	20.3	27.5	35.5	69.1	20.0	.0	8.0	.0	72.0	.0

Exhibit 11.22

Long-Term/Short-Term Asset Allocation: Composite Statistics (60-Month Horizon)

Strategy	Annual expected return	Annual standard deviation	Annual expected yield	Probability of annual return less than					
				.0%	8.0%	10.0%	12.0%	20.0%
1	7.17%	1.848%	6.87%	.0%	84.7%	100.0%	100.0%	100.0%
2	7.50	1.903	6.89	.0	72.8	99.8	100.0	100.0
3	8.00	2.024	6.94	.0	50.8	98.6	100.0	100.0
4	8.50	2.182	7.00	.0	31.2	93.9	100.0	100.0
5	9.00	2.368	7.05	.0	17.7	83.3	99.8	100.0
6	9.50	2.573	7.11	.0	9.9	67.7	98.5	100.0
7	10.00	2.847	7.16	.0	6.0	51.2	94.4	100.0
8	10.50	3.268	7.17	.0	4.5	37.8	85.4	100.0
9	11.00	3.859	7.30	.0	4.2	29.3	73.1	100.0
10	11.50	4.518	7.52	.0	4.3	24.1	61.5	100.0
11	12.00	5.214	7.74	.0	4.5	20.8	52.1	99.7
12	12.50	5.941	7.82	.0	4.7	18.6	44.8	99.0
13	13.00	6.751	7.71	.0	5.2	17.3	39.5	97.4
14	13.50	7.607	7.81	.0	5.7	16.6	35.6	94.8
15	14.00	8.484	7.83	.0	6.1	16.1	32.7	91.5
16	14.50	9.412	7.63	.0	6.7	15.8	30.5	87.6
17	15.00	10.390	7.43	.0	7.3	15.8	29.0	83.6
18	15.50	11.405	7.23	.1	7.9	15.9	27.8	79.6
19	16.00	12.448	7.03	.1	8.5	16.1	27.0	75.9
20	16.50	13.511	6.82	.2	9.1	16.3	26.3	72.4
21	17.00	14.599	6.72	.4	9.7	16.6	25.9	69.2
22	17.50	15.744	6.72	.5	10.3	16.9	25.6	66.4
23	18.00	16.937	6.72	.8	11.0	17.4	25.5	66.3
24	18.01	16.973	6.72	.8	11.0	17.4	25.5	

A pension fund is a prime example. The plan sponsor is concerned with performance of the assets and maintenance of acceptable levels of downside risk as measured by the standard deviation. But this is not the only concern. The other concern is the performance of the fund's surplus (i.e., the difference between the market value of the assets and the present value of the liabilities) and the maintenance of acceptable levels of downside risk for the surplus. By considering the surplus as specified by FASB 87—hence the liabilities—a better asset allocation can be achieved than in models that simply consider assets.

A "shortfall" approach strikes a balance between asset performance and the maintenance of acceptable levels of its downside risk, and surplus performance and the maintenance of acceptable levels of its downside risk. This model has also been applied to the asset allocation problem faced by property and casualty insurance companies required to maintain a statutory surplus.[9]

An important insight is that those involved in the asset allocation decision should not lump together all fixed income securities into one asset class. Rather, within an asset/liability framework, there is a continuum of fixed income instruments, each with a different duration. Since liabilities are often interest-rate sensitive and therefore have a duration, the variety of durations of bonds is hidden by lumping them into one asset class. Asset allocation models that consider liabilities and a continuum of fixed income instruments along the yield curve will be superior to those considering only assets and that lump all fixed income securities together as one asset class.

USING FUTURES TO IMPLEMENT AN ASSET ALLOCATION DECISION

The product of an asset allocation decision is the asset mix. A mix necessitates the shifting of funds among the asset classes. Funds can be shifted in one of two ways. The most obvious is by buying or selling the amount specified in the asset mix in the cash market. The costs associated with shifting funds in this manner are transactions costs such as commissions, bid-ask spreads, and market impact. Shifting will also disrupt the activities of the money managers who are managing funds for each asset class.

9 Alfred Weinberger, "Allocation for Property/Casualty Insurance Companies: A Going Concern Approach," Salomon Brothers Inc., New York, July 1991.

For example, a pension sponsor typically engages one set of money managers for managing equity funds and a different set for managing bond funds. An asset allocation decision requiring the reallocation of funds will necessitate the withdrawal of funds from some managers and the placement of funds with others. If the shift is temporary as a result of a tactical asset allocation decision, there will be a subsequent revision of the asset allocation, further disrupting the activities of money managers.

An alternative approach is to use the futures market to change an exposure to an asset class. As we explain in Chapter 10, buying futures contracts increases exposure to the asset class underlying the futures contract, while selling futures contracts reduces it.

The advantages of using financial futures contracts are: (1) transactions costs are lower; (2) execution is faster in the futures market; (3) market impact costs are avoided or reduced as the sponsor has more time to buy and sell securities in the cash market; and (4) activities of the managers employed by the pension sponsor are not disrupted. A strategy of using futures for asset allocation to avoid disrupting the activities of managers is sometimes referred to as an *overlay strategy*. Futures contracts involving stock indexes and interest rates of non-U.S. markets have been particularly useful for U.S. portfolio managers investing in these markets.

The major disadvantage of using futures contracts is that the futures contract may be mispriced; more specifically, the futures contract of the asset class that is being purchased may be too expensive relative to its fair value, and/or the futures contract of the asset class that is being sold may be too cheap relative to its fair value.

FORECAST-FREE ASSET ALLOCATION

The asset allocation models we have discussed are based on traditional mean-variance analysis. They require that the investor formulate a set of inputs, including specifications of expected returns for each asset, standard deviations of return, the correlation between each pair of assets, and perhaps a set of investment policy constraints. These inputs are then analyzed by a quadratic optimization program to find the set of efficient portfolios that offer minimum risk for given levels of expected return.

Less doctrinaire approaches may be less structured; many asset allocation strategies, for example, rely on historical patterns or relationships that are perceived to generate expected returns. Both formal and informal approaches, however, rely on a set of return or interest rate expectations. Those who have superior skills in accurately and reliably predicting returns will realize superior investment results. But investors may not believe they have superior forecasting ability, or they may sometimes lack conviction in a particular expectation. There will thus be times when it is undesirable to rely on strategies driven by return expectations.

Moreover, and perhaps more important, an investor may prefer a strategy that is not symmetric with respect to its upside potential and its downside risk. A mean-variance efficient portfolio provides a return equal to the weighted average of its individual assets' returns. If one of the assets performs very well, this exceptional performance will be less than fully reflected in the performance of the total portfolio, because a limited percentage of funds is allocated to that asset. If one of the assets does extremely poorly, its negative performance will affect the total portfolio to the extent that the portfolio is invested in that asset. The portfolio's exposure to the upside and the downside is symmetrical.

Suppose one could devise an asset allocation strategy that promised performance equal to the return on the best-performing of several assets, less a fixed and known return percentage. The portfolio would have almost full exposure to exceptionally good performance of any one asset, but would not be affected at all if one of the assets performed exceptionally poorly. Its exposure to the upside and the downside of any one asset's performance would not be symmetrical: Upside potential would be unabridged, while downside risk would be limited.

A dynamic asset allocation strategy that does this is called *multiple asset performance* (MAP for short).[10] The MAP strategy does not require knowledge of expected returns. The total portfolio achieves the return of the best-performing asset, less some predetermined percentage cost, whatever the assets' realized returns. The portfolio's exposure to the upside performance of any one asset exceeds its exposure to the downside.

---

10 For an application of MAP to the allocation of funds to various international equity markets, see H. Gifford Fong and Oldrich A. Vasicek, "Forecast-Free International Asset Allocation," *Financial Analysts Journal* (March-April 1989), pp. 29–33.

The MAP strategy does not rely on any historical relationships among realized returns. Because it is based on option pricing theory, it is consistent with the efficient market hypothesis.

The Strategy

The objective of MAP strategy is to achieve a return on the total investment equal to the return of the best-performing asset, less the predetermined strategy cost. Suppose investment funds are allocated across three asset classes (using a representative portfolio for each market). If asset class 1 happens to perform the best, the return on the strategy will equal the return on asset class 1 less the known cost. If asset class 2 performs best, the return will equal the return on asset class 2, less the cost.

The objective of the strategy can be expressed as:

$$(1) \qquad R_p = \max (R_1, R_2, \ldots, R_n) - c$$

where R_p = the total portfolio return over a chosen investment horizon

R_i = the individual asset class returns (all assumed to be continuously compounded)

n = the number of assets in the allocation problem

c = the strategy cost expressed as a return difference, or lag

Note that if one of the assets—say, n—has a fixed return over the investment horizon, the strategy also guarantees a minimum return of, in this case:

$$R_{min} = R_n - c$$

It is possible to think of the MAP strategy as the purchase of a new type of call option, one that covers several assets and has no exercise price. At the expiration date of the option, the option holder will claim one of the assets covered by the option (obviously, the most valuable one).

Such an option would trade for an amount—say, V—that will equal the present value of the option's expected benefit. The benefit will depend on the payout from the option at expiration—that is, the value of the asset chosen at expiration by the option holder.

If we denote the values of the assets at the expiration date by A_k^* (k = 1, 2, . . ., n), then the payout at expiration is:

$$\max_{1 \leq k \leq n} A_k^*$$

The expected value of this payout is discounted to its present value at the risk-free rate, R_F, to determine the value, V, of the option:

(2) $$V = e^{-R_F T} \, (E) \max_{1 \leq k \leq n} A_k^*$$

where T is the time to the option's expiration. The expectation (E) must be evaluated, in accordance with modern option pricing theory, under the assumption that the value of each asset grows at the risk-free rate from its current value, A_k^*:

(3) $$(E) A_k^* = e^{-R_F T} A_k; k = 1, 2, \ldots, n$$

Equation (2) can be used to produce a valuation formula for the multiple-asset option. The formula will depend only on the current value of the assets, and on the covariance matrix of the n-dimensional stochastic process that characterizes the assets over the investment period. For diffusion processes, the valuation formula involves a sum of (n–1)-dimensional cumulative normal distribution functions with covariance matrixes that are transformations of the n-dimensional instantaneous covariance matrix of the assets, integrated over the horizon. The famous Black-Scholes formula is a special case of the valuation equation for two assets, one risky and one riskless.[11] Margrabe has provided a formula for two risky assets,[12] and Stulz has derived an equation for one riskless and two risky assets.[13]

---

11 Fischer Black and Myron Scholes, "The Pricing of Options and Corporate Liabilities," *Journal of Political Economy* (May-June 1973), pp. 637–659.

12 William Margrabe, "The Value of an Option to Exchange One Asset for Another," *Journal of Finance* (March 1978), pp. 177–186.

13 René Stulz, "Options on the Minimum or the Maximum of Two Risky Assets," *Journal of Financial Economics* (May 1982), pp. 161–185.

COST

At the beginning of the investment period, the assets are defined to have a unit value so that:

$$A_k = 1; k = 1, 2, \ldots, n$$

The initial value of the option, V, evaluated from equation (2), can be used to calculate the strategy cost. The relationship is given by:

(4) $$V = e^{cT}$$

The cost of the strategy will increase with the number of assets involved. Besides the number of assets, the cost will depend on the riskiness of the assets (the riskier the assets, the higher the cost), the correlation between the assets (the more correlated, the lower the cost), and the length of the investment horizon (the cost per year decreases with increasing horizon length).

Exhibit 11.23 shows MAP strategy costs, as annual percentage return differences, by the number of assets involved and by the length of the investment horizon. The standard deviations for all assets are assumed to be 18% annually, and the correlation between any two assets is assumed to be .3.

These costs represent the price for getting the best out of a number of asset returns. Suppose the values of the parameters chosen are descriptive of the asset classes in Exhibit 11.23. It is possible to implement a strategy whose realized return will equal the highest of four separate asset classes over a five-year period, less 6.4% annually. No

Exhibit 11.23

MAP Strategy Costs (annual percentage)

Investment horizon	Number of assets				
	2	3	4	5	6
1 Year	8.1	12.3	15.0	16.9	18.5
2 Years	5.6	8.5	10.4	11.8	12.9
5 Years	3.4	5.2	6.4	7.2	7.9

prediction is needed as to which of these markets will have the highest return or what the expected return of each is.

The more diverse the realized returns of the underlying asset classes, the more the benefits from the MAP strategy. The greater the diversity, the more likely return (equal to the highest individual return less costs) is to outperform a more traditional fixed asset allocation. The MAP strategy lets the investor capture the return variability of the underlying assets.

Strategy Implementation

A multiple-asset option such as that described above is not available in the market. The MAP strategy accomplishes its objective by creating such an option synthetically.

The strategy is executed by an active allocation of the investment funds among n assets in such a fashion that the value of the investment is at all times equal to the calculated value of the option, V. Because at the terminal date the value of the option is equal to that of the most valuable asset, this strategy will yield the return on the best-performing asset less the cost of purchasing the option.

To ensure that the investment value stays equal to the calculated value of the option, we must ensure that any change in the value of the investment (resulting from changes in the asset values) is always the same as a corresponding change in the option value, V. For a given percentage change in the value of an asset, A_k, the percentage response in the value of the option equals the partial derivative $\partial V / \partial A_k$ multiplied by the ratio A_k / V. The proportion of total funds invested in an individual asset is thus maintained equal to:

$$(5) \qquad P_k = \frac{A_k}{V} \times \frac{\partial V}{\partial A_k} \qquad k = 1, 2, \ldots, n$$

The required allocations change continuously as a function of the asset performance to date and the remaining time to expiration.

SUMMARY

There are several dimensions to the asset allocation decision. Policy asset allocation can be characterized as a long-term decision, in that the investor seeks to assess an appropriate long-term "normal" asset mix that represents an ideal blend of controlled risk and enhanced return. Dynamic asset allocation strategies involve shifting the asset mix mechanically in response to changing market conditions so as to reshape the return distribution. Portfolio insurance is the best-known strategy of this sort. Tactical asset allocation refers to active strategies that seek to enhance performance by shifting the asset mix of a portfolio to take advantage of the changing patterns of reward available in the capital markets.

Asset allocation optimization models are based on the Markowitz portfolio framework, replacing individual assets with asset classes. The basic Markowitz model has been embellished to provide investors with information about the risks associated with achieving a specified expected return. Other models allow for multiple scenarios and for short-term/long-term asset allocations. The basic inputs for all of these models are the expected returns, expected cash yields, risk estimates, and correlations (or covariances) for each asset class included in the analysis. Optimization models should consider not only asset distributions, but also the distribution of liabilities.

An asset allocation decision can be implemented in either the cash market or the futures market. The advantages of using futures rather than the cash market are reduced transactions costs, speed of execution, and avoidance of disruption of manager activity. The disadvantage is that the futures contract may be mispriced so that it will reduce the return on the portfolio compared to transacting in the cash market.

The multiple asset performance (MAP) strategy is a form of dynamic asset allocation that uses option pricing theory to allocate portfolio assets across major asset classes; it does not require forecasts of expected returns. The return on the MAP portfolio will be the return on the best-performing asset, less a predetermined percentage cost.

Chapter 12

Bond Performance and Attribution Analysis

In this chapter we will see how to measure and evaluate the investment performance of a fixed income portfolio manager. *Performance measurement* involves calculation of the return realized by a portfolio manager over some time interval that we call the *evaluation period*. *Performance evaluation* has two aims. The first is determination of whether the manager added value by outperforming the established benchmark. The second is determination of how the manager achieved the calculated return—that is, by which active strategy. Decomposition of performance results to explain why the results were achieved is called *performance analysis* or *return attribution analysis*.

There are three desired requirements of a bond performance and attribution analysis process. The first is that the process be accurate. While there are several ways of measuring portfolio return, the process should recognize the time when each cash flow actually occurs, in order to measure actual portfolio performance accurately. The second requirement is that the process be informative. It should be capable of assessing the skills that go into fixed income portfolio management. In order to be informative, the process must effectively address the key managerial skills, and explain how these are expressed in terms of realized performance. The final requirement is that the process be simple. Whatever its format, the output of the process should be understood by the manager and client, and by any others who may be concerned with performance. These requirements should be kept in mind as we explain the process for analyzing bond performance in this chapter.

FUNDAMENTAL ISSUES IN THE ANALYSIS OF RETURNS

There are six fundamental issues in bond portfolio performance and analysis.

1. *Total portfolio return measurement.* Return is generally measured in terms of a period rate of return on the average value of the funds invested during that time period. For a portfolio, the value of the funds invested changes over a period with (1) cash inflows representing a return on investment (dividends and interest) and new contributions to the fund, and (2) cash outflows for payments to beneficiaries (in the case of a pension fund) or a net redemption of shares (in the case of a mutual fund). The impact of cash flows that are beyond a manager's control must be taken into consideration.

2. *Internal environment versus management contribution.* To investigate the performance of a manager, it is necessary first to identify the macro sources of return. This requires decomposing the total portfolio return into (1) the portion attributable to the external environment, and therefore not under the control of management, and (2) the portion that was under the control of management, and that therefore represents the manager's contribution.

3. *Specific management skill.* After identifying the portion of the total portfolio return that represents management contribution, it is necessary to define the micro components of return. These include maturity (or duration) management, spread/quality management, and individual security selection. Suppose a manager expects interest rates are going to drop, and purchases long telephones. The choice of long bonds is a maturity or duration decision. The choice of telephones is a sector decision;

selection of particular issues within the telephone sector is an individual security decision. The process used to analyze performance should identify return attributable to these three individual management skills.

4. *Individual security returns.* It is also necessary to identify how each individual security has performed over the security evaluation period. The security evaluation period is the period for which a particular security is held. It will differ from the portfolio evaluation period for securities that are purchased or sold during the portfolio evaluation period. We can look at both total security returns and security returns decomposed into the various components that we have identified for the portfolio as a whole.

5. *Effect of transactions.* To evaluate transactions, the marginal impact of each purchase, sale, and swap should be examined. Did a purchase or sale add to or detract from the overall portfolio performance?

6. *Cash account and portfolio value.* The process should allow for a monitoring of the cash account balance as the result of earnings and transactions and the monitoring of the portfolio market value as the result of capital gains/losses, interest accrual, and contributions/withdrawals.

PERFORMANCE MEASUREMENT

The starting point for evaluating the performance of a manager is measurement of return. As we will see, there are several important issues to be addressed in developing a methodology for calculating a portfolio's return. Because different methodologies can lead to quite disparate results, it is admittedly difficult to compare the performances of managers. It is easy to misunderstand the meaning of the data that managers provide their current and prospective clients. This has led to abuses when some managers report performance results that are better than actual performance. To mitigate this problem, the Committee for Performance Standards of the Association of Investment Management and Research has established criteria for calculating performance results and presenting them.

Alternative Return Measures

To begin with the basic concept, the dollar return realized on a portfolio for any evaluation period (such as a year, month, or week) is equal to the sum of (1) the difference between the market value of the portfolio at the end of the evaluation period and the market value at the beginning, and (2) any distributions made from the portfolio. It is important to include any capital or income distributions from the portfolio to a client or beneficiary.

The rate of return, or simply return, expresses the dollar return in terms of the amount of the market value at the beginning of the evaluation period. Thus, the return can be viewed as the amount (expressed as a fraction of the initial portfolio value) that can be withdrawn at the end of the evaluation period while keeping the initial market value of the portfolio intact.

In equation form, the portfolio's return can be expressed as follows:

(1)
$$R_P = \frac{MV_1 - MV_0 + D}{MV_0}$$

where R_p = the return on the portfolio
     MV_1 = the portfolio market value at the end of the evaluation period
     MV_0 = the portfolio market value at the beginning of the evaluation period
     D = the cash distributions from the portfolio to the client during the evaluation period

To illustrate this calculation, assume a pension plan has a portfolio market value of $25 million at the beginning and $28 million at the end of the evaluation period. During the evaluation period, $1 million is distributed to the plan sponsor from investment income. Thus:

MV_1 = $28,000,000
MV_0 = $25,000,000
D = $1,000,000

then,

$$R_P = \frac{\$28{,}000{,}000 - \$25{,}000{,}000 + \$1{,}000{,}000}{\$25{,}000{,}000} = .16 = 16\%$$

There are three assumptions in measuring return according to equation (1). First, cash is assumed to flow into the portfolio from interest income during the evaluation period and to be reinvested in the portfolio. For example, if during the evaluation period $2 million is received from interest income, this amount is reflected in the market value of the portfolio at the end of the period.

The second assumption is that any distributions from the portfolio occur at the end of the evaluation period, or are held in the form of cash until the end of the evaluation period. In the example, when did the $1 million distributed to the plan sponsor actually occur? To understand why the timing of the distribution is important, consider two extreme cases: (1) the distribution is made at the end of the evaluation period, as assumed by equation (1), and (2) the distribution is made at the beginning of the evaluation period. In the first case, the manager has the use of the $1 million to invest for the entire evaluation period. In the second case, the manager loses the opportunity to invest the funds until the end of the evaluation period. Consequently, the timing of the distribution will affect the return, but this is not considered in equation (1).

The third assumption is that there is no cash paid into the portfolio by the client. Suppose that some time during the evaluation period, the plan sponsor gives an additional $1.5 million to the manager to invest; the $28 million market value of the portfolio at the end of the evaluation period would thus include a contribution of $1.5 million. Equation (1) does not indicate that the ending market value of the portfolio may be affected by cash paid in. The timing of this cash inflow, like the timing of distributions, will affect the calculated return.

Thus, while equation (1) is useful to determine return for an evaluation period of any length of time, from a practical point of view these assumptions limit its application. The longer the evaluation period, the more likely the assumptions will not be met. Over five years, for example, it is highly likely there will be more than one distribution and more than one contribution. Return calculations made over a long period of time are not very reliable because of the assumption that all cash payments and inflows occur at the end of the period.

These narrow assumptions mean it is difficult to compare the returns of two managers over some evaluation period. They also make the formula not useful for evaluating performance over different periods. For example, equation (1) cannot provide reliable performance information to compare a one-month evaluation period and a three-year evaluation period. To make such a comparison, the return must be expressed per unit of time, for example, per year.

The way to handle these practical issues is to calculate return for a short unit of time such as a month or a quarter. We call return so calculated the *subperiod return*. To get the return for the evaluation period, the subperiod returns are then averaged. If the evaluation period is one year and 12 monthly returns are calculated, the monthly (subperiod) returns are averaged to get the one-year return. If a three-year return is sought, and 12 quarterly returns can be calculated, quarterly returns are the subperiod returns, and they are averaged to get the three-year return. The three-year return can then be converted into an annual return by a straightforward procedure described later.

Three methodologies are used in practice to calculate the average of the subperiod returns: (1) the arithmetic average rate of return, (2) the time-weighted rate of return (also called the geometric rate of return), and (3) the dollar-weighted return.

Arithmetic Average Rate of Return: The *arithmetic average rate of return* is an unweighted average of the subperiod returns. The general formula is:

$$R_A = \frac{R_{P1} + R_{P2} + \cdots + R_{PN}}{N}$$

where R_A = the arithmetic average rate of return
R_{Pk} = the portfolio return for subperiod k as measured by equation (1), k = 1, . . ., N
N = the number of subperiods in the evaluation period

For example, if the portfolio returns [as measured by equation (1)] are −10%, 20%, and 5% in months July, August, and September, respectively, the arithmetic average monthly return is 5%, as shown below:

$$N = 3, R_{P1} = -.10, R_{P2} = .20, \text{ and } R_{P3} = .05$$

$$R_A = \frac{-.10 + .20 + .05}{3} = .05 = 5\%$$

There is a major problem with using the arithmetic average rate of return. To see the problem, suppose the initial market value of a portfolio is $28 million. At the end of one month, the market value is $58 million, and at the end of the next month $28 million, with no distributions to or cash inflows from the client for either month. Then using equation (1) the subperiod return for the first month (R_{P1}) is 100% and the subperiod return for the second month (R_{P2}) is –50%. The arithmetic average rate of return is then 25%—not a bad return! But remember that the portfolio's initial market value was $28 million, and its market value at the end of two months is again $28 million. The return over this two-month evaluation period is therefore zero. Yet, the arithmetic average rate of return says it is a whopping 25%.

Clearly it is improper to take the arithmetic average rate of return to be a measure of the average return over an evaluation period. A proper interpretation is that it is the average value of the withdrawals (expressed as a fraction of the initial portfolio market value) that can be made at the end of each subperiod while keeping the initial portfolio market value intact. In the first example, where the average monthly return is 5%, the investor must add 10% of the initial portfolio market value at the end of the first month, can withdraw 20% of the initial portfolio market value at the end of the second month, and can withdraw 5% of the initial portfolio market value at the end of the third month. In the second example, the average monthly return of 25% means that 100% of the initial portfolio market value ($28 million) can be withdrawn at the end of the first month and 50% must be added at the end of the second month.

Time-Weighted Rate of Return: The *time-weighted rate of return* measures the compounded rate of growth of the initial portfolio market value during the evaluation period, assuming that all cash distributions are reinvested in the portfolio. This is also referred to as the *geometric rate of return* because it is computed by taking the geometric average of the portfolio subperiod returns computed from equation (1). The general formula is:

$$R_T = [(1 + R_{P1}) (1 + R_{P2}) \cdots (1 + R_{PN})]^{1/N} - 1$$

where R_T is the time-weighted rate of return and R_{Pk} and N are as defined earlier.

Assume again the portfolio returns are –10%, 20%, and 5% in July, August, and September. The time-weighted rate of return is:

$$R_T = [(1 + (-.10))\,(1 + .20)\,(1 + .05)]^{1/3} - 1$$
$$= [\,(.90)\,(1.20)\,(1.05)]^{1/3} - 1 = .043$$

At a time-weighted rate of return of 4.3% per month, one dollar invested in the portfolio at the beginning of July would have grown at a rate of 4.3% per month during the three-month evaluation period.

The time-weighted rate of return in the second example is 0%, as expected, as shown below:

$$R_T = [(1 + 1.00)\,(1 + (-.50))]^{1/2} - 1 = [(2.00)\,(.50)]^{1/2} - 1 = 0\%$$

In general, the arithmetic and time-weighted average return methods will give different values for the portfolio return over some evaluation period. This is because computation of the arithmetic average rate of return assumes that the amount invested is maintained (through additions or withdrawals) at its initial portfolio market value. The time-weighted return, on the other hand, is the return on a portfolio that varies in size because of the assumption that all proceeds are reinvested.

In general, the arithmetic average rate of return will exceed the time-weighted average rate of return. The exception is in the special situation where all the subperiod returns are the same, in which case the averages are identical. The magnitude of the difference between the two averages is smaller, the less the variation in the subperiod returns over the evaluation period.

For example, suppose that the evaluation period is four months, and that the four monthly returns are as follows:

$$R_{P1} = .04,\ R_{P2} = .06,\ R_{P3} = .02,\ \text{and}\ R_{P4} = -.02$$

The average arithmetic rate of return is 2.5%, and the time-weighted average rate of return is 2.46%—not much of a difference. In the example where we calculate an average rate of return of 25% but a time-weighted average rate of return of 0%, the large discrepancy is due to the substantial variation in the two monthly returns.

Dollar-Weighted Rate of Return: The *dollar-weighted rate of return* is computed by finding the interest rate that makes the present value of the cash flows from all the subperiods in the evaluation period plus the terminal market value of the portfolio equal to the initial market value of the portfolio. The cash flow for each subperiod reflects the difference between the cash inflows attributable to investment income (coupon interest) and client contributions to the portfolio and the cash outflows reflecting distributions to the client. Notice that it is not necessary to know the market value of the portfolio for each subperiod to determine the dollar-weighted rate of return.

The dollar-weighted rate of return is simply an *internal rate of return* calculation, which is another name for it. The general formula for the dollar-weighted return is:

$$V_0 = \frac{C_1}{(1 + R_D)} + \frac{C_2}{(1 + R_D)^2} + \cdots + \frac{C_N + V_N}{(1 + R_D)^n}$$

where V_0 = the initial market value of the portfolio
$\quad\quad C_k$ = the cash flow for the portfolio (cash inflows minus cash outflows) for subperiod k, $\quad$ k = 1, 2, ..., N
$\quad\quad R_D$ = the dollar-weighted rate of return
$\quad\quad V_N$ = the terminal market value of the portfolio

Consider a portfolio with a market value of $100,000 at the beginning of July; capital withdrawals of $5,000 at the end of months July, August, and September; no cash inflows from the client in any month; and a market value at the end of September of $110,000. Then V_0 = $100,000, N = 3, $C_1 = C_2 = C_3$ = $5,000, and V_3 = $110,000, and R_D is the interest rate that satisfies the equation:

$$\$100,000 = \frac{\$5,000}{(1 + R_D)} + \frac{\$5,000}{(1 + R_D)^2} + \frac{\$5,000 + \$110,000}{(1 + R_D)^3}$$

It works out that the interest rate that satisfies this expression is 8.1%. This, then, is the dollar-weighted return.

The dollar-weighted rate of return and the time-weighted rate of return will produce the same result if no withdrawals or contributions occur over the evaluation period, and if all investment income is reinvested. The problem with the dollar-weighted rate of return is that it is affected by factors that are beyond the control of the manager. Specifically, any contributions made by the client or withdrawals that the client requires will influence the calculated return. This makes it difficult to compare the performance of two managers.

To see this, suppose that a pension plan sponsor engages two managers, A and B, and gives $10 million to A to manage and $200 million to B. Suppose that (1) both managers invest in identical portfolios (that is, the two portfolios have the same securities and are held in the same proportion), (2) for the first two months the rate of return on the two portfolios is 20% for month 1 and 50% for month 2, and (3) the amount received in investment income is in cash. Also assume that the plan sponsor does not make an additional contribution to the portfolio of either manager. Under these assumptions, it is clear that the performance of both managers would be identical.

Suppose, however, that the plan sponsor withdraws $4 million from A at the beginning of month 2. This means that A could not invest the entire amount at the end of month 1 and capture the 50% increase in the portfolio value. A's net cash flow for month 1 would be –$2 million; $2 million is realized in investment income and $4 million is withdrawn by the plan sponsor. The dollar-weighted rate of return is then calculated as follows:

$$\$10 = \frac{-\$2}{(1+R_D)} + \frac{\$12}{(1+R_D)^2} \longrightarrow R_D = 0\%$$

For B, the cash inflow for month 1 is $40 million ($200 million times 20%), and the portfolio value at the end of month 2 is $360 million ($240 million times 1.5). The dollar-weighted rate of return is:

$$\$200 = \frac{\$40}{(1+R_D)} + \frac{\$330}{(1+R_D)^2} \longrightarrow R_D = 38.8\%$$

These are quite different results for two managers we agreed have identical performance. For manager A, however, the withdrawal by the plan sponsor and the size of the withdrawal relative to the portfolio value have a significant effect on the calculated return. Withdrawal of $4 million from B at the beginning of month 2 would not have had as significant an impact. The same problem occurs if we assume that the return in month 2 is –50%, and that instead of withdrawing $4 million from A, the plan sponsor contributes $4 million.

Despite this limitation, the dollar-weighted rate of return does provide information. It indicates information about the growth of the fund, which a client will find useful. This is not growth that is attributable to the performance of the manager, however, because of contributions and withdrawals.

Annualizing Returns

Typically, return measures are reported as an average annual return, although the evaluation period may be shorter or longer than one year. This requires the annualization of the subperiod returns. Subperiod returns are typically calculated for a period of less than one year for the reasons described earlier. The subperiod returns are then annualized using the formula:

$$\text{Annual return} = (1 + \text{Average period return})^{\text{Number of periods in year}} - 1$$

Suppose the evaluation period is three years, and a monthly period return is calculated. Suppose further that the average monthly return is 2%. Then the annual return would be:

$$\text{Annual return} = (1.02)^{12} - 1 = 26.8\%$$

Suppose now that the period used to calculate returns is quarterly, and the average quarterly return is 3%. Then the annual return is:

$$\text{Annual return} = (1.03)^{4} - 1 = 12.6\%$$

AIMR Performance Presentation Standards

If there are subtle issues in calculating the return over the evaluation period, there are also industry concerns as to how managers should present results to clients and how managers should use performance data when they seek funds to manage. According to Claude N. Rosenberg, Jr., Chairman of the Committee for Performance Presentation Standards (CPPS) of the Association for Investment Management and Research (AIMR):

> There is little consistency within the investment management industry in the presentation of performance data and records. There certainly has been a great deal of confusion about what should be reported to clients and prospects. The investment management industry has pretty much operated on an honor system, and although there is a great deal of honor in our

industry, there are too many approaches that make this whole subject a real hornet's nest. Because there has been confusion, there has been misuse, and some of the misuse must, bluntly, be recognized as deception, and in some cases—we hope not too many—misuse has been motivated by outright dishonesty.[1]

While the Securities and Exchange Commission has established standards for reporting performance results, they are not very specific. Standards adopted by the AIMR that went into effect in 1993 "are a set of guiding ethical principles intended to promote full disclosure and fair representation by investment managers in reporting their investment results."[2] A secondary objective is to ensure uniformity in the presentation of results so as to facilitate performance comparisons. It is important to emphasize that the AIMR standards deal with the presentation of the data and what must be disclosed, not with how the manager should be evaluated.

In developing these standards, the CPPS recognizes that in practice there is no single ideal set of performance presentation standards that is applicable to all users. They are intended to provide guidelines and recommendations for reporting. Our discussion highlights (1) the requirements and mandatory disclosures for compliance and (2) practices recommended.

Requirements and Mandatory Disclosures: To be considered in compliance with the standards, managers must:

- Calculate performance on a total return basis.

- Use accrual accounting rather than cash accounting in calculating return.

- Calculate return using the time-weighted rate of return methodology, with valuation on at least a quarterly basis and geometric linking of period returns. (We discuss this further below.)

- Include all actual fee-paying, discretionary portfolios in one composite or aggregate measure. This prevents a manager from

---

1 Claude N. Rosenberg, Jr., panel discussion, as reported in *Performance Measurement: Setting Standards, Interpreting the Numbers* (Charlottesville, VA: The Institute for Chartered Financial Analysts, 1989), p. 15.

2 *Performance Presentation Standards: 1993* (Charlottesville, VA: Association for Investment Management and Research, 1993).

showing only the performance of selected accounts (those that have performed well) to a potential client. The number of portfolios and amount of assets in the composite, and the percentage of the firm's total assets the composite represents, must be disclosed. The firm must also disclose the existence of any minimum size below which portfolios are excluded from a composite and the inclusion of any nonfee-paying portfolios in the composite.

- Not link the results of simulated and model portfolios with actual portfolio performance. That is, only actual portfolio performance can be reported, not the performance that would have been realized if a certain strategy had been employed.

- Deduct all trading costs in calculating the return.

- Disclose whether the performance results are calculated gross or net of management fees. If net results are reported, the average weighted management fee must be disclosed.

- Disclose the tax rate assumption if the results are reported after taxes.

- Present at least a 10-year performance record. If the firm has been in existence for less than 10 years, the performance since inception must be reported.

- Present annual returns for all years.

- Provide a complete list and description of all the firm's composites.

Other required practices and disclosures deal with the reporting of results of accounts that have been terminated, the treatment of new portfolios added to a composite, and the handling of international and real estate portfolios.

Recommended Guidelines and Disclosures: The AIMR encourages a manager to:

- Revalue a portfolio whenever cash flows in or out of the portfolio and market action combine to distort performance. We focus on this practice below when we discuss the return calculation under the standards.

- Disclose performance gross of management fees in one-on-one presentations to clients.[3] The results also should be presented before taxes.

- Treat convertible and other hybrid securities consistently across and within composites.

- Disclose external risk measures such as standard deviation of composite returns across time.

- Disclose benchmarks that parallel the risk or investment style the client is expected to track. We discuss benchmarks later in this chapter.

- Disclose results for leveraged portfolios on an unleveraged basis where possible.

There are specific recommended guidelines and disclosures for international portfolios.

Calculating Returns under the Standards: In our illustrations of the various ways to measure portfolio return, we used the same length of time for the subperiod (e.g., a month or a quarter). The subperiod returns are then averaged, with the preferred method being geometric averaging. The AIMR standards require that the return measure minimize the effect of contributions and withdrawals so that cash flow beyond the control of the manager is minimized. Calculating the subperiod return daily is one way to minimize the impact of contributions and withdrawals. The time-weighted return measure can then be calculated from the daily returns.

From a practical point of view, the problem is that calculating a daily return requires that the market value of the portfolio be determined at the end of each day. While this is no problem for a mutual fund that must calculate the net asset value of the portfolio each business day, it is time-consuming for other managers. Moreover, there are asset classes for which the determination of daily prices would be difficult (e.g., certain fixed-income securities, securities in emerging markets, and real estate).

---

3 This is also acceptable to the SEC for one-on-one presentations to clients. If information is distributed to more than one client, the SEC requires that the returns be reported after deducting management fees.

An alternative to the time-weighted rate of return is the dollar-weighted rate of return, which as we noted earlier is less desirable for comparing the performance of managers because of the effect of withdrawals and contributions beyond the control of the manager. The advantage of this method from an operational perspective, however, is that market values do not have to be calculated daily. The effect of withdrawals and contributions is minimized, moreover, if they are small compared to the length of the subperiod. Whenever the cash flow is over 10% at any time, the AIMR standards require that the portfolio be revalued on that date.[4]

Once the subperiod returns in an evaluation period are calculated, they are compounded. The AIMR standards specify that for evaluation periods of less than one year returns should *not* be annualized. Thus, if the evaluation period is seven months, and the subperiod returns calculated are monthly, the seven-month return should be reported by calculating the compounded seven-month return instead.

RETURN ATTRIBUTION ANALYSIS

So how do we evaluate the performance of a manager to determine if the manager added value beyond what could have been achieved by some passive strategy? How do we know whether that performance is due to skill or luck?

Benchmark Portfolios

To evaluate the performance of a manager, a client must specify a benchmark against which the manager will be measured. Two types of benchmarks have been used in evaluating fixed income portfolio managers: (1) market indexes published by dealer firms and vendors, and (2) normal portfolios. We discuss the various types of market indexes in Chapter 8. The other types of benchmarks are discussed here.

A *normal portfolio* is a customized benchmark that includes "a set of securities that contains all of the securities from which a manager normally chooses, weighted as the manager would weight them in a

---

4   For a further discussion of implementation of the AIMR standards, see Deborah H. Miller, "How to Calculate the Numbers According to the Standards," in *Performance Reporting for Investment Managers: Applying the AIMR Performance Presentation Standards* (Charlottesville, VA: AIMR, 1991).

portfolio."[5] Thus, a normal portfolio is a specialized index. Some argue that normal portfolios are more appropriate benchmarks than market indexes because they control for investment management style, thereby representing a passive portfolio against which a manager can be evaluated.

The construction of a normal portfolio for a particular manager is no simple task.[6] The objective is to construct a portfolio that, given the historical portfolios held by the manager, will reflect that manager's style in terms of assets and the weighting of those assets. The construction of a normal portfolio for a manager requires (1) defining the universe of fixed income securities to be included in the normal portfolio, and (2) determining how these securities should be weighted (i.e., equally weighted or capitalization-weighted).

Defining the set of securities to be included in the normal portfolio begins with discussions between the client and the manager to determine the manager's investment style. Then the universe of all publicly traded securities is reduced to a subset that includes those securities that the manager considers eligible, given his or her investment style.

The next question is how these securities should be weighted in the normal portfolio. The two choices are equal-weighting or capitalization-weighting of each security. Various methodologies can be used to determine the weights. These methodologies typically involve a statistical analysis of the historical holdings of a manager and the risk exposure contained in those holdings.

Plan sponsors work with pension consultants to develop normal portfolios for a manager. The consultants use vendor systems that have been developed for performing the needed statistical analysis and the necessary optimization program to create a portfolio exhibiting similar factor positions to replicate the "normal" position of a manager. A plan sponsor must recognize that there is a cost to developing and updating the normal portfolio.

There are some who advocate leaving the responsibility of developing normal portfolios to the manager. Yet many clients are reluctant to let their managers control the construction of normal portfolios because they believe the managers will produce easily beaten, or "slow

5 Jon Christopherson, "Normal Portfolios and Their Construction," in Frank J. Fabozzi (ed.), *Portfolio and Investment Management* (Chicago: Probus Publishing, 1989), p. 382.

6 See Mark Kritzman, "How to Build a Normal Portfolio in Three Easy Steps," *Journal of Portfolio Management* (Spring 1987), pp. 21–23.

rabbit," benchmarks. Bailey and Tierney demonstrate that under reasonable conditions there is no long-term benefit for the manager to construct a "slow rabbit" benchmark and explain the disadvantage of a manager pursuing such a strategy.[7] They recommend that clients should let managers control the benchmarks, and focus instead on monitoring the quality of the benchmarks and the effectiveness of the managers' active management strategies.

Purpose of Return Attribution Analysis

Fixed income attribution analysis seeks to identify the factors that contribute to the realized performance and to give a quantitative assessment of the contribution of each factor to the total return. The total portfolio return is partitioned into components representing the effect of each factor.

The performance attribution we describe is that of Gifford Fong Associates. The particular system that monitors and evaluates the performance of a fixed income portfolio as well as the individual securities held in the portfolio is called BONDPAR. BONDPAR decomposes return into (1) elements beyond the manager's control, such as the interest rate environment and client-imposed duration policy constraints, and (2) elements that the management process contributes to, such as interest rate management, sector/quality allocations, and individual bond selection.

BONDPAR answers six questions:

1. How does each element of the manager's return compare to the same elements of return of the benchmark?

2. What is the cost of being in the bond market?

3. What effect do client policies have on portfolio returns?

4. Has the manager successfully anticipated interest rate changes?

5. Has the manager been successful at selecting the issuing sector and quality groups that enhance the portfolio's performance?

6. Has the manager improved returns by selecting individual bonds because of company fundamentals?

---

7 Jeffrey V. Bailey and David E. Tierney, "Gaming Manager Benchmarks," *Journal of Portfolio Management* (Summer 1993), pp. 37–40.

Analysis of Return

The analysis of fixed income portfolio performance continues to evolve. From its early beginnings, when total return calculation was emphasized, to the first attempts at the attribution of returns, the methodology of performance analysis has developed, with the objective being to understand the process responsible for the return achieved.[8] As the complexity of fixed income strategies has grown, and security types exploded, so has the need for refining the performance measurement and analysis activity.

The most basic framework for developing a return attribution model for fixed income portfolios partitions the total portfolio return into components, each component representing the effect of a given factor. The first level of this decomposition aims at distinguishing between the effect of the external interest rate environment and the management contribution. Separating the effect of circumstances that are outside the control of the portfolio manager from the effect of the portfolio management process is the first step to gain valuable insight into the nature of the portfolio performance. Denoting the total realized portfolio return by R, such a partition can be written as:

(2) $$R = I + C$$

where I = the effect of the external interest rate environment
           beyond the portfolio manager's control
       C = the contribution of the management process

If the portfolio had no element of management, the return would be I, or the return due to the environment.

A portfolio without management can be considered to be randomly selected from an available universe of fixed income securities. As a proxy for this management-free randomly selected portfolio, we can use the total of all default-free securities, best approximated by all outstanding U.S. Treasury issues. These are the only available securities that are truly fixed income securities in the sense that the promised payments are expected with virtual certainty. Including corporate, municipal, or agency issues constitutes an element of the management

---

8 Gifford Fong, Charles Pearson, and Oldrich Vasicek, "Bond Performance: Analyzing Sources of Return," *Journal of Portfolio Management* (Spring 1983), pp. 46–50.

process: It involves a decision to accept a degree of default risk in exchange for the higher yields typically expected on lower-quality securities. The standard for identification of the effect of the internal interest rate environment is thus a value-weighted Treasury index.[9]

We can achieve a more refined analysis of the external factor component by partitioning the actual holding-period return on the Treasury index into two sources: interest rate level and interest rate change. Higher interest rate levels mean higher holding-period returns, on which the effect of interest rate changes is then superimposed. The effect of the interest rate environment thus consists of two components: return that would be realized if interest rates did not change, and return attributable to the actual interest rate change.

To assign a precise meaning to the assumption of no change in interest rates, we use the term structure analysis technique, which is discussed in Chapter 4 and Technical Appendix A. This technique provides a market-implicit forecast. One can therefore define the effect of the current level of interest rates as the return on Treasury bonds under the assumption of no change in the current forward rates. The effect of the interest rate change is then defined as the difference between the actual realized return on the Treasury index and the return under the market-implicit forecast. Now we can decompose the effect of I, the external interest rate environment, as:

$$(3) \qquad\qquad I = E + U$$

where E = return on the default-free securities under the market-implicit scenario of no change in the forward rates
      U = return attributable to the actual change in forward rates

We can interpret the component E as the expected return on a portfolio of default-free Treasury securities. The component U is then the unexpected part of the actual return on the Treasury index, which

---

9 One might argue that the relevant portfolio bogey should vary according to investor preference. In the determination of the investor's investment objectives, individual preferences are certainly appropriate. The intent here, however, is to measure the interest rate effect on a universe that involves no other aspect, such as credit risk or spread relationships. That does not mean that a comparison of the portfolio return to a broader bond market index is inappropriate. Such comparison is in fact an integral part of the performance analysis. It is achieved by performing the return analysis for the chosen bogey as well, thus allowing a direct comparison of the resulting components of return of the actual portfolio and the specialized bogey.

is due to the forward rate change. The sum I of these components is the actual return on the Treasury index. Finally, we can attribute the difference between the actual portfolio return and the actual Treasury index return, C, to the management process.

In evaluating the management contribution, C, consider the means by which the management process can affect the portfolio. Three principal management skills that have an effect on performance include maturity management, sector/quality management, and selection of the individual securities. A partitioning of the management contribution is thus:

(4) $C = M + S + B$

where M = return from maturity management
        S = return from spread/quality management
        B = return attributable to the selection of specific securities

Maturity management (which might more correctly be called duration management) is an important tool of a bond portfolio manager, and one that typically has the largest impact on performance. The successful application of this skill is related to the ability of the manager to anticipate interest rate changes. Holding long-duration portfolios during periods of decreasing interest rates and short-duration portfolios during periods of rate increases will typically result in superior performance. Being short when rates decline or long when rates go up will have a negative impact on performance.

Sector and quality management refers to allocation of the portfolio among the alternative issuing sectors and quality groups of the bond market in order to exploit spread relationships among the individual sector/quality groups. Portfolio concentration in high-quality industrial issues, for instance, during a period when high-quality industrials are performing better than other sectors, would increase the portfolio return. The ability to select the "right" issuing sector and quality group at the right time constitutes sector/quality management skill.

Selectivity, or individual bond picking, is the skill of selecting specific securities within a given sector/quality group to enhance the portfolio return. Individual securities show specific returns over and above the average performance of their sector/quality group. Selectivity means concentrating on the bonds within a segment whose specific returns are the most advantageous. As with the other two management skills, selectivity comes into play in initial portfolio construction as well as in subsequent activities such as purchases, sales, or swaps within a sector/quality group.

The three component skills of portfolio management all have a timing dimension. That is, timing is not a separate skill, but rather an aspect of each of the skills. Timing the shift of the portfolio from short- to long-duration or vice versa is really an element of maturity management, rather than an independently exercised ability. Without timing, there would be no maturity management. Similarly, timing is an essential element of sector/quality management and a part of choosing the proper bonds within a given sector/quality group. To provide a meaningful analysis of the portfolio return, the timing aspect must be included in the calculation of the return components.

Measurement of Return Components

We can measure the return components by security repricing. Consider maturity management first. If all securities held during the evaluation period are Treasury issues, and if each issue is consistently priced exactly on the term structure of default-free rates (so that there are no specific returns on any security), the maturity management component M of the total return would be equal to the difference between the realized total return R and the effect I of the external environment. In other words, if the sector/quality effect and the selectivity effect are eliminated, the total management contribution can be attributed to maturity management. This means we can reprice each security as if it is a Treasury issue priced from the term structure, measure the total return under such pricing, and subtract the external effect component I to obtain the effect of maturity management

Practically, this is accomplished by estimating the term structure of default-free rates from the universe of Treasury issues as of each valuation date throughout the evaluation period. The default-free price of each security held on that date is then calculated as the present value of its payments discounted by the spot rates corresponding to the maturity of that payment. The total return over the evaluation period is calculated using the default-free prices, but otherwise maintaining all actual activity in the portfolio, including all transactions, contributions and withdrawals, cash account changes, and the like. Finally, the actual Treasury index return over the evaluation period is subtracted to arrive at the maturity management component M.

To determine the spread/quality management component S of the total return, each security is priced as if it is exactly in line with its own sector/quality group (that is, with no specific returns). Next the total return under such prices is calculated, and the total of the external component I and the maturity management component M is subtracted.

One must be careful to determine the sector/quality prices correctly. It is not correct to base sector/quality pricing on sector/quality indexes, because the differences in actual performance among various sector/quality indexes are primarily due to the different maturity composition of the market segments. For instance, telephone issues generally perform poorly during periods of increasing interest rates, not because they are telephones, but because they are longer than the bond market as a whole. The correct approach is first, to define a meaningful classification of the bond market by sector/quality groups. Then the term structure of default-free rates from U.S. Treasury issues is estimated using the term structure analysis methodology. Next, for each valuation date, the default-free prices for all securities existing in the market at that date are calculated. The spreads, or yield premiums, for each security are then calculated as the difference between the actual yield and yield determined from the default-free price. These yield premiums are averaged over all securities in the given sector/quality group to determine the average yield premium for the sector/quality group as of the given date. After all this is done, the sector/quality prices of the securities in the given portfolio can be calculated by determining their default-free prices from the term structure, calculating the yield, adding the appropriate average yield premium depending on the sector/quality of that security, and converting this yield back to price.

When all securities in the portfolio have been priced according to their sector/quality group at each of the valuation dates, the total portfolio return with the sector/quality prices can be calculated. Again, the portfolio return with these prices is calculated including all actual purchases, sales, swaps, contributions, and withdrawals. The sector/quality component S of the portfolio management is then obtained by subtracting the external effect component and the maturity management component from the return calculated on the sector/quality prices.

Finally, to determine the selectivity component of the management contribution, the actual prices, which reflect the specific returns on each security, are used. The selectivity component B is thus calculated by subtracting the total of all previously determined components from the actual total portfolio return.

In this way, we can partition the total portfolio return into five components as follows:

(5)
$$R = \underbrace{E + U}_{I} + \underbrace{M + S + B}_{C}$$

These components are the effect of interest rate level (E), the effect of interest rate change (U), maturity management (M), sector/quality management (S), and selectivity (B). The first component can also be interpreted as the expected return on default-free securities, and the second as the unexpected component of the actual return on the default-free Treasury market index. The first two components are the effect of external factors beyond the control of the portfolio manager, namely, the interest rate environment. Their sum is the actual return on the Treasury index. The last three components reflect factors within the control of the manager; that is, management skill. Together they add up to the total management contribution. The sum of all five components is the actual return on the portfolio.

An alternative way of looking at the composition of the total return, which will reflect the way these components are actually calculated, is to consider the cumulative totals. The first total, E, is the expected return on a randomly selected portfolio of Treasury issues, calculated assuming no change in interest rates. The second total, E + U, is the actual return on a randomly selected portfolio of Treasury issues. The third total, E + U + M, is the return on the actual portfolio (including all activity) as if all securities are Treasury issues priced on the term structure (that is, no sector/quality effects and no specific returns). The fourth total, E + U + M + S, is the return on the actual portfolio as if all securities are priced according to their issuing sector and quality (that is, no specific returns). Finally, the fifth total, E + U + M + S + B, is the actual portfolio return. The decomposition of the total return into its components as specified in equation (5) provides a meaningful and informative analysis of the portfolio performance.

The effect of transactions costs is also included by this analysis. As a transaction is made, the cost is reflected in the price paid for a purchase and the price received for a sale. This in turn is captured in the return due to the selectivity component. Hence, excessive turnover of the portfolio will be reflected in the selectivity component of the portfolio.

After we have calculated components of return for the portfolio being analyzed, we can repeat the same return decomposition for a total bond market index such as the Lehman Government/Corporate Bond Index. The return components of the bond index provide benchmarks against which we can compare the return components of the portfolio.

Risk Adjustments

Before we illustrate the process for bond portfolio performance and analysis, a discussion of risk adjustments is in order. For equity portfolios, it is customary to calculate a risk-adjusted return, defined as the actual portfolio beta. Crude attempts at a similar adjustment for bond portfolios have been made by substituting the bond portfolio duration relative to an index for the beta of a stock portfolio. This is incorrect, because duration measures the portfolio response only if interest rates always change by parallel shifts of the forward rates.

It turns out that the correct adjustment for interest rate risk is actually the maturity management component, M, as defined earlier. Similarly, the sector/quality component, S, is an adjustment for the second source of risk in the bond market, namely, default risk. If the investment policy of a fund constrains the manager as to the maturity composition and/or sector and quality composition of the portfolio, it may be appropriate to consider the maturity and/or the sector/quality return components risk adjustments. For instance, if both maturity and sector composition of the portfolio are specifically prescribed by policy, the risk-adjusted return is equal to the selectivity component, E. In general, however, interpretation of the maturity and sector/quality components as risk adjustments means removing the principal sources of return from the observed performance.

The maturity management component seeks to measure the effect of overall changes in interest rates relative to the bogey chosen (all-Treasury index). The net difference in maturity between the portfolio and the index is evaluated to determine the impact of this difference on return. This component is measured by the difference between the risk-free rate of return of the portfolio and the index return. For managers concerned only with the direction of interest rates, this is an appropriate analysis; if the overall shift in the term structure is of concern, a more refined measurement procedure is called for.

Duration measures the effects of a parallel shift in the yield curve. If the yield curve change is not parallel, the magnitude of the yield curve shift will vary depending upon where the measurement is made. Consistent with the concept of using the Treasury index to measure the unmanaged interest rate effect, we use the duration of the Treasury index as the point for measuring the amount of the parallel yield shift.

The duration return component of interest rate management can then be expressed as:

$$(6) \qquad R_{Dp} = -(D_p - D_i) \times S_{Di}$$

where R_{Dp} = duration return component of interest rate management effect for the portfolio

D_p = beginning-of-month average adjusted portfolio duration

D_i = beginning-of-month average adjusted Treasury index duration

S_{Di} = shift in Treasury yield at Treasury index duration

As part of the maturity management analysis, a regression of the changes of the spot rate yield curve is computed. The shift in rates for the Treasury index is then:

$$(7) \qquad S_{Di} = a + b \times D_i$$

where S_{Di} = shift in Treasury yield at Treasury index duration

a = intercept of the regression of the changes of the spot rate yield curve

b = slope of the regression line of the changes of the spot rate yield curve

D_i = beginning-of-month average adjusted Treasury index duration

The convexity management return component of interest rate management actually results from two effects. The first effect is from the change in the level of interest rates. Duration can be thought of as measuring the effect of minute (or local) changes in rates on price (a first-order effect), while convexity can be thought of as measuring the change in duration as rates shift (a second-order measure).

This second-order yield shift effect is calculated as:

(8) $R_{Csp} = (C_p - C_i) \times (.5 \times a^2)$

where R_{Csp} = convexity return component from the shift in the
                     level of interest rates
       C_p = adjusted convexity of the portfolio at the beginning of
                     the month
       C_i = adjusted convexity of the Treasury index at the
                     beginning of the month
       a   = intercept of the regression of the changes of the spot
                     rate yield curves

   The other effect measured by convexity can be thought of as a
"twist" effect (i.e., the effect of rotation in the yield curve). This twist
effect is calculated as:

(9) $R_{Ctp} = [-(C_p - C_i) \times b] + [(D_p - D_i) \times b \times D_i]$

where R_{Ctp} = convexity return component from the twist in interest
                     rate change
       C_p = adjusted convexity of the portfolio at the beginning of
                     the month
       C_i = adjusted convexity of the Treasury index at the
                     beginning of the month
       b   = slope of the regression line of the changes of the spot
                     yield curve
       D_p = beginning-of-month average adjusted portfolio
                     duration
       D_i = beginning-of-month average adjusted Treasury index
                     duration

   The sum of the above two effects is the convexity effect.
   The parameters of duration and convexity do not measure effects
resulting from changes in the shape of the yield curve (i.e., a downward-sloping curve changing to a "humped" curve). We classify such
effects as "yield curve shape changes" rather than duration and convexity effects. Yield curve shape change ends up being the residual
component of the maturity management component after elimination
of duration and convexity effects.

Exhibit 12.1 illustrates the refinement of the maturity management component using the spot rate yield curves from October 31, 1988, and November 30, 1988. The surprising realization is that yield curve shape changes can be a very significant factor in total return. This is true not only for the isolated example in Exhibit 12.1, but for actual portfolios as well.

Illustration

Here we illustrate the return attribution model using a hypothetical portfolio for the period February 28, 1990, to March 31, 1990. We show particularly how it answers the six questions about management.

Exhibit 12.2 shows the holdings of the portfolio and the transactions during the period. Also shown for each security are the beginning and ending par amount, proceeds, accrued value, interest paid during the evaluation period, and capital gain or loss.

Exhibit 12.3 shows the results of the performance attribution analysis for the portfolio in Exhibit 12.2. The Evaluation Period Return column is the return and components of return for the portfolio over the evaluation period. The Bond Equivalent Annualized Return column is the annualized return and components of return for the portfolio over the evaluation period. The Market Index column shows the evaluation period return of a market index (benchmark). The index selected for this example is the Salomon BIG index.

The decomposition of the evaluation period return is shown in the sections labeled I, II, III, and IV. Section I, Interest Rate Effect, is the return over the evaluation period of the full Treasury index. We can interpret this return as the cost of being in the bond. Therefore, this component of return is considered out of the manager's control. Here we use the Salomon Brothers' Treasury Index for the interest rate effect; other Treasury indexes can be used when appropriate. The interest rate effect is further decomposed into two subcomponents: the *expected* interest rate effect and the *unexpected* interest rate effect. The former is the return on default-free securities under the market-implicit scenario of no change in the forward rates. This simulates the effect of return from rolling down the spot rate curve. The unexpected interest rate effect is the return attributable to the actual change in forward rates.

Section II shows the policy effect. This is an option that allows an analysis of a duration policy constraint specified by the manager's client. BONDPAR calculates the portion of the total return due to the

---

Exhibit 12.1

Illustration of Refinement of the Maturity Management Component

Based on spot rate curves from October 31, 1988, and November 30, 1988

Using the 10-year zero, the following effects were calculated:

$D_p = 9.585;$ $D_i = 4.525;$ $C_p = .965;$ $C_i = .4408;$ $a = .005277;$ $b = -.0001446$

Interest rate management effect =

> Return of the 10-year zero – Return of the Treasury index
>
> $= -2.31\% - (-1.22\%)$
>
> $= -1.09\%$

Duration effect $= -(D_p - D_i) \times S_{Di}$
> $= [-(D_p - D_i)] \times [a + b \times D_i]$
> $= [-(9.585 - 4.525)] \times [.005277 + (-.0001446 \times 4.525)]$
> $= -.0233908 = -2.34\%$

Convexity effects:

Yield curve shift $= [(C_p - C_i) \times (.5 \times a^2)] \times 100$
> $= [(.965 - .4408) \times (.5 \times (.005277)^2)] \times 100$
> $= .000729$

Twist $= [-100 \times (C_p - C_i) \times b] + [(D_p - D_i) \times b \times D_i]$
> $= [-100 \times (.965 - .4408) \times (-.0001446)] + [(9.585 - 4.525) \times (-.0001466) \times 4.525]$
> $= .0075799 - .0033108 = .004269$

Total convexity $=$ Duration shift + Twist
> $= .000729 + .004269$
> $= .004998 = .50\%$

Yield curve shape change effect =

> Interest rate management effect – (Duration effect + Convexity effect)
>
> $= -1.09\% - (-2.34\% + .50\%)$
>
> $= .76\%$

Exhibit 12.2

Bond Performance Analysis: Individual Security Listing and Transactions

CUSIP	Bond description	Initial/ last date	Beg/ end par value ($000)	Beg/ end price (%)	Beg/ end account ($000)	Interest paid ($000)	Capital gain/ loss ($000)
041033BM	ARKANSAS POWER & LIGHT CO						
1	14.125% 11/ 1/14 E4	2/28/90	24500.000	98.689	1124.70		
		3/31/90	20000.000	98.765	1177.08	.00	17.99
161610BA	CHASE MANHATTAN CORP						
2	9.750% 9/15/99 F3	2/28/90	25000.000	99.969	1103.65		
		3/31/90	30000.000	100.080	130.00	1462.50	69.05
172921CT	CITICORP MORTGAGE SECS INC						
3	9.500% 1/ 1/19 PS	2/28/90	76151.720	86.250	542.58		
		3/31/90	76151.720	85.031	602.87	602.87	−928.29
3024519X	FHA INSURED PROJECT MORTGAGE						
4	7.400% 2/ 1/21 PS	2/28/90	73071.970	84.438	405.55		
		3/31/90	73071.970	83.875	450.61	450.61	−411.40
313400KK	FEDERAL HOME LOAN MTG CORP						
5	12.250% 3/15/95 AG	2/28/90	30600.000	106.250	1718.93		
		3/31/90	30600.000	105.813	162.98	1874.25	−133.72
4581829H	INTER-AMERICAN DEVELOPMENT						
6	11.000% 12/11/92 X1	2/28/90	5600.000	103.313	131.76		
		3/31/90	5600.000	102.813	188.22	.00	−28.00
674599AW	OCCIDENTAL PETROLEUM CORP						
7	11.750% 3/15/11 04	2/28/90	34000.000	102.875	1808.85		
		3/31/90	34000.000	102.500	177.56	1997.50	−127.50
912827TQ	UNITED STATES TREASURY NOTES						
8	7.375% 5/15/96 TR	2.28/90	93500.000	94.156	2000.11		
		2/31/90	93500.000	93.594	2590.62	.00	−525.47
912827WM	UNITED STATES TREASURY NOTES						
9	9.250% 8/15/98 TR	3/13/90	92000.000	102.531	658.23		
		3/31/90	92000.000	102.969	1034.36	.00	402.96
912827XM	UNITED STATES TREASURY NOTES						
10	9.000% 5/15/92 TR	2/28/90	85900.000	101.031	2242.42		
		3/10/90	.000	100.750	2498.69	.00	−241.38

Exhibit continues

Exhibit 12.2 Concluded

Transaction Report

CUSIP	Bond description	Type of trans.	Trade date	Settle date	Par value ($000)	Account ($000)	Price (%)	Cost/ proceeds ($000)
041033BM	ARKANSAS POWER & LIGHT CO							
1	14.125% 11/ 1/14 E4	Sale	3/ 5/90	3/12/90	4500.000	231.30	98.751	4675.1
161610BA	CHASE MANHATTAN CORP							
2	9.750% 9/15/99 F3	Purchase	3/ 6/90	3/13/90	5000.000	241.04	99.254	5203.7
912827XM	UNITED STATES TREASURY NOTES							
10	9.000% 5/15/92 TR	Termsale	3/10/90	3/12/90	85900.000	2498.69	100.750	89042.9
912827WM	UNITED STATES TREASURY NOTES							
9	9.250% 8/15/98 TR	Purchase	3/13/90	3/15/90	92000.000	658.23	102.531	94986.8

policy constraint and separates it from the Interest Rate Management Effect. This effect, shown in Section III, shows the option-adjusted default-free return for the portfolio. This component of return shows whether the manager has successfully anticipated interest rate changes. The interest rate management effect is broken into three subcomponents: (1) duration effect, which is the effect on the return due to the magnitude of the yield curve shift;[10] (2) convexity effect, which is the return component of managing the convexity of the portfolio; and (3) yield curve shape change effect, which is the return due to the change in the shape of the yield curve (i.e., the residual return component not measured by duration and convexity).

Other Management Effects are shown in Section IV, divided into three effects. The sector/quality effect is the return component, which shows whether the manager successfully selected the sector and quality groups that performed better over the evaluation period. The bond selectivity effect is the return component due to the selection of individual bonds in the portfolio. Transactions cost refers to the hypothetical effect of transactions on the portfolio's return.

The last two sections, V and VI, provide summary information. Total Return is the time-weighted total return for the evaluation period.

---

10 Consistent with the concept of using the Treasury index to measure the unmanaged interest rate effect, this component is measured relative to the duration of the Treasury index.

This is the sum of the Interest Rate Effect, Policy Effect, Interest Rate Management Effect, and Other Management Effects. The Sources of Return section separates the return into capital gains (the change in price) and interest income.

While Exhibit 12.3 shows the decomposition of return for the entire portfolio, the same analysis can be done for each security. This is shown in Exhibit 12.4.

SUMMARY

Performance measurement involves calculation of the return realized by a manager over some evaluation period. Performance evaluation is determination of whether a manager adds value by outperforming an established benchmark and of how the manager achieves the calculated return.

Return or performance attribution models identify the sources of return. In the fixed income area, returns are attributed to (1) elements beyond the manager's control, such as the interest rate environment and duration policy constraints imposed by a client, and (2) elements that the management process contributes to, such as interest rate management, sector/quality allocations, and individual bond selection. To refine the return attribution of a fixed income portfolio, a breakdown of the maturity management component may be accomplished, which further reveals the sources of management skill. For fixed income strategies that rely upon the use of these specialized approaches, this framework can be a useful monitoring tool.

Exhibit 12.3

Performance Attribution Analysis for a Portfolio with BONDPAR

	Evaluation period return (%)	Bond-equivalent annualized return (%)	Market index evaluation period return (%)
I. Interest rate effect (Salomon Treasury Index)			
1. Expected	.66	7.93	.66
2. Unexpected	−.57	−6.87	−.57
Subtotal	.09	1.06	.09
II. Policy effect			
3. Portfolio duration requirement	.01	.07	.01
(4.60 years)			
III. Interest rate management effect			
4. Duration	.06	.69	.00
5. Convexity	−.07	− .84	−.10
6. Yield curve shape change	−.15	−1.78	.10
Subtotal (options adjusted)	−.16	−1.93	.00
IV. Other management effects			
7. Sector/Quality	.18	2.15	.10
8. Bond selectivity	.32	3.79	.00
9. Transactions cost	−.03	−.38	.00
Subtotal	.47	5.56	.10
V. Total return	.41	4.76	.20
VI. Sources of return			
1. Capital gains	−.44	−5.20	
2. Interest income	.85	9.96	
Total return	.41	4.76	

Exhibit 12.4

Performance Attribution Analysis for Each Security with BONDPAR

Initial face value ($000)	Bond description	Initial date	Last date	Market performance		Portfolio management				Total return (%)	Return source	
				Market expect	Rate change	Int rate	Sector /Qual	Selec- tivity	Trans cost		Capital gains	Interest Income
24500.0	ARKANSAS POWER & LIGHT CO 14.125% 11/ 1/14 E4 — 1 041033BM	2/28/90	3/31/90	.66	-.57	.37	.69	.25	-.07	1.88	.07	1.25
25000.0	CHASE MANHATTAN CORP 9.75% 9/15/99 F3 — 2 16610BA	2/28/90	3/31/90	.66	-.57	-.19	.01	1.12	-.04	.98	.11	.88
76151.7	CITICORP MORTGAGE SECS INC 9.500% 1/ 1/19 PS — 3 172921CT	2/28/90	3/31/90	.66	-.57	-.04	.25	-.70	.00	-.40	-1.31	.91
73072.0	FHA INSURED PROJECT MTG 7.400% 2/ 1/21 PS — 4 3024519X	2/28/90	3/31/90	.66	-.57	-.55	.70	-.10	.00	.14	-.59	.73
30600.0	FEDERAL HOME LOAN MTG CORP 12.250% 3/15/95 AG — 5 313400KK	2/28/90	3/31/90	.66	-.57	-.08	.06	.50	.00	.57	-.39	.96
5600.0	INTER-AMERICAN DEVELOPMENT 11.000% 12/11/92 X1 — 6 458182 9H	2/28/90	3/31/90	.66	-.57	.05	-.03	.37	.00	.48	-.47	.95
	7 674599AW											

Exhibit continues

Exhibit 12.4 Concluded

Initial face value ($000)	Bond description	Initial date	Last date	Market performance		Portfolio management				Total return (%)	Return source	
				Market expect	Rate change	Int rate	Sector /Qual	Selec- tivity	Trans cost		Capital gains	Interest Income
34000.0	OCCIDENTAL PETROLEUM CORP 11.750% 3/15/11 04 8 912827TQ	2/28/90	3/31/90	.66	-.57	-.31	.05	.84	.00	.68	-.35	1.02
93500.0	UNITED STATES TREASURY NOTE 7.375% 5/15/96 TR 9 912827WM	2/28/90	3/31/90	.66	-.57	-.19	.00	.17	.00	.07	-.58	.66
92000.0	UNITED STATES TREASURY NOTE 9.250% 8/15/98 TR 10 912827XM	3/13/90	3/31/90	.39	-.33	-.15	.00	.99	-.06	.82	.42	.40
85900.0	UNITED STATES TREASURY NOTE 9.000% 5/15/92 TR	2/28/90	3/10/90	.21	-.18	.13	.00	-.08	-.06	.02	-.27	.29

The *Individual Security Performance* report lists the return components for all individual securities held during the evaluation period.

- *Initial Face Value* indicates in ($000) the beginning holding position for the bond.
- *Bond Description* displays the security's portfolio bond number, CUSIP number, coupon, maturity date, and sector/quality.
- *Initial Date and Last Date* display the evaluation period for the security being analyzed.
- The remaining columns break down the components of return for the individual security over the evaluation period.

Section IV

Technical Appendices

Technical Appendix A

Term Structure Modeling*

In Chapter 4 we discussed term structure analysis and showed the products of a term structure model. In this technical appendix, we explain how the term structure model works.

In specification of the model proposed for estimation of the term structure, we use the notation:

t = time to payment (measured in half years)

D(t) = the discount function; that is, the present value of a unit payment due in time t

R(t) = spot rate of maturity t, expressed as the continuously compounded semiannual rate. The spot rates are related to the discount function by the equation

$$D(t) = e^{-tR(t)}$$

F(t) = continuously compounded instantaneous forward rate at time t. The forward rates are related to the spot rate by the equation

$$R(t) = \frac{-d}{dt} \log D(t)$$

---

* This appendix is adapted from Oldrich A. Vasicek and H. Gifford Fong, "Term Structure Modeling Using Exponential Splines," *Journal of Finance* (May 1982), pp. 339–348.

n   = number of bonds used in estimation of the term
        structure
T_k = time to maturity of the kth bond, measured in half
        years
C_k = the semiannual coupon rate of the kth bond,
        expressed as a fraction of the par value
P_k = price of the kth bond, expressed as a fraction of the
        par value

The basic model can be written in the form:

(1) $$P_k + A_k = D(T_k) + \sum_{j=1}^{L_k} C_k D(T_k - j + 1) - Q_k - W_k + \epsilon_\kappa$$

$$k = 1, 2, \ldots, n$$

where $A_k = C_k(L_k - T_k)$ = the accrued interest portion of the market
                        value of the kth bond
       $L_k = [T_k] + 1$ = the number of coupon payments to be
                        received
       Q_k = the price discount attributed to the effect
                        of taxes
       W_k = the price discount due to call features
       ϵ_k = a residual error with $E(\epsilon_k) = 0$

The model specified by equation (1) is expressed in terms of the
discount function, rather than the spot or forward rates. The reason for
this specification is that the price of a given bond is linear in the
discount function, while it is nonlinear in either the spot or forward
rates. Once the discount function is estimated, the spot and forward
rates can easily be calculated.

An integral part of the model specification is a characterization of
the structure of the residuals. We will postulate that the model be
homoscedastic in yields, rather than in prices. This means that the variance of the residual error on yields is the same for all bonds. The reason
for this requirement is that a given price increment, say, $1 per $100
face value, has a very different effect on a short bond than on a long
bond. Obviously, an error term in price on a 3-month Treasury bill
cannot have the same magnitude as that in price of a 20-year bond. It

is, however, reasonable to assume that the magnitude of the error term would be the same for yields.

With this assumption, the residual variance in equation (1) is given as

(2) $$E(\epsilon_k^2) = \sigma^2 \omega_k, \quad k = 1, 2, \ldots, n$$

where

(3) $$\omega_k = \left(\frac{dP}{dY}\right)_k^2$$

is the squared derivative of price with respect to yield for the kth bond, taken at the current value of yield. The derivative dP/dY can easily be evaluated from time to maturity, the coupon rate, and the present yield. In addition, we will assume that the residuals for different bonds are uncorrelated:

$$E(\epsilon_k \epsilon_l) = 0, \quad \text{for } k \neq l$$

In specification of the effect of taxes, we will assume that the term Q_k is proportional to the current yield C_k/P_k on the bond:

(4) $$Q_k = q \frac{C_k}{P_k} \left(\frac{dP}{dY}\right)_k, \quad k = 1, 2, \ldots, n$$

For the call effect, the simplest specification is to introduce a dummy variable I_k, equal to 1 for callable bonds and to 0 for noncallable bonds, and put

(5) $$W_k = w I_k, \quad k = 1, 2, \ldots, n$$

Although more complicated specifications (such as those based on option pricing) are possible, equation (5) seems to work well with Treasury bonds, which invariably have the same structure of calls five years prior to maturity at par.

We now need to specify the discount function D(t). Earlier approaches fit the discount function by means of polynomial splines of the second or third order.[1] While splines constitute a very flexible family of curves, there are several drawbacks to their use in fitting discount functions. The discount function is principally of an exponential shape,

$$D(t) \sim e^{-\gamma t}, \quad 0 \leq t < \infty$$

Splines, being piecewise polynomials, are inherently ill-suited to fit an exponential type curve. Polynomials have a different curvature from exponentials, and although a polynomial spline can be forced arbitrarily to be close to an exponential curve by choosing a sufficiently large number of knot points, the local fit is not good.

A practical manifestation of this phenomenon is that a polynomial spline tends to "weave" around the exponential, resulting in highly unstable forward rates (which are the derivatives of the logarithm of the discount function). Another problem with polynomial splines is their undesirable asymptotic properties. Polynomial splines cannot be forced to tail off in an exponential form with increasing maturities.

It would be convenient if we can work with the logarithm log $D(t)$ of the discount function, which is essentially a straight line and can be fitted very well with splines. Unfortunately, the model given by equation (1) would then be nonlinear in the transformed function, which necessitates the use of complicated nonlinear estimation techniques.[2]

There is a way out of this dilemma. Instead of using a transform of the function $D(t)$, we can apply a transform to the *argument* of the function. Let α be some constant and put

(6) $$t = -\frac{1}{\alpha}\log(1 - x), \quad 0 \leq x < 1$$

Then $G(x)$ defined by

(7) $$D(t) = D\left(-\frac{1}{\alpha}\log(1 - x)\right) \equiv G(x)$$

---

1   See, for example, J. Huston McCulloch, "Measuring the Term Structure of Interest Rates," *Journal of Business* (January 1971), pp. 19–31; and J. Huston McCulloch, "An Estimate of the Liquidity Premium," *Journal of Political Economy* (February 1975), pp. 95–118.

2   Terence C. Langetieg and Stephen J. Smoot, "An Appraisal of Alternative Spline Methodologies for Estimating the Term Structure of Interest Rates," working paper, University of Southern California, December 1981.

is a new function with the following properties: (1) $G(x)$ is a decreasing function defined on the finite interval $0 \le x \le 1$ with $G(0) = 1$, $G(1) = 0$; (2) to the extent that $D(t)$ is approximately exponential,

$$D(t) \sim e^{-\gamma t}, \quad 0 \le t < \infty$$

the function $G(x)$ is approximately a power function,

$$G(x) \sim (1 - x)^{\gamma/\alpha}, \quad 0 \le x \le 1$$

(3) the model specified by equation (1) is linear in G. Thus, we have replaced the function $D(t)$ to be estimated by the approximate power function $G(x)$, which can be very well-fitted by polynomial splines, while preserving the linearity of the model. Moreover, desired asymptotic properties can easily be enforced.

If $G(x)$ is polynomial with $G'(1) \ne 0$, then the parameter α constitutes the *limiting value of the forward rates:*

$$\lim_{t \to \infty} F(t) = \alpha$$

Indeed, in that case

$$G(x) = - G'(1)(1 - x) + o(1 - x)$$

and consequently

$$D(t) = - G'(1) e^{-\alpha t} + o(e^{-\alpha t})$$

as $t \to \infty$. Using polynomial splines to fit the function $G(x)$ will thus assure the desired convergence of the forward rates. The limiting value α can be fitted to the data together with the other estimation parameters.

Let $g_i(x)$, $0 \le x \le 1$, $i = 1, 2, \ldots, m$ be a base of a polynomial spline space. Any spline in this space can be expressed as a linear combination of the base. If $G(x)$ is fitted by a function from this space,

(8)
$$G(x) = \sum_{i=1}^{m} \beta_i g_i(x), \quad 0 \le x \le 1$$

the model of equation (1) can be written as

$$P_k + A_k = \sum_{i=1}^{m} \beta_i \left(g_i(X_{k1}) + \sum_{j=1}^{L_k} C_k g_i(X_{kj}) \right) - q \frac{C_k}{P_k} \left(\frac{dP}{dY} \right)_k - w I_k + \epsilon_k$$

(9) $\quad E(\epsilon_k) = 0, \quad E(\epsilon_k^2) = \sigma^2 \omega_k, \quad E(\epsilon_k \epsilon_l) = 0 \text{ for } k \neq l$

where

$$X_{kj} = 1 - e^{-\alpha(T_k - j + 1)} \quad j = 1, 2, \ldots, L_k$$

The model described by equation (9) is used in the estimation of the term structure. It is linear in the parameters $\beta_1, \beta_2, \ldots, \beta_m, q, w$, with residual covariance matrix proportional to

$$\Omega = \begin{vmatrix} \omega_1 & & & & \\ & \omega_2 & & & \\ & & \cdot & & \\ & & & \cdot & \\ & & & & \omega_n \end{vmatrix}$$

If we write

$$U_k = P_k + A_k$$

$$Z_{ki} = g_i(X_{k1}) + \sum_{j=1}^{L_k} C_k g_i(X_{kj}), \quad i = 1, 2, \ldots, m$$

$$Z_{k,m+1} = - \frac{C_k}{P_k} \left(\frac{dP}{dY} \right)_k$$

$$Z_{k,m+2} = -I_k$$

for $k = 1, 2, \ldots, n$, then the least-squares estimate of $\beta = (\beta_1, \beta_2, \ldots, \beta_m, q, w)'$ conditional on the value of α can be directly calculated by the generalized least-squares regression equation

$$\hat{\beta} = (Z'\Omega^{-1}Z)^{-1}Z'\Omega^{-1}U$$

where $U = (U_k)$, $Z = (Z_{ki})$. The sum of squares

$$S(\alpha) = U'\Omega^{-1}U - \hat{\beta}'Z'\Omega^{-1}U$$

is then a function of α only. We can then find the value of α that minimizes $S(\alpha)$ by use of numerical procedures, such as the three-point Newton minimization method.

Once the least-squares values of the regression coefficients β_1, β_2, ..., β_m, q, w and the parameter α are determined, the fitted discount function is given by

(10)
$$\hat{D}(t) = \sum_{i=1}^{m} \hat{\beta}_i g_i (1 - e^{-\hat{\alpha}t}), \quad t \geq 0$$

As for the spline space, cubic splines are selected as the lowest odd order with continuous derivatives. The boundary conditions are $G(0) = 1$, $G(1) = 0$. The base $(g_i(x))$ should be chosen to be reasonably close to orthogonal, in order that the regression matrix

$$Z'\Omega^{-1}Z$$

can be inverted with sufficient precision.

Although the model is fitted in its transformed version given by equation (9), it may be illustrative to rewrite it in the original parameter t. In any interval between consecutive knot points, $G(x)$ is a cubic polynomial, and therefore $D(t)$ takes the form

$$D(t) = a_0 + a_1 e^{-\alpha t} + a_2 e^{-2\alpha t} + a_3 e^{-3\alpha t}$$

on each interval between knots. The function $D(t)$ and its first and second derivatives are continuous at the knot points. This family of curves, used to fit the discount function, can be described as the *third-order exponential splines*.

Least-squares methods are highly sensitive to wrong data, so a screening procedure should be used to identify and exclude outliers.

Observations with residuals larger than four standard deviations should be excluded, and the model fitted again. This procedure should be repeated until no more outliers are present.

Technical Appendix B

Derivation of Risk Immunization Measures

In Chapter 9, we presented a measure of immunization risk against an *arbitrary interest rate change*. In this appendix, we derive the measure of immunization risk in the single-horizon and multiple liabilities cases. The risk measure represents the variance of the time to payments, and therefore the exposure of the portfolio to relative changes of rates of different maturities. The risk measure developed here is based on second-order conditions for the term structure change (first-order conditions define the duration).

Consider a portfolio at time $t_0 = 0$ immunized with respect to a given horizon H against parallel rate changes. Let the payments on the portfolio be $C_1, C_2, \ldots, C_m$, paid out at times $s_1, s_2, \ldots, s_m$, and denote by I_0 the initial value of the investment,

$$(1) \qquad I_0 = \sum_{j=1}^{m} C_j P_0(s_j)$$

Here $P_0(t)$ is the discount function under the current interest rates. In terms of the instantaneous forward rates $i(t)$, $t \geq 0$, the discount function can be written as

$$P_0(t) = \exp\left(-\int_0^t i(\tau)\,d\tau\right)$$

Suppose now that the forward rates change from $i(t)$ to $i'(t) = i(t) + \Delta i(t)$. The discount function then becomes

$$P_0'(t) = \exp\left(-\int_0^t i'(\tau)\,d\tau\right)$$

$$= P_0(t)\exp\left(-\int_0^t \Delta i(\tau)\,d\tau\right)$$

The change ΔI_H in the end-of-horizon value of the portfolio due to the change $\Delta i(t)$ in the forward rates is then obtained as

$$\Delta I_H = \sum_{j=1}^m C_j P_0'(s_j)/P_0'(H) - \sum_{j=1}^m C_j P_0(s_j)/P_0(H)$$

$$= \sum_{j=1}^m C_j \exp\left(\int_{s_j}^H \Delta i(\tau)\,d\tau\right) P_0(s_j)/P_0(H) - \sum_{j=1}^m C_j P_0(s_j)/P_0(H)$$

or

(2) $$\Delta I_H = \sum_{j=1}^m f(s_j)C_j P_0(s_j)/P_0(H) - I_0/P_0(H)$$

where

(3) $$f(t) = \exp\left(\int_t^H \Delta i(\tau)\,d\tau\right)$$

By expansion of $f(t)$ into a Taylor series around the duration $D = H$ of the portfolio, we have approximately

$$(4) \qquad f(t) = -(t-H) \cdot \Delta i(H) - \tfrac{1}{2}(t-H)^2 \cdot \left(\frac{d(\Delta i)}{dt} - (\Delta i)^2 \right)_{t=H}$$

After substitution for $f(t)$ into equation (2), the change of the end-of-horizon investment value can be written as

$$(5) \qquad \Delta I_H = -\Delta_s \cdot \sum_{j=1}^{m} (s_j - H)^2 C_j P_0(s_j) / P_0(H)$$

It follows that

$$(6) \qquad \frac{\Delta I_H}{I_H} = -M^2 \Delta_s$$

where

$$(7) \qquad M^2 = \sum_{j=1}^{m} (s_j - H)^2 C_j P_0(s_j) / I_0$$

and

$$(8) \qquad \Delta_s = \tfrac{1}{2} \left(\frac{d(\Delta i)}{dt} - (\Delta i)^2 \right)_{t=H}$$

Equation (7) is the risk immunization measure for the single horizon case.

Note that the term proportional to $\Delta i(H)$ in equation (4) does not appear in equation (5) for the terminal value change. This is because the portfolio duration is equal to the horizon length H. Thus, any shift component of the rate change has no first-order effect on immunized portfolios.

The quantity Δ_s can be interpreted as the change in the slope of the spot rates (the twist of the yield curve). Indeed, the change in the spot rates is related to the change in the instantaneous forward rates as follows:

$$\Delta R(t) = \frac{1}{t} \int_0^t \Delta i(\tau) \, d\tau$$

If the change in the forward rates is approximately linear,

$$i(t) = a + bt$$

the change in the spot rates is also linear with half the slope.

$$R(t) = a + \tfrac{1}{2}bt$$

We thus have approximately

(9)
$$\Delta\left(\frac{dR}{dt}\right) = \frac{d(\Delta R)}{dt} = \tfrac{1}{2}\frac{d(\Delta i)}{dt} = \Delta_s$$

the last approximation being justified by the negligible magnitude of $(\Delta i)^2$.

In the case of multiple liabilities, again let ΔI_H denote the change in the value of the investment at time $H = t_n$ (the date of the last liability), resulting from an arbitrary change $\Delta i(t)$ in the forward rates. After a derivation similar to the one leading to equation (2), the terminal value change can be written as

(10)
$$\Delta I_H = \sum_{j=1}^{m} f(s_j)C_jP_0(s_j)/P_0(H) - \sum_{i=1}^{n} f(t_i)A_iP_0(t_i)/P_0(H)$$

where $f(t)$ is again given by equation (3). Expanding $f(t)$ into a Taylor series around the portfolio duration D (which is now in general not equal to the horizon length H) and substituting into equation (10) yields

(11)
$$\Delta I_H = -\Delta_s M^2 I_0/P_0(H)$$

where

(12)
$$M^2 = \sum_{j=1}^{m} (s_j - D)^2 C_jP_0(s_j)/I_0 - \sum_{i=1}^{n} (t_i - D)^2 A_iP_0(t_i)/I_0$$

where D is the duration of the portfolio equal to the duration of the liability stream given by

$$D = \sum_{j=1}^{m} S_j C_j P_0(s_j)/I_0 = \sum_{i=1}^{n} t_i A_i P_0(t_i)/I_0$$

and

(13) $$\Delta_s = \tfrac{1}{2} \exp\left(\int_{D}^{H} \Delta i(\tau)d\tau\right)\left(\frac{d(\Delta i)}{d\tau} - (\Delta i)^2\right)t = D$$

Equation (12) is the risk immunization measure for the multiple liabilities case and reduces to equation (8) in the single-horizon case. The approximate interpretation of Δ_s as the change in the slope of the yield curve is still appropriate.

Note that while the expansion of f(t) into a finite Taylor series and the consequent results such as equations (5) or (11) are approximations, equations (2) and (10) are exact.

Technical Appendix C

Valuation and Risk Measures for Interest Rate Futures

In Chapter 10, we described how the theoretical futures price is determined using the arbitrage model. In this appendix, we explain how to determine the theoretical price of the Treasury bond and note futures contract, given the prices of Treasury bonds and notes in the cash market. We explicitly derive the values of the delivery options embedded in the futures contract (the quality (swap) option, the timing option, and the wild card option), as well as the risk parameters of the futures contract such as the price variability, duration, and convexity.

The model we describe can be used to determine whether futures are cheap or expensive relative to cash at any given time, for forward simulations of futures contract behavior under scenarios of interest rate changes, and to determine the contribution of futures to the duration and convexity of fixed income portfolios in immunization or asset allocation strategies.

THE FUTURES EQUATION: LAST TRADING DAY

The notation is

$F(t)$	=	Treasury bond futures contract price at time t
$P_i(t), i = 1, 2, \ldots, m$	=	prices of deliverable bonds at time t

$a_i, i = 1, 2, \ldots, m$ $\qquad = \quad$ conversion factors for deliverable bonds

Times are defined as follows:

$t_{C1}, t_{C2}, \ldots, t_{Cn}$ $\qquad$ times of close of trading from the first position day to the last position day (the last day of trading)

$t_{N1}, t_{N2}, \ldots, t_{Nn-1}$ $\qquad$ the corresponding notice times (t_{Nn} is undefined)

$t_{I1}, t_{I2}, \ldots, t_{In}$ $\qquad$ the corresponding invoice times

Consider the futures price $F(t_{Cn})$ on the last day of trading, assuming the contract is still alive. The short has to deliver a qualifying bond by the last invoice date t_{In}, and the long is then obliged to pay the price $F(t_{Cn})$ times the appropriate conversion factor, plus accrued interest. If the ith bond is delivered, the short receives the value

$$a_i F(t_{Cn}) - P_i(t_{In})$$

Because the short will choose the cheapest-to-deliver bond, the gain will be

$$\max_{1 \le i \le m} [a_i F(t_{Cn}) - P_i(t_{In})]$$

At the close of trading, the expected present value of the gain must equal zero for the contract to find both a buyer and a seller. This yields an equation for $F(t_{Cn})$ as follows:

(1) $$E_{tCn} \max_{1 \le i \le m} [a_i F(t_{Cn}) - P_i(t_{In})] = 0$$

The expectations in this and all subsequent equations are mathematical expectations defined as the integral over all possible outcomes weighted by the probability function. The stochastic behavior of bond prices is described by the equation

$$P_i(s) = P_i(t) - P_i(t)D_i(t)[R(s) - R(t)] + P_i(t)r(t)(s-t) - C_i(s-t)$$

where r(t) and R(t) are the short and long rates, respectively, and $D_i(t)$ and C_i are the duration and coupon, respectively, of the ith bond.

Equation (1) is solved for the last closing price $F(t_{Cn})$ as a function of rates at time t_{Cn}.

THE FUTURES EQUATION: PRIOR DAYS

Now consider the close of trading t_{Ck}, $1 \leq k < n$, on any given day prior to the last trading day. At the corresponding notice time t_{Nk}, the short is faced with the choice of giving the notice to deliver, for an expected gain of

$$E_{tNk} \quad \max_{1 \leq i \leq m} \quad [a_i F(t_{Ck}) - P_i(t_{Ik})]$$

or to carry the position for another day for an expected gain of

$$E_{tNk} \ [F(t_{Ck}) - F(t_{Ck+1})]$$

The short will choose the more profitable action, and the expected gain will thus be the larger of the two quantities. The closing price $F(t_{Ck})$ at the time t_{Ck} is then such that the expected gain to the seller is zero. This provides an equation for $F(t_{Ck})$ as

$$(2) \qquad E_{tCk} \ \max \left[E_{tNk} \ \max_{1 \leq i \leq m} \ (a_i F(t_{Ck}) - P_i(t_{Ik}), \right.$$

$$\left. E_{tNk} \ [F(t_{Ck}) - F(t_{Ck+1})] \right] = 0 \ , 1 \leq k < n$$

Equation (2) is solved recursively, starting with the next-to-last day t_{Cn-1}. At each step, the price $F(t_{Ck})$ is determined as a function of rates at that time. This function is then used in calculating the mathematical expectation that is present in the equation for the previous day.

Prior to the delivery month, the futures contract price is given by the basic equation

$$(3) \qquad F(t) = E_t \ F(t_{C1}) \quad \text{for } t \leq t_{C1}$$

Together equations (1), (2), and (3) completely describe the pricing of futures contracts.

THE OPTION VALUES

The futures contract price $F(t)$ includes the values of the embedded options. We would like to identify these separately, so we can write

(4) $$F(t) = F_0(t) - V_S(t) - V_T(t) - V_W(t)$$

where $F_0(t)$ is the price of the futures contract if the seller has no delivery options, $V_S(t)$ is the value of the swap option (the right to choose which bond to deliver), $V_T(t)$ is the value of the timing option (choosing the day of delivery), and $V_W(t)$ is the value of the wild card delivery option (the opportunity to decide until time t_{Nk} whether to give the notice to deliver, while the settlement price $F(t_{Ck})$ has been fixed at an earlier time $t_{Ck} < t_{Nk}$). We group the values of the timing and wild card options together, as the wild card option cannot exist without the timing option.

We will define $F_0(t)$ as the futures contract price if the delivery consists of the current cheapest-to-deliver bond, and takes place on the last delivery date. The no-option component is then given by the equation

$$F_0(t) = \min_{1 \le i \le m} \ E_t\, P_i(t_{In})/a_i \quad \text{for } t \le t_{Cn}$$

Now define $F_S(t)$ as the price of the futures contract if the seller can choose which bond to deliver, but delivery must still take place on the last day. Then $F_S(t)$ must satisfy equation (1) and therefore

$$F_S(t_{Cn}) = F(t_{Cn})$$

but equation (2) no longer applies. Instead, we have

$$F_S(t) = E_t\, F_S(t_{Cn}) \qquad \text{for all } t \le t_{Cn}$$

The value of the swap option is then determined as

$$V_S(t) = F_0(t) - F_S(t)$$

and the value of the timing and wild card options is calculated as

$$V_T(t) + V_W(t) = F_S(t) - F(t)$$

DURATION AND CONVEXITY

To calculate the duration and convexity of the futures contract (and of the components in equation (4), if desired) modify the current rate $R(t)$ to $R_+(t) = R(t) + h$ and $R_-(t) - h$, calculate the corresponding futures prices $F_+(t)$ and $F_-(t)$, respectively, and put

$$D_F(t) = \frac{F_+(t) - F_-(t)}{2\,h\,F(t)}$$

$$C_F(t) = \frac{F_+(t) + F_-(t) - 2F(t)}{h^2\,F(t)}$$

for duration and convexity, respectively. The variability of the futures contract price is then

$$\sigma_F = \sigma D_F(t)$$

where σ is the variability of interest rate changes.

Technical Appendix D

Mathematical Programming Techniques

Mathematical programming refers to management science techniques that may be used to find optimal solutions to problems requiring resources to be allocated so as to attain a maximum or minimum value for an objective function subject to specified constraints. Linear programming, quadratic programming, integer programming, and dynamic programming are all mathematical programming techniques.

Throughout this book, we have cited examples of seeking to maximize or minimize an objective function subject to a set of constraints. The optimal solutions to those problems are obtained using primarily two mathematical programming techniques, linear programming or quadratic programming. In this appendix, we describe these two techniques.

THE GENERAL MATHEMATICAL PROGRAMMING PROBLEM IN PORTFOLIO MANAGEMENT

In all mathematical programming problems in portfolio management, there are four steps. The first step is to define the variables about which a decision must be made. These variables are referred to as *decision variables*.

The second step is to specify the objective that the portfolio manager seeks to optimize in mathematical terms. This mathematical expression is termed the *objective function*. The form of the objective function is what differentiates linear and quadratic programming. In the former, the objective function is linear, while in the latter it is quadratic. Immunization strategies and cash flow matching, both described in Chapter 9, are examples of portfolio management applications using linear programming. Examples of quadratic programming are the asset allocation problem described in Chapter 11, the methodology for tracking a bond index described in Chapter 8, and the variance/covariance approach for constructing an optimal bond portfolio described in Chapter 7. The objective function may be maximized in applications involving expected return or minimized in applications involving some measure of risk.

The third step in mathematical programming is to establish the constraints under which the objective function is to be optimized. The final step is to solve the mathematical programming model. Computer programs to solve linear and quadratic programming problems with linear constraints can be purchased from commercial software vendors.

LINEAR PROGRAMMING FORMULATION FOR PORTFOLIO MANAGEMENT PROBLEMS

The general linear programming model used in portfolio management problems involving the maximization of expected portfolio return can be stated as follows.

Let R_p = the expected return on the portfolio
          r_i = the expected return on security i
          X_i = the proportion of the portfolio invested in security i
          N = the number of potential securities

The objective function is then:

$$R_p = r_1 X_1 + r_2 X_2 + \ldots + r_N X_N$$

In all applications, there is a constraint restricting the total allocation of funds to be equal to one. That is,

$$X_1 + X_2 + \cdots + X_N = 1$$

Furthermore, if no short selling is permitted, the following constraints must be imposed:

$$X_i \geq 0 \qquad \text{for } i = 1, \ldots, N$$

The other constraints will vary from application to application. For example, there may be constraints imposed on the maximum or minimum concentration that may be allocated to a particular industry or quality sector.

In general, we can express these constraints as follows:

$$C_{1,1}X_1 + C_{1,2}X_2 + \cdots + C_{1,N}X_N \leq b_1$$
$$C_{2,1}X_1 + C_{2,2}X_2 + \cdots + C_{2,N}X_N \leq b_2$$

$$\cdot \qquad \cdot \qquad \qquad \cdot \qquad \cdot$$

$$C_{K,1}X_1 + C_{K,2}X_2 + \cdots + C_{K,N}X_N \leq b_K$$

where $C_{j,i}$ = the constraint coefficient for security i with respect to the jth constraint

b_j = the concentration limit for the jth constraint

K = the number of constraints

For example, if constraint k is that the total allocated must equal one, then

$$C_{k,1} = C_{k,2} = \cdots = C_{k,N} = b_k = 1$$

If a maximum is imposed on the amount that may be allocated to a security, then the constraint coefficient for that security is one, all others are zero, and b_k is the maximum amount.

It is convenient to express this model in matrix notation. To do so, we shall use the following notation:

x = a column vector with the elements X_i

r = a column vector with the elements r_i

b = a column vector of constraints b_j

C = a matrix of constraint coefficient elements $C_{j,i}$

That is,

$$C = \begin{bmatrix} C_{1,1} & C_{1,2} & \cdots & C_{1,N} \\ C_{2,1} & C_{2,2} & \cdots & C_{2,N} \\ \cdot & \cdot & & \cdot \\ \cdot & \cdot & & \cdot \\ \cdot & \cdot & & \cdot \\ C_{K,1} & C_{K,2} & & C_{K,N} \end{bmatrix}$$

Then, letting a prime (') denote a matrix or vector transpose, the linear programming problem can be expressed as follows:

Maximize:

$$R_p = r'x$$

Subject to:

$$Cx \le b$$

QUADRATIC PROGRAMMING FORMULATION FOR PORTFOLIO MANAGEMENT PROBLEMS

The general quadratic programming model used in portfolio management problems involves the minimization of portfolio variance. This can be stated as follows:

Let σ_p^2 = the variance of the portfolio
       Σ = the variance/covariance matrix

Then the general quadratic programming problem can be expressed as:

Minimize:

$$\sigma_p^2 = x'\Sigma x$$

Subject to:

$$Cx \le b$$

where one of the constraints is a minimum expected portfolio return, $\hat{R}_p$, to be well-defined. That is,

$$\hat{R}_p \leq r_1X_1 + r_2X_2 + \cdots + r_NX_N$$

In the case of the asset allocation problem and the variance/covariance approach to bond portfolio optimization, it is necessary to generate an efficient frontier to obtain the optimal allocation of funds. This is accomplished by sequentially varying the minimum expected return and finding the minimum-variance portfolio consistent with that return. In this way, the entire set of minimum-variance portfolios may be traced out. The efficient frontier is then the positively sloped segment of the set of minimum-variance portfolios including, of course, the global minimum-variance portfolio itself.

Technical Appendix E

Risk of Loss Analysis for Asset Allocation Model

In the process of locating points on the efficient frontier for the asset allocation model described in Chapter 11, the standard deviation of the optimal portfolio at each point can also be obtained. These values form the basis for determining the probabilities of loss associated with these mixes. In this appendix we shall explain this process, which we call *risk of loss analysis*.

If the optimal mixes associated with M values of R are called x_m (m = 1,2, . . . , M), associated with R_m, the corresponding minimum standard deviations can be called σ_m. Using the matrix notation adopted in Appendix D, these are related according to

$$R_m = r'x_m$$

and

$$\sigma_m = \sqrt{x_m' \sum x_m}$$

Thus R_m and σ_m represent the total expected return and total standard deviation, respectively, based on the individual components r and Σ given for a single time period.

The probability of not achieving the expected return level L with the constrained optimal portfolio with an expected return of R_m,

$$Q = \Pr\{R \le L \mid x_m\}$$

may now be determined.

This computation requires some assumption about the shape of the distribution of periodic returns R. Assume that the periodic portfolio returns are lognormally distributed with mean R_m and variance σ_m so that the variable z given by

$$z = \ln(1 + R)$$

will be normally distributed with mean

$$\mu_{z_m} = \ln(1 + R_m) - \frac{1}{2}\sigma_{z_m}^2$$

and variance

$$\sigma_{z_m}^2 = \ln\left[\frac{\sigma_m^2 + (R_m + 1)^2}{(R_m + 1)^2}\right]$$

Under this assumption, the probability of loss for this optimal mix (expected return R_m) with the loss threshold L may be obtained as follows:

$$Q_m = \Pr\{z_m \equiv \ln(1 + R) \le \ln(1 + L) \mid x_m\}$$
$$= \tfrac{1}{2} + \tfrac{1}{2}\,\mathrm{erf}\left[\frac{\ln(1 + L) - \mu_{z_m}}{\sqrt{2}\,\sigma_{z_m}}\right]$$

where "erf" is the error functional defined as

$$\mathrm{erf}(x) = \int_0^x e^{-t^2}dt$$

The probability of loss over t time periods can be obtained using the random walk assumption discussed in Chapter 11. It will be

$$Q_m(t) = \tfrac{1}{2} + \tfrac{1}{2}\,\mathrm{erf}\left[\frac{\ln(1 + L) - \mu_{z_m}^t}{\sqrt{2t}\,\sigma_{z_m}}\right]$$

which represents the probability of not achieving at least the total return L in t time periods using the optimal mix x_m, which has a total expected return R_m (or tR_m for t time periods) and standard deviation σ_m (or $\sigma_m \sqrt{t}$).

Technical Appendix F

Multiple Scenario Extension for Asset Allocation Model

In Chapter 11, we describe how the basic asset allocation model can be extended to multiple scenarios. In this appendix, we describe this approach.

Suppose the forecast of the course of future events is to be expressed in terms of N possible scenarios, which are discrete or mutually exclusive, and to each of which a probability of occurrence P_n, $n = 1, 2, \ldots, N$, is assigned. Suppose, in addition, that the joint distribution of asset returns under each of these possible scenarios is given by $f_n(z)$, where z is the vector of future returns of the J assets over the time period of the forecast. Just as in the case of a single scenario, the expected return of the nth scenario, $\hat{R}_n$, given its occurrence, will be

$$\hat{R}_n = E_n[R(z)] = \iint \ldots \int x'z f_n(z) dz_1 dz_2 \ldots dz_J$$

$$= x' E_n(z)$$

and its standard deviation will be

$$\hat{\sigma}^2_{R_n} = E_n[(R(z) - \hat{R}_n)^2]$$

$$= \iint \ldots \int (R_n(z) - R_n)^2 f_n(z) dz_1 dz_2 \ldots dz_J$$

$$= x' \sum_n x$$

where x is a column vector whose elements are the allocation of the portfolio to security i, and where Σ_n is the covariance matrix among the J assets given the occurrence of the nth scenario. Consider the unconditional distribution (i.e., without knowledge of which scenario will occur), which can be called the composite distribution, identified with the scenario subscript denoted by an asterisk (*). Since the scenarios are assumed to be mutually exclusive, the composite joint distribution may be written merely as a superposition of the joint distributions of the individual scenarios:

$$f_*(z) = \sum_n P_n f_n(z)$$

This yields immediately the unconditional (or composite) expected return:

$$\hat{R}_* = \iint \ldots \int x'z \left[\sum_n f_n(z) \right] dz_1 dz_2 \ldots dz_J$$

$$= \sum_n P_n \hat{R}_n$$

The variance of the composite distribution requires slightly more effort but may be reduced to

$$\hat{\sigma}_*^2 = E[(R - R_*)^2]$$

$$= \iint \ldots \int \left(\sum_{j=1}^J x_j z_j - \hat{R}_* \right) \left(\sum_{k=1}^J x_k z_k - \hat{R}_* \right)$$

$$\times \left[\sum_n f_n(z) \right] dz_1 dz_2 \ldots dz_J$$

$$= \sum_n P_n \sum_{j=1}^{J} \sum_{k=1}^{J} x_j x_k \left[cov_n(z_j, z_k) - (\hat{z}_{jn} - \hat{z}_{j*})(\hat{z}_{kn} - \hat{z}_{k*}) \right]$$

where $cov_n(z_j, z_k)$ represents the conditional covariance between the assets j and k given the occurrence of scenario n. $\hat{z}_{jn}$ represents the mean return of the jth asset with the nth scenario, and $\hat{z}_{j*}$ is the mean return of the jth asset with the composite scenario, or

$$\hat{z}_{j*} = \sum_n P_n \hat{z}_{jn}$$

The quadratic form $\hat{\sigma}_*^2$ may now be minimized to obtain the constrained optimal mixes at each return level for the composite scenario just as for a single scenario.

The unconditional probability of loss may be readily estimated, assuming that the distribution of total portfolio returns for each scenario is lognormal. Since the scenarios are mutually exclusive, the distribution of portfolio returns will be the sum of the conditional distributions weighted by the probability of occurrence of each:

$$g_*(z) = \sum_n P_n g_n(z)$$

It follows immediately from the expressions derived for the individual scenarios that the probability of not achieving at least the total return L in t time periods using the optimal mix (for the composite scenario) x_{m*}, which has a total expected return $t\hat{R}_{*m}$ and standard deviation $\hat{\sigma}_{*m}\sqrt{t}$, will be

$$Q_{*m}(t) = \tfrac{1}{2} + \tfrac{1}{2} \sum_n P_n erf \left[\frac{t\ln(1+L) - \mu_{nz_m} t}{\sqrt{2t}\ \sigma_{nz_m}} \right]$$

where

$$\mu_{nz_m} = \ln(1 + \hat{R}_{nm})$$

and

$$\sigma_{nz_m} = \ln\left[\frac{\hat{\sigma}_{nm}^2 + (\hat{R}_{nm} + 1)^2}{(\hat{R}_{nm} + 1)^2}\right]$$

$\hat{R}_{nm}$ represents the portfolio expected return level for the nth scenario assumptions using the mth optimal mix for the composite portfolio and $\hat{\sigma}_{nm}$ the corresponding portfolio return standard deviation.

Index

Active/immunization combination, 209-10
Active management strategies, 5-7, 127-57
  expectational inputs and, 8-9
  maturity spacing strategies, 155-56
  overview of process, 128-29
  portfolio optimization, 153-54
    variance/covariance approach, 153-54
    worst case approach, 154
  risk and, 8
  sensitivity analysis and, 10, 132-33
  techniques of, 130-53
    interest rate anticipation strategies, 130-41
    relative return analysis, 141-50
    sector/security strategies, 150-53
  timing, 146-47
  trades or exchanges, 154-55
Active/passive combination, 209-10
Adjustable-rate mortgage, 105-6
Adjustable-rate passthroughs, 27, 105-6
AIMR performance presentation standards, 291-95
Alpha, in stock valuation, 6 n.

Asset allocation models, 230, 243-79
  categories of, 243
  forecast-free asset allocation, 273-78
    cost, 277-78
    strategy, 275-76, 278
  futures and, 272-73
  liabilities considered, 266-72
  multiple scenarios and, 253-64
  N-asset allocation model, 249-52
  risk-of-loss and, 252-53
  short-term/long-term asset allocation, 264-66
  two-asset class allocation model, 245-49
Asset/liability management, and swaps, 237
Assets, selecting, 4-5
Association for Investment Management and Research (AIMR), 291-95
Attribution analysis. *See* Bond performance measurement

B

Bailey, Jeffrey V., 297
Barbell structure, 155-56, 192-93
Benchmark portfolio, 128, 295-97

351